ROMARE BEARDEN

Photographs by **FRANK STEWART**

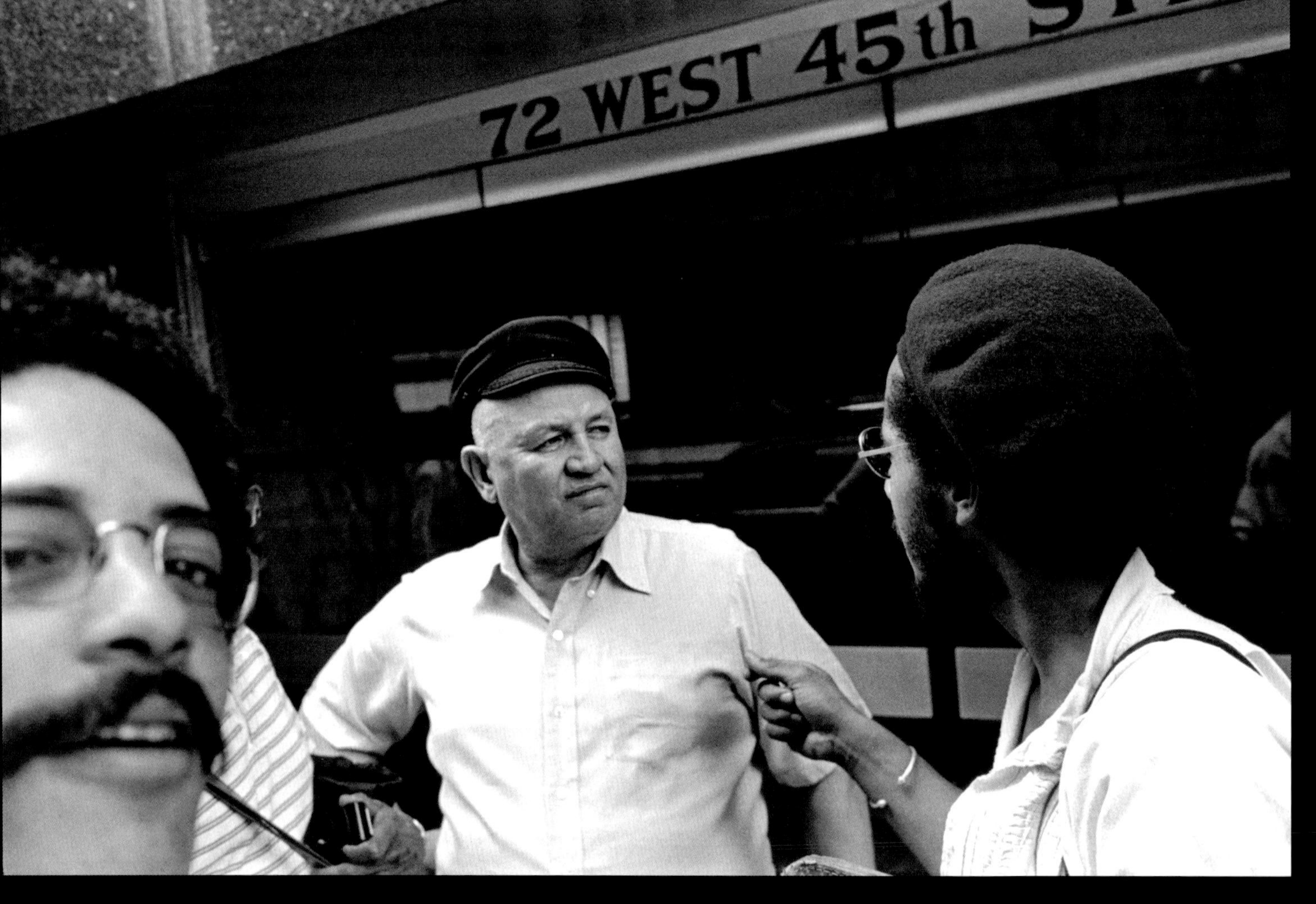
72 WEST 45th

ROMARE BEARDEN

Photographs by **FRANK STEWART**

Foreword DAVID C. DRISKELL

Introduction RUTH FINE

Pomegranate

San Francisco

in association with BLACK LIGHT PRODUCTIONS

Published by Pomegranate Communications, Inc.
Box 808022, Petaluma CA 94975
800 227 1428; www.pomegranate.com

Pomegranate Europe Ltd.
Unit 1, Heathcote Business Centre, Hurlbutt Road
Warwick, Warwickshire CV34 6TD, U.K.
[+44] 0 1926 430111

Library of Congress Control Number: 200404589

ISBN 0-7649-2979-8

Pomegranate Catalog No. A762

Designed by Tamako Okamura

Printed in China

13 12 11 10 09 08 07 06 05 04 10 9 8 7 6 5 4 3 2 1

Dedicated to William Edward-Lee Lathan
in hopes that the world is a better place for him to grow up in,
and that he makes a difference in it.
—Frank Stewart

FOREWORD

While an undergraduate at Howard University I became aware of Romare Bearden after viewing an exhibition of his art at the Barnett Aden Gallery in Washington, D.C., where I was an assistant to gallery owners Alonzo Aden and James V. Herring. I first met the artist in 1954, and then became more familiar with his work during the 1960s, when I returned to Howard University to teach in the Department of Art. Thereafter I visited with Bearden and his wife, Nanette, from time to time when I traveled to New York City. We exchanged numerous letters throughout the 1970s, and kept in touch by phone in the 1980s.

I was one of many artists of the 1960s who found their personal creative voice by studying the accomplished artistry of Bearden, Jacob Lawrence, and other black masters whose art was beginning to indelibly imprint upon the visual arts what was being thought of as a black aesthetic. As early as the 1930s, Bearden's writings addressed the issue of a black ethos in art that took into account the social and political climate. Perhaps more than any artist of his generation, Bearden garnered the attention of the art world by being both a spokesman for black artists and an innovator when working with experimental media. He also revolutionized the medium of collage, winning it a deserved painterly respect for the first time since its formative years of the twentieth century. When he turned almost exclusively to using collage as his principal medium, I carefully examined his style and methodology, hoping to acquire more knowledge of how he managed to transform the bits and pieces of colored paper with which he worked into such visually engaging images. Few would argue that his mastery of stylistic techniques with a medium once considered child's play moved his artistry solidly onto the significant path of Modernism. That Bearden was always able to produce quality art while experimenting across media testifies to his profound blending of form and content in a previously unparalleled manner.

Equally important during Bearden's abundantly creative career were the bonds and associations he made with other artists, particularly young writers, musicians, and photographers. He reached out to photographers at first in search of visual images to provide the content for the compositions he arranged as collages and photomontages in the 1960s, and later to help him record the images he often hastily sketched as subjects. These recorded ideas became sources for later compositions.

Frank Stewart was first introduced to Bearden in 1975, when I asked the documentary film-maker Carlton Moss to interview Bearden on camera for the film *Two Centuries of Black American Art*, an adjunct to the 1976 eponymous exhibition at the Los Angeles County Museum of Art. Stewart served as recording photographer for the film. (He credits the development of his special photographic abilities to Moss and to John W. Simmons, Moss' most successful protégé in the field of cinematography.) He continued working with Bearden for the remainder of the artist's life, documenting his creative activities, accompanying him to the guest appearances he made as lecturer around the nation, and recording the numerous exhibition openings they attended. The wonderful creative exchange that developed—with Stewart using the camera as a medium of communication and Bearden mentoring in return—enabled Stewart to witness the lineage of Bearden's artistry during the artist's most prolific period.

From this enduring and supportive friendship came hundreds of Stewart's photographs of Bearden, a wealth of which are showcased in this book. Taken from the late 1970s until his death in 1988, they suitably combine biographical and documentary aspects, and in a fresh and creative way, they illustrate Bearden's passion for art and reveal his mature, father-figure persona in the presence of other artists. Each photograph uniquely captures the warmth of Bearden's personality and thrusts the history of the moment and the progression of Bearden's cultural agenda into the viewer's realm.

Romare Bearden provides a rare opportunity to witness how two artists interacted with each other while both were involved with their individual crafts, often under public scrutiny. For Bearden, the making of friendships often went hand in hand with the making of art. He cherished sharing his artistry with those who sought his wise counsel, a gift that people of his genius rarely bestow. For Stewart, it is obvious that the collaboration inspired him, and in turn he afforded Bearden an environment in which the artist felt comfortable under the scrutiny of the camera. Stewart deftly captured Bearden's elusive side, his private side; he managed to grab his off-moments and telling gazes. Collectively these photographs offer a deeply personal and comprehensive portrait.

Frank Stewart has admirably rallied to the call to extend the pictorial canon of the black experience in American culture, and he has done so in a manner that reflects positively on the life, the art, and the times of a great American icon. With verve and insightful passion, Frank Stewart presents an important aspect of the legacy of a great American artist: Romare Bearden.

—David C. Driskell

INTRODUCTION

PORTRAIT OF A FRIENDSHIP: ROMARE BEARDEN AND FRANK STEWART

As a young photographer, Frank Stewart searched vigorously for African American mentors, artists who were working within the culture of his community. He knew "as well as the Bible" the handful of books representing the work of black photographers that was available at the time.[1] Among the most important of these books was the Roy DeCarava/Langston Hughes collaboration, *Sweet Flypaper of Life*, a highly personal account of Harlem that became and remains one of Stewart's inspirations.

Stewart's professional engagement with photography dates to 1967, when he was eighteen, during a brief period at Middle Tennessee State College. Enrolled on an athletic scholarship in track and field, he was one of very few black students at the recently integrated school. He rapidly learned the limitations of this so-called culture of equality when traveling to track meets with the team. Lingering racist attitudes forced the black athletes to eat in restaurant kitchens; indeed, "sometimes we couldn't even go into the restaurants," Stewart remembers.

The situation on campus wasn't terribly friendly either, and Stewart soon realized that he was far more comfortable on the Fisk University campus—about twenty-five miles away—where his cousin, Adrian Jenkins, was studying painting with David C. Driskell, and John W. Simmons, a friend from his hometown of Chicago, was an assistant to the photography instructor, Robert Senstack. Stewart tells how he "would run track in the morning, then go to Nashville and audit classes at Fisk . . . just hang out and learn photography." He regards Senstack as his first teacher.

Stewart's informal association with Fisk lasted just a semester, after which he returned to Chicago. While in Tennessee, however, the budding photographer had the good fortune to meet California filmmaker Carlton Moss, who as a visiting artist at Fisk each month taught the three-day course "The Image of the Black Man in American Film." Through his cousin, Adrian, Stewart also met Driskell, who taught art history as well as painting, and was running the university art gallery.[2] Driskell remembers that Stewart essentially was part of the Fisk family, joining in on field trips and other university events. During the following decade, Driskell, Moss, and Simmons would be instrumental in bringing Romare Bearden into Stewart's artistic life.

Stewart went on to study photography with Gary Winogrand at The Art Institute of Chicago during the summer of 1972 and to earn a BFA degree in photography from The Cooper Union for the Advancement of Science and Art in Manhattan (1975), where Roy DeCarava was teaching. Meeting DeCarava was one of Stewart's major objectives when he decided to move from Chicago to New York to study photography. In addition to the Americans DeCarava and Winogrand, Stewart's early mentors were two European masters, Henri Cartier-Bresson and André Kertész, both of whose work is marked by a sense of immediacy that stems from their use of a handheld 35mm camera. Working in the reportage tradition—taken from life—Stewart describes a major aspect of his project as placing himself (to borrow Cartier-Bresson's phrase) "in a position to get the decisive moment." He embraced this stance quite early in his career, while working out of Chicago as a documentary photographer for the African American press from 1970 to 1980.

During his childhood, Bearden's name had become familiar to Stewart through his mother, Dorothy Johnson, who introduced her son to the importance of cultural concerns. "A ceramist, a painter, a seamstress, she designed clothes, made hats, did all kinds of things. [Bearden] was as famous as Dwight Eisenhower; the chances of meeting this guy were very remote." Yet meet him Stewart did, in 1975, when he joined the trio of friends from Fisk—Driskell, Moss, and Simmons—to shoot *Two Centuries of Black American Art*, a film made to accompany the eponymous exhibition that Driskell had organized for the Los Angeles County Museum of Art.

Prior to shooting *Two Centuries of Black American Art*, Stewart had worked informally with Moss and Simmons on other documentaries about African American culture, for example, *The Life of Frederick Douglass: The Slave Contribution to the Plantation System.* Stewart's role was to shoot the necessary still photographs while work on the film progressed. In a 2003 Black Entertainment Television documentary, *Frank Stewart: Journey with Jazz at Lincoln Center*, several of the people interviewed discussed Stewart's adaptability to virtually any situation.[3] It would appear that this was true by the mid-seventies when he was a young photographer and that his mild manner led Bearden to take an immediate liking to him: when the day's shoot for *Two Centuries of Black American Art* ended, Bearden asked if Stewart could return the following day to photograph some of his recently completed works of art. "Romie said we needed a big view camera. I had never used one [and] I didn't know anything about shooting art, but I borrowed a camera and read some books right quick." Predictably, these first transparencies of Bearden's collages came out underexposed, but "Romie just looked at me and said we had to do them again. So I corrected my mistake and from then on I knew how to shoot art. . . . And that started our relationship."[4] Stewart was in his mid-twenties, Bearden in his mid-sixties.

Around 1978 the two men bought a car together—this joint ownership provided Stewart with a vehicle and Bearden with a ready and willing driver whenever he needed one. The arrangement worked well for them both. While continuing to document Bearden's art throughout these years, Stewart also recognized that this friendship offered other photographic opportunities. "There was never a time when Romie asked me to take pictures of him. I just started taking pictures because we were hanging out together. I'm a photographer; he looked like a willing subject." Until Bearden's death in 1988, Stewart was that proverbial fly on the wall in situations both public and private, creating thousands of photographic images of the artist, his family and friends, his studio practices and professional relationships, his exhibitions and teaching stints.

Stewart divided the some 100 photographs in this book into eight important segments of Bearden's life.[5] The book begins and ends in a loft building at 357 Canal Street in lower Manhattan, where Bearden and his wife, Nanette Rohan Bearden, lived from 1956—two years after their marriage—until the end of their life together. At first they occupied the fifth floor of the walkup, but around 1986, when Bearden's health prevented him from climbing that high, they rented another space on the second floor. Shifts of mood from Stewart's early "Canal Street" photographs to those under the heading "Canal Street: Last Days" offer a heartbreakingly poignant view of Bearden's evolution from good health and virility to his battle with the ravages of cancer.

Images of Nanette Bearden form a secondary thread to that of Romare throughout the book, from the first "Canal Street" segment to the last. The presence as well in both these sections of Stewart's young daughters, Sing and Bining, and Bearden's beloved cats of the moment, Count Rustikoff (Rusty), King Tut (Tuttie), and Michelangelo (Mikie), likewise suggests the affection shared among Bearden and the children and Bearden and his cats. The Canal Street photographs also offer important information about Bearden's lifestyle and about his essential character. The paintings on view where he lived were the abstract expressionist works he had made between 1956 and 1962, before undertaking the collages rooted in the African American experience for which he is best known. Stewart's photographs further show us that Bearden continued to make art on Canal Street during the years he maintained a studio in Long Island City. The artist's scholarly nature is keenly captured in images showing walls of books and journals; multiple shots of Bearden on the telephone (at Canal Street and in Long Island City) suggest the importance of this mode of communication in his life.

Revealing visual details about the Beardens' environment are compelling as well: a corner filled with plants and an ornamental elephant made from decorative Indian fabric; striped slipcovers covered with plastic, presumably as protection from the cats who obviously had the run of the place; transparent window curtains that permitted light to pervade the loft. Similar domestic details appear in the "Staten Island" section, the place where Nanette's family lived in a community formed by immigrants like themselves, from the Caribbean island of St. Martin.

Stewart's "Long Island City" images were taken at 23-03 45th Road, in the second studio Bearden rented in that area. These photographs reveal that Bearden generally worked standing at a table rather than at an easel, and they provide glimpses of his materials (inks and dyes) and tools (a small roller to reinforce the glue used to attach collage pieces). Also visible in the studio are notes the artist tacked to the wall, and a remarkable photograph of his elegantly dressed great-grandparents, the Kennedys, seated together on their porch in Mecklenburg County,

North Carolina.[6] Here and at a table in the Beardens' Caribbean home, Stewart documented the artist making additional versions of his earlier compositions, based on reproductions of these collages in books and exhibition catalogs.

Apparent from the range of individuals Bearden welcomed to his studio is his penchant for friendship, to say nothing of his desire for intellectual stimulation, and possibly even to escape the rigors of work. Many of his visitors were writers. Included in the "Long Island City" section—and in other sections—is Albert Murray, who over a period of many years provided Bearden with the titles for his collages. The two men had met in Paris in 1950. During that same European trip—the artist's first—Bearden met painter Herbert Gentry, who also visits "Long Island City." Others Stewart photographed in this studio are writers Harry Henderson—with whom Bearden collaborated on two books about African American artists—Halima Taha, and Ntozake Shange.[7]

June Kelly was Bearden's manager beginning in 1975. She was responsible for exhibitions held outside New York City, for his print publications, and for his numerous commissions. Kelly is present here in multiple contexts in "The World of Art" and "Friends."[8] Several other people are also included in both of these sections, suggesting the seamless nature of Bearden's life, with professional matters and friendship often inseparable. "The World of Art" focuses primarily on opening celebrations for exhibitions, Bearden's own and those of artists he admired. Stewart captures him talking with writers Barrie Stavis and Nelson Breen at a decade retrospective organized by the Mint Museum in Charlotte, North Carolina, *Romare Bearden: 1970–1980.* Breen was the director and, with Billie Allen (who appears here in the "Friends" section), the co-author of *Bearden Plays Bearden,* 1980, an hour-long documentary film with which Stewart also was actively involved.

Filmmaker/photographer Sam Shaw, whom Bearden met back in the 1940s, and artists Betye Saar and Raymond Saunders are pictured at the time of Bearden's first solo show in southern California (1980), at the Art Garden. Stewart's formal composition of this exhibition space early in the day of the exhibition preview—almost empty of people—emphasizes the geometry of the architecture, in stark contrast to another shot, made later in the day during the opening, when the room was filled with Bearden's admirers, in which the element of reportage holds sway. Painters Ernest Critchlow, Gwendolyn Knight Lawrence, Jacob Lawrence, and Norman Lewis, most of them friends from Bearden's youth in Harlem, are pictured at Manhattan's Terry Dintenfass Gallery, where paintings by Lawrence and Horace Pippin might be seen. Dintenfass herself is present in this compilation, too, embracing Bearden, who in another shot is deep in conversation with Hugh McKay, the man responsible for the publication of several of Bearden's screenprints, including the *Odysseus* series.

Stewart also portrayed photographer James VanDerZee with Bearden, as well as several artists of a younger generation: Benny Andrews, Frederick J. Brown, and Tei Sing Smith. African art and Diego Rivera's murals—two subjects of considerable interest to Bearden—are part of "World of Art," as are various stages of Bearden's work on a mosaic mural commission for the city of Baltimore. The "Friends" section is filled with luminaries in their fields: Alvin Ailey, Addison Bates, Count Basie, Dizzy Gillespie, Diane McIntyre, and Cecil Taylor from the worlds of dance and music; Wole Soyinka, Aimé Césaire, and Vernon Jordan from the worlds of politics and the struggle for human rights.

That Stewart organized his photographs to include a section titled "Lectures and Teaching" speaks to the photographer's understanding of the importance of education within Bearden's artistic life. Although he rarely used them formally, Bearden's natural skills as a teacher had an impact on many artists with whom he came into contact, and Stewart was among the most fortunate of these, given his opportunity to spend large blocks of time with Bearden. Any direct influence of Bearden's art on Stewart's photographs is not readily apparent, but a transfer of ideas by virtual osmosis presumably played a role in their relationship.

Aesthetic concepts, thoughts about motifs to consider, working methodologies, and perhaps most importantly, notions of how an artist functions in the world were in the air as Stewart and Bearden spent time together. They enjoyed both wordless communication and conversations as Bearden made collages and Stewart shot photographs. Stewart's photographs of Bearden's lectures at a Manhattan community center and at Vassar College about his own work; lectures at Yale University and the Mint Museum about other artists' work; and lectures at a gallery program—which also included art historian Mary Schmidt Campbell[9]—about collecting African American art document more formal teaching situations.

The "St. Martin" section reveals the degree to which Stewart became a member of Bearden's family, able to photograph the artist at ease in the place he considered most rejuvenating. Stewart was present when Bearden bathed in the sea, stood tall against the lush diversity of the tropical landscape, and visited with friends such as poet/playwright Derek Walcott and cultural historian Richard Long, both of whom had traveled to the island to visit Bearden. We also see Bearden lecturing to a captivated audience of listeners as well as painting watercolors. One of the most poignant photographs in the book is of Bearden looking, longingly perhaps, into his unfinished St. Martin studio, probably already aware that he had only a few years left to work in it. The vista in the distance shows the grandeur of the island, the hilly landscape that Bearden depicted in his many collages and watercolors of St. Martin.

Bearden and Stewart shared concerns regarding subject matter and the formalist impulses of their art. First and foremost is the culture as Stewart so often refers to it: the life of black people in the South of both artists' roots; in the North, especially New York; and in the Caribbean. While Bearden never went to Africa, a place of considerable importance to Stewart, African art and culture were joint enthusiasms; well before meeting Bearden, Stewart had a deep interest in the history of both African and world art. Because of Stewart's intuitive affinity with Bearden (and his other important teacher, DeCarava), his photographs tend to have a compositional understructure, in keeping with the point of view Bearden elaborated in his 1969 essay, "The Geometric Structure of My Montage Paintings," in the journal *Leonardo.* And of course there was their shared, although very different, engagement with film. Bearden's collages, in their use of photographic images, their documentary approach, and the cinematic cuts and juxtapositions that are among their strongest characteristics, together suggest the significant role that photography played in his art.

Stewart's photographic portrait of Bearden unwittingly, perhaps, served as his apprenticeship for other long-term, more formally conceived projects, first with the Wynton Marsalis Septet and now as senior photographer for Jazz at Lincoln Center, traveling with the talented musicians in the Lincoln Center Jazz Orchestra. As he was with Bearden's intimate circle, Stewart has become part of the orchestra's family, functioning as an ambassador for jazz music and, when abroad, as an ambassador for the United States.[10] Stewart is currently working on his second book with Marsalis as well as on two books rooted in Cuba and Ghana.[11] Stewart's love of both Africa and the Caribbean is profound (as was Bearden's), growing from his concern "with seeking out the roots of black culture, where the slaves came from, where the rhythms of African Americans came from . . . how [the culture] got to be what it is, from West Africa through South America and the Caribbean."

Frank Stewart has called photography a method that was "born grown," suggesting that the photographer's task is to explore "the inherent intelligence of the medium." His photographic portrait of Romare Bearden does just that. Reflecting his experiences with two of the great twentieth-century American artists, as an undergraduate at Cooper Union with Roy DeCarava and the thirteen years spent in the studio with Romare Bearden, Stewart's art reveals his intellectual rigor, formalist aesthetic, and humanistic concerns. Like the photographs and collages created by his mentors, Stewart's photographs of Romare Bearden present a rich tapestry of African American life and culture, conveyed by the eye of the artist, the tool of the camera, and the universally understood medium of light.

—Ruth Fine

NOTES

1. All quotations are from a November 1, 2003, taped conversation with Frank Stewart. Much of the content of this essay also is based on that and other conversations about various subjects I have had with Stewart during the past four years. I am grateful for the friendship and generosity of spirit he brought to these conversations. I also thank Susan Sillins for her orchestration of this book, and Mary Lee Corlett for her assistance in various matters.

2. In conversation April 2, 2004, David C. Driskell generously provided information about Fisk University and Frank Stewart's early years as a photographer.

3. *Frank Stewart: Journey with Jazz at Lincoln Center*, Black Entertainment Television, 2003.

4. Stewart subsequently photographed art for The Studio Museum in Harlem, several New York galleries, and major book projects, including David C. Driskell, *The Other Side of Color: African American Art in the Collection of Camille O. and William H. Cosby Jr.* (San Francisco: Pomegranate Communications, Inc., 2001).

5. A well-known multipart photographic portrait that provides a context for this idea is the one Alfred Stieglitz took over the years of his lover, who then became his wife, Georgia O'Keeffe. The notion of the deep respect and love one human being feels for another is evident in the warmth with which Stewart conveys Bearden's diversity and complexity.

6. Deborah Willis, ed., *Picturing Us: African American Identity in Photography* (New York: New Press, 1994) highlights the importance of family photographs in the lives of African Americans.

7. The books co-written by Bearden and Henderson are *Six Black Masters of American Art* (New York: Doubleday & Co., Inc., 1972) and *A History of African-American Artists: From 1792 to the Present* (New York: Pantheon Books, 1993) (although published posthumously, it was completed within Bearden's lifetime). Shange's collaboration with Bearden (published posthumously as well) is *I Live in Music* (New York: Welcome Enterprises Inc., 1994). Among Halima Taha's publications is *Collecting African American Art: Works on Canvas and Paper* (New York: Crown Books, 1998).

8. Another person of key importance to Bearden's professional life was Arne Ekstrom, the principal in Cordier & Ekstrom, Inc., who previously had played a role in the Michael Warren Gallery, renamed Daniel Cordier & Michael Warren, Inc. Bearden first showed at Michael Warren in 1960, at Cordier & Warren in 1961, and at Cordier & Ekstrom beginning in 1964 for the rest of his life. According to Nicolas Ekstrom, Arne's son, the elder Mr. Ekstrom did not like to be photographed; he does not appear in this book.

9. Mary Schmidt Campbell was the first art historian to produce a book-length scholarly study about Bearden's art. See her 1982 PhD dissertation for Syracuse University, "Romare Bearden: A Creative Mythology."

10. Robert O'Meally commented on the orchestra as ambassadors in *Frank Stewart: Journey with Jazz at Lincoln Center.*

11. Stewart's two publications are Wynton Marsalis, *Sweet Swing Blues on the Road* (New York: W. W. Norton & Co., 1994), documenting the travels and the performances of the Wynton Marsalis Septet from 1989 through 1992; and Lolis Eric Elie, *Smokestack Lightning: Adventures in the Heart of Barbecue Country* (New York: Farrar, Straus & Giroux, 1996). In progress, in addition to the second collaboration with Marsalis, are *Sweet Breath of Life*, edited by Frank Stewart, text by Ntozake Shange, photographs by The Kamoinge Workshop, forthcoming from Simon & Schuster; *Tu Tumbao/Cuban Rhythm*, in association with Petra Richterova; and *Clock of the Earth*, text by art historian George N. Preston, with whom Stewart has been traveling to Africa since 1974.

CANAL STREET

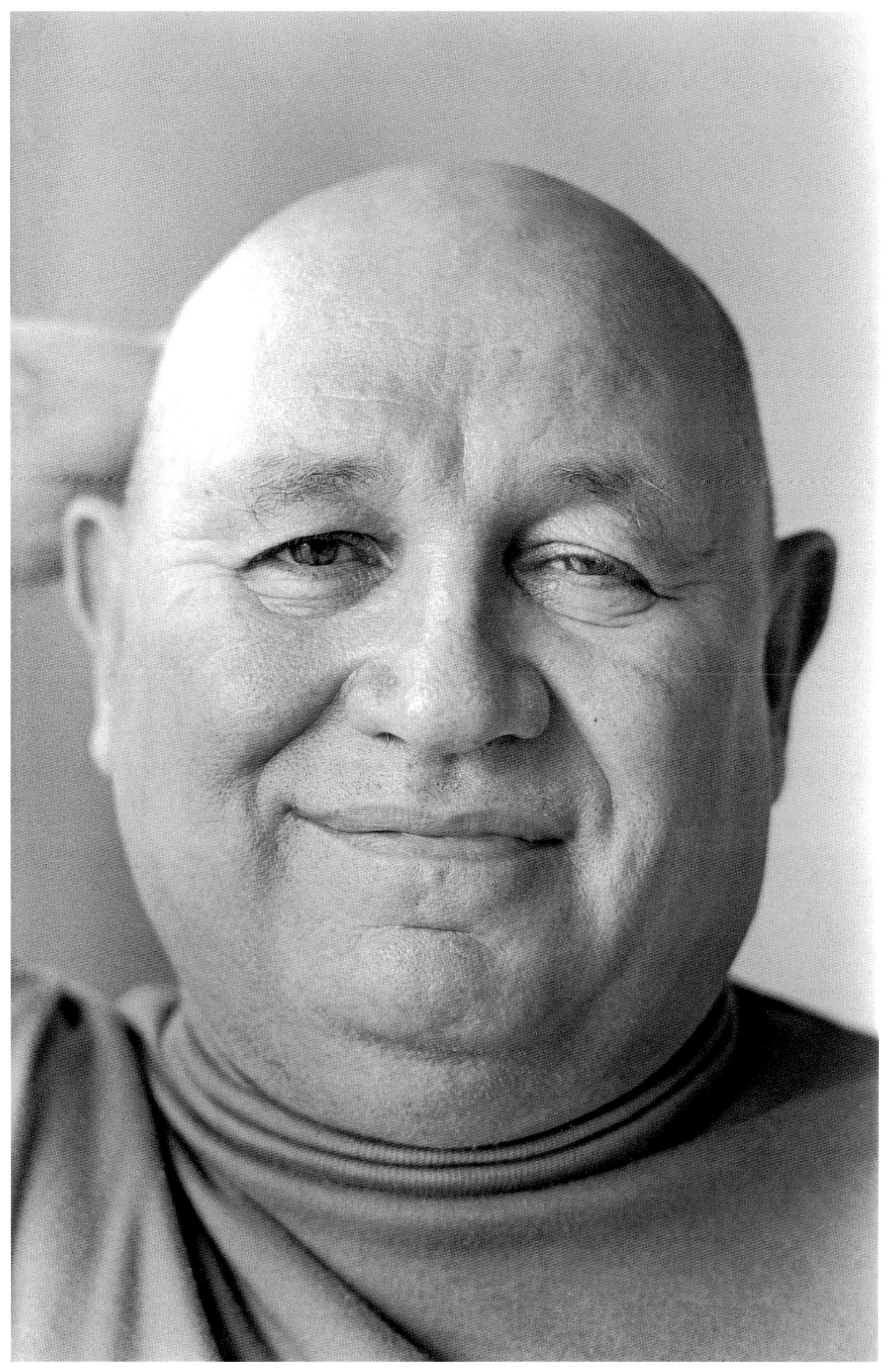

Romare Bearden. 1975

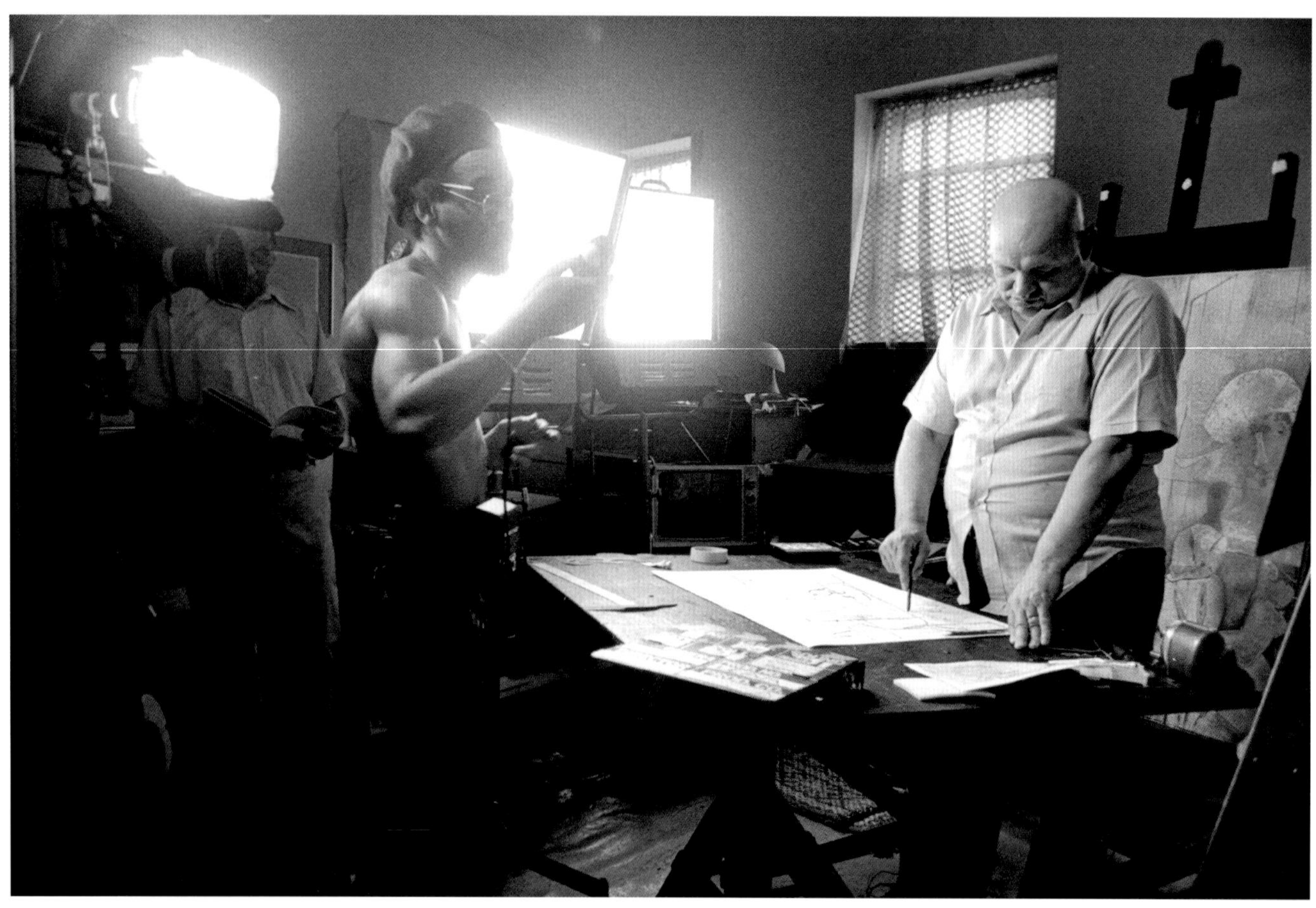

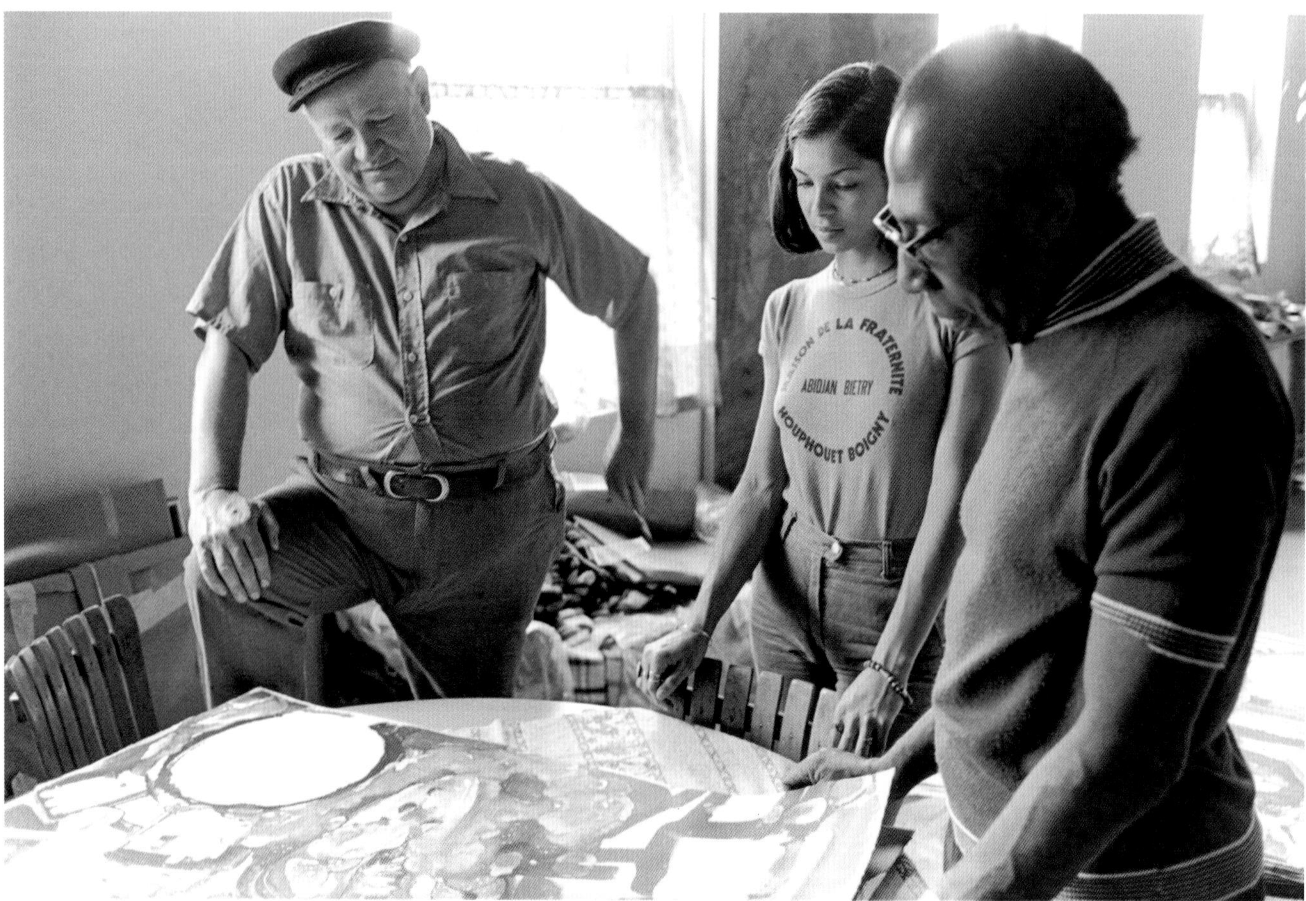

Carlton Moss, John W. Simmons, and Romare Bearden. Our first day of shooting *Two Centuries of Black American Art* was with Bearden, in New York, in July. Toward the end of what may have been the hottest day of the year, Romie started getting testy, saying "It's hot in here; can we wrap this up?" 1975

Bob Blackburn (Romie's printer) and Jeanne Moutoussamy inspecting a new group of monotypes. 1975

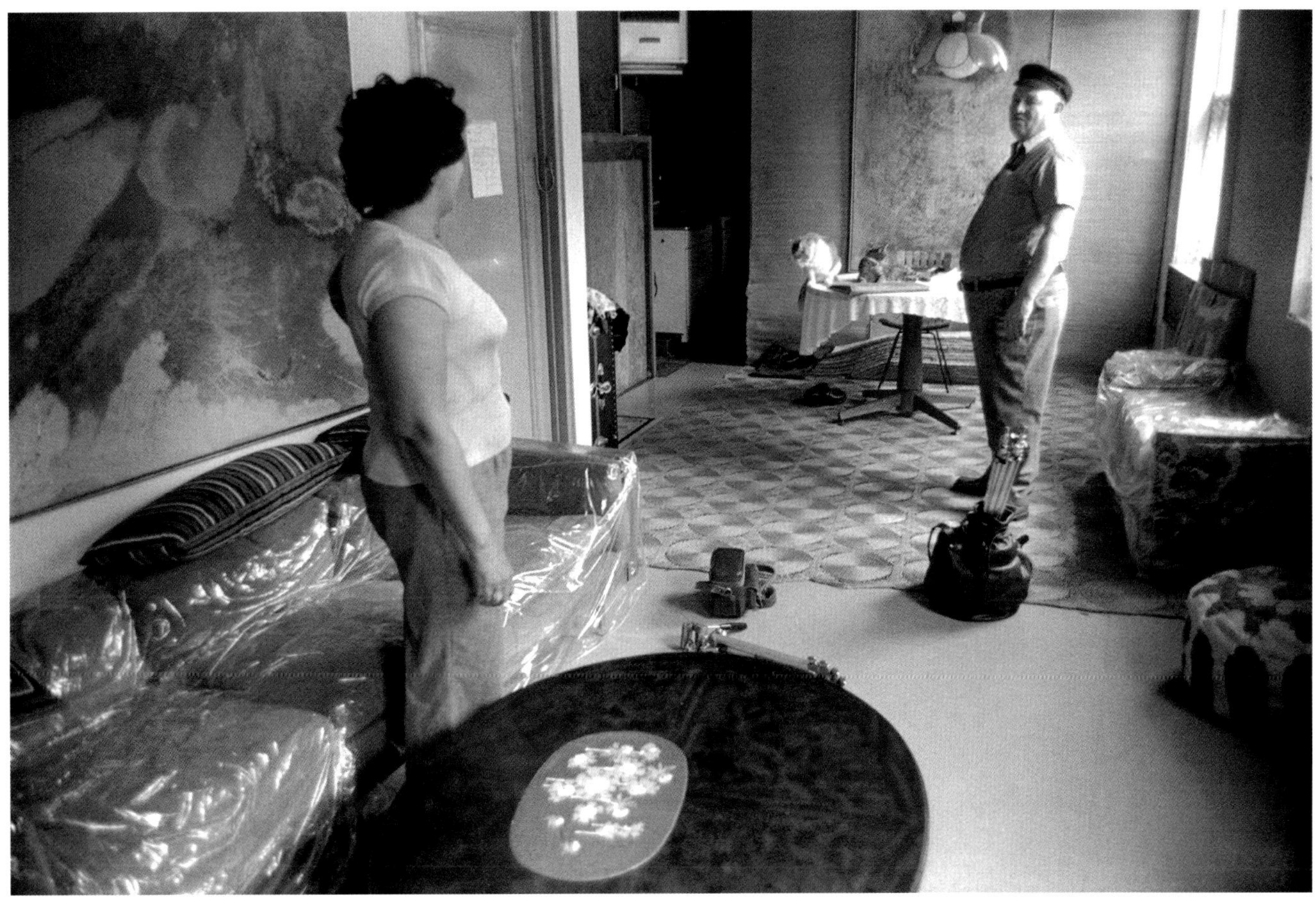

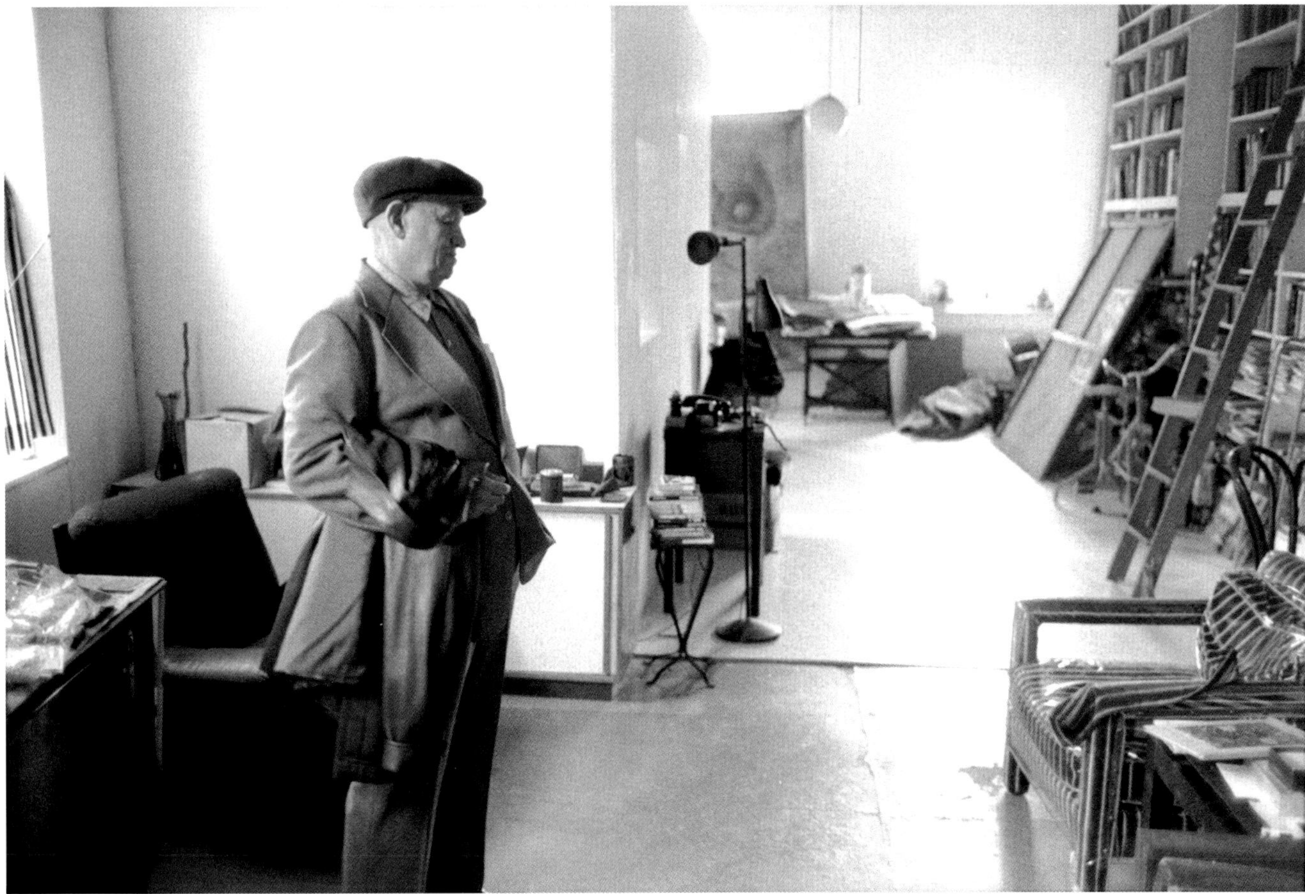

Nanette and Romie lived five flights up in a loft building with maybe fourteen-foot ceilings, so the stairs had to go all the way up those fourteen feet of room space. By the time you got to Romie's place, you were out of breath. I don't know how they did it all those years. 1975

There was a room that was both studio and living space on Canal Street. Romie worked there a little bit even after he had the Long Island City studio. 1976

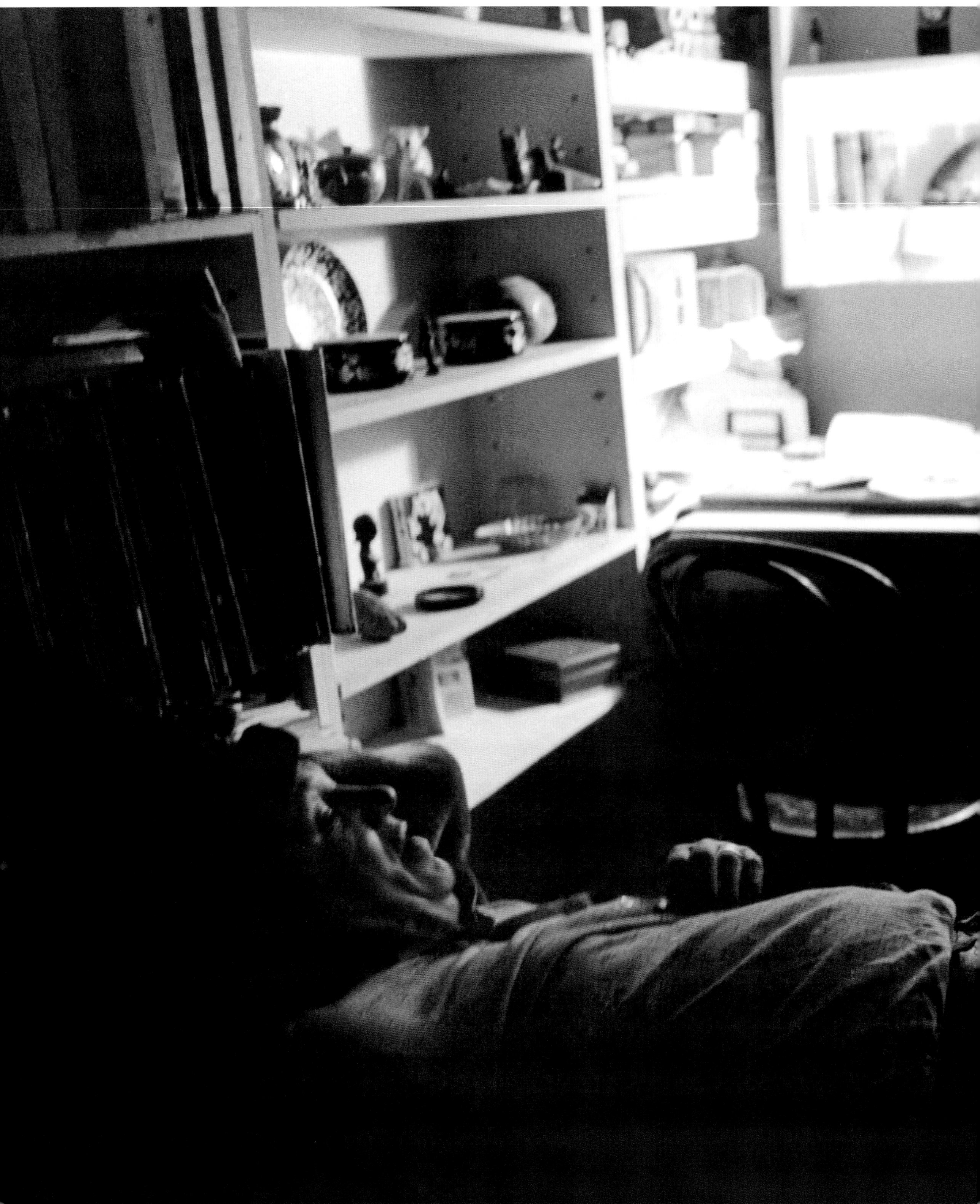

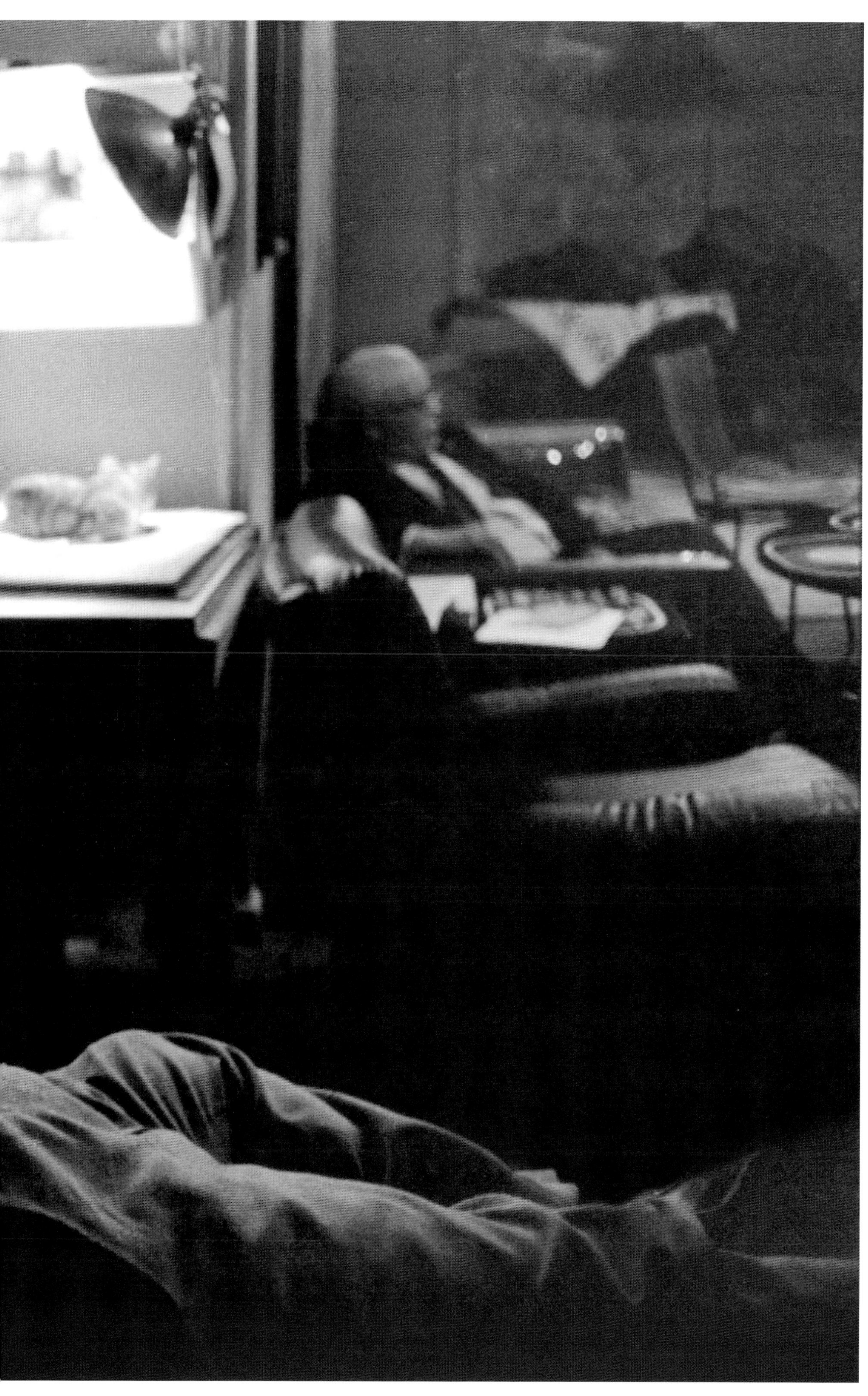

Romie's looking at TV
in his repose position,
with his cousin, Major
Edward Morrow. 1979

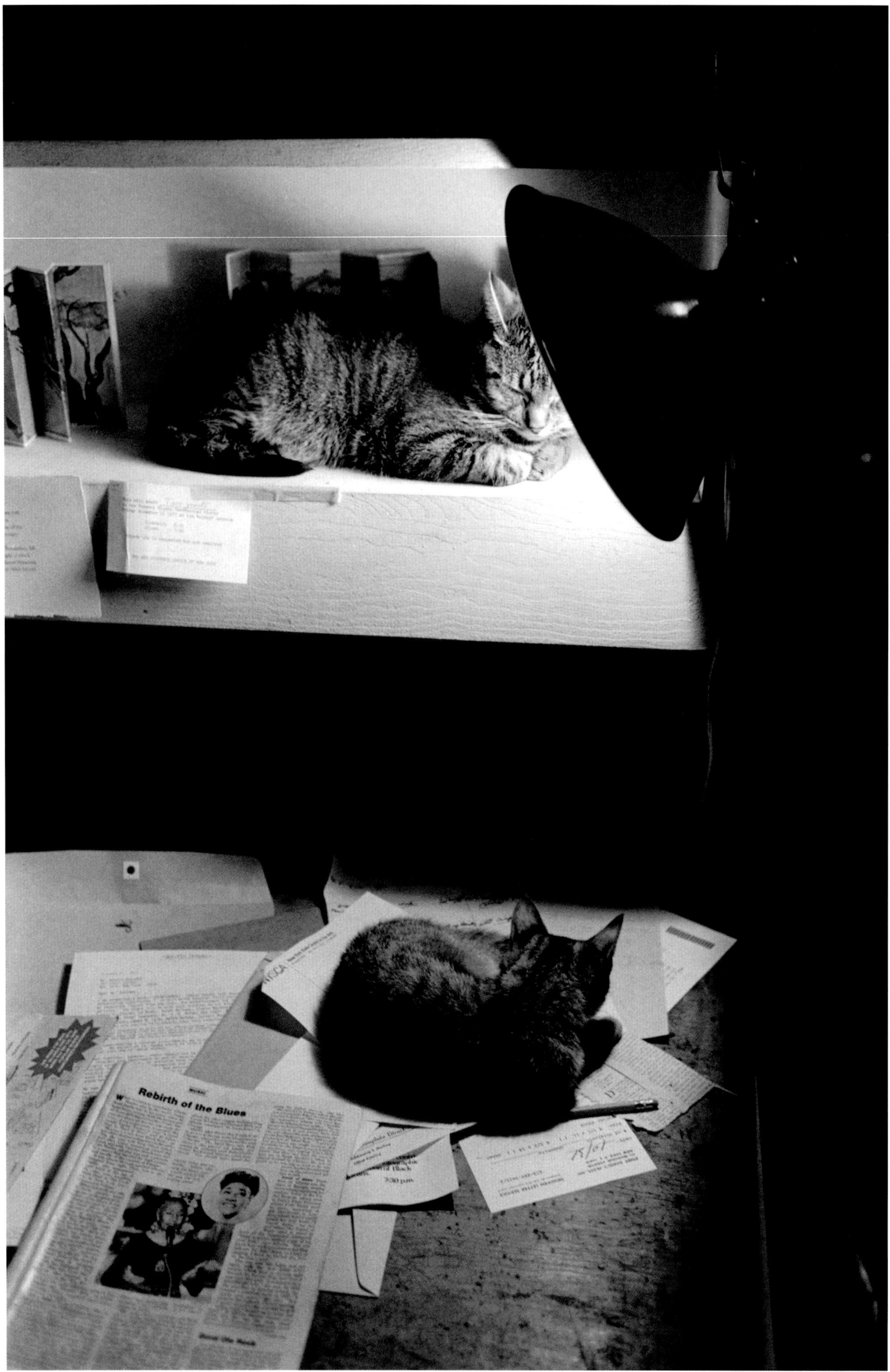
Rebirth of the Blues

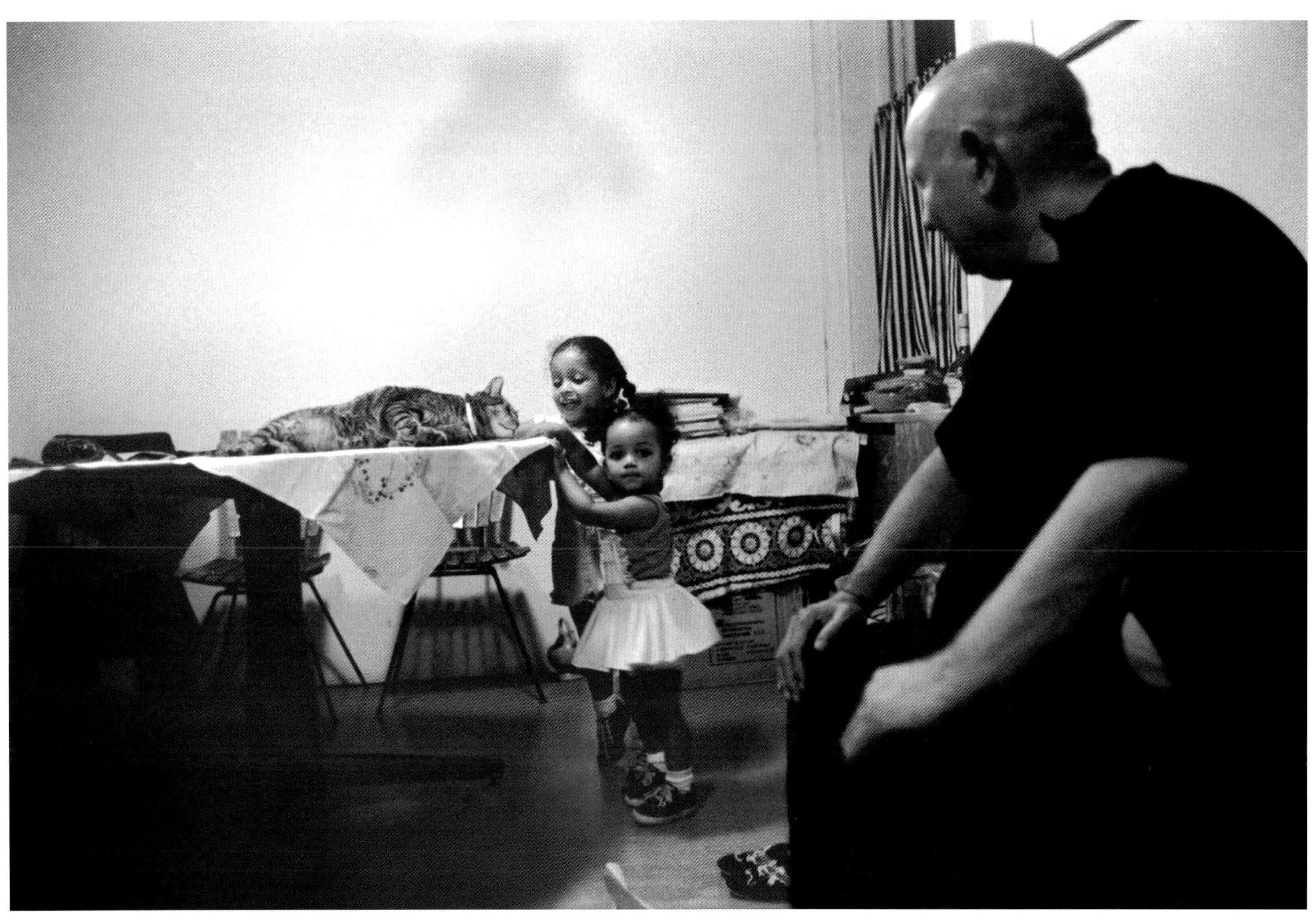

These are my daughters, Sing and Bining Stewart, with King Tut and Romie. Romie would tell me that cats could see spirits: "Have you ever watched a cat and all of a sudden it stops, and it turns its head, and it's looking around the room? It's seeing a ghost." 1983

FACING PAGE
King Tut (top) and Michelangelo. The cats had the run of the house. They were on everything. Romie said North American tabby cats were artists' cats because the lofts in New York were very cold, and tabbies were the only cats that wouldn't catch pneumonia. 1979

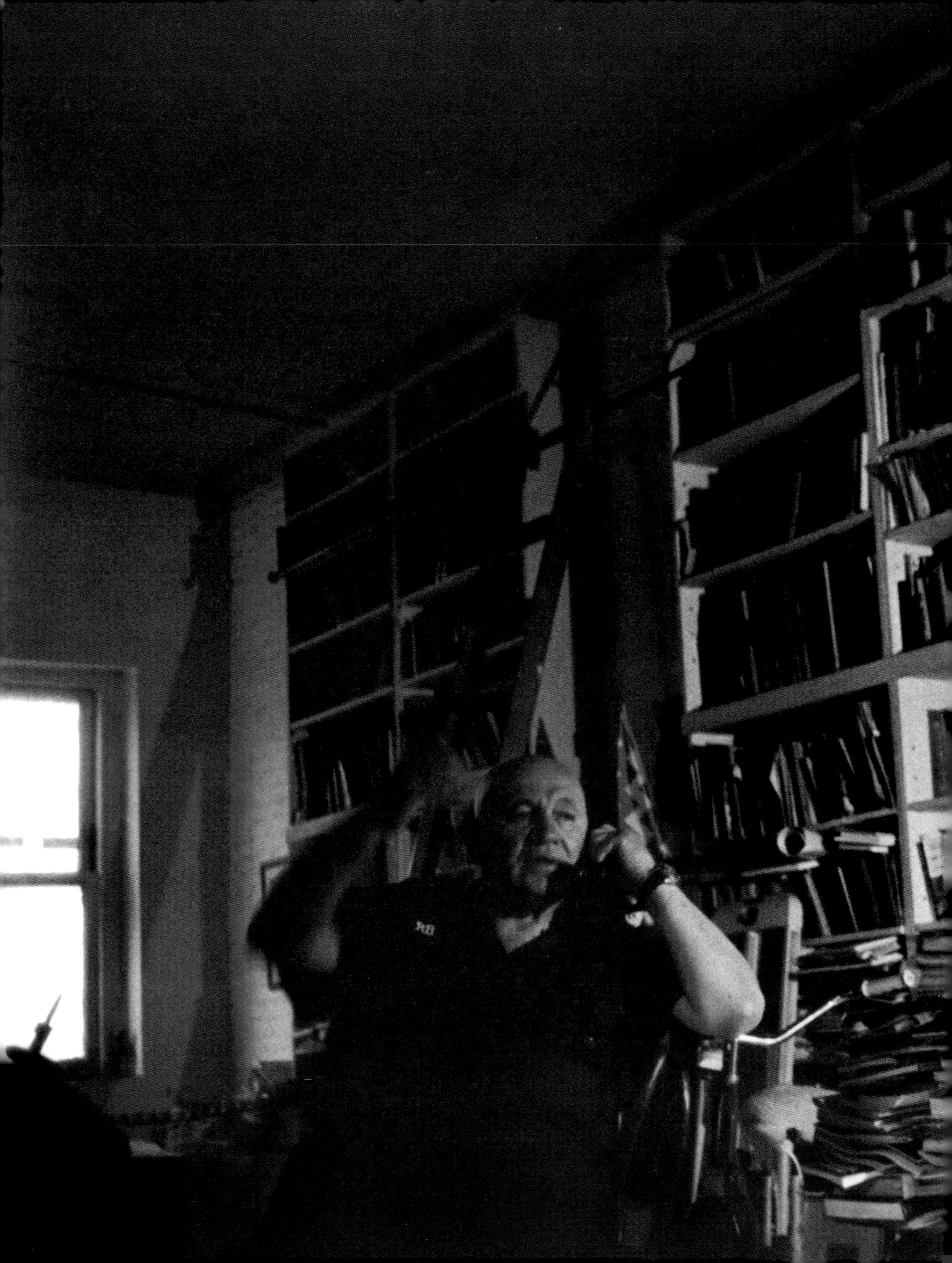

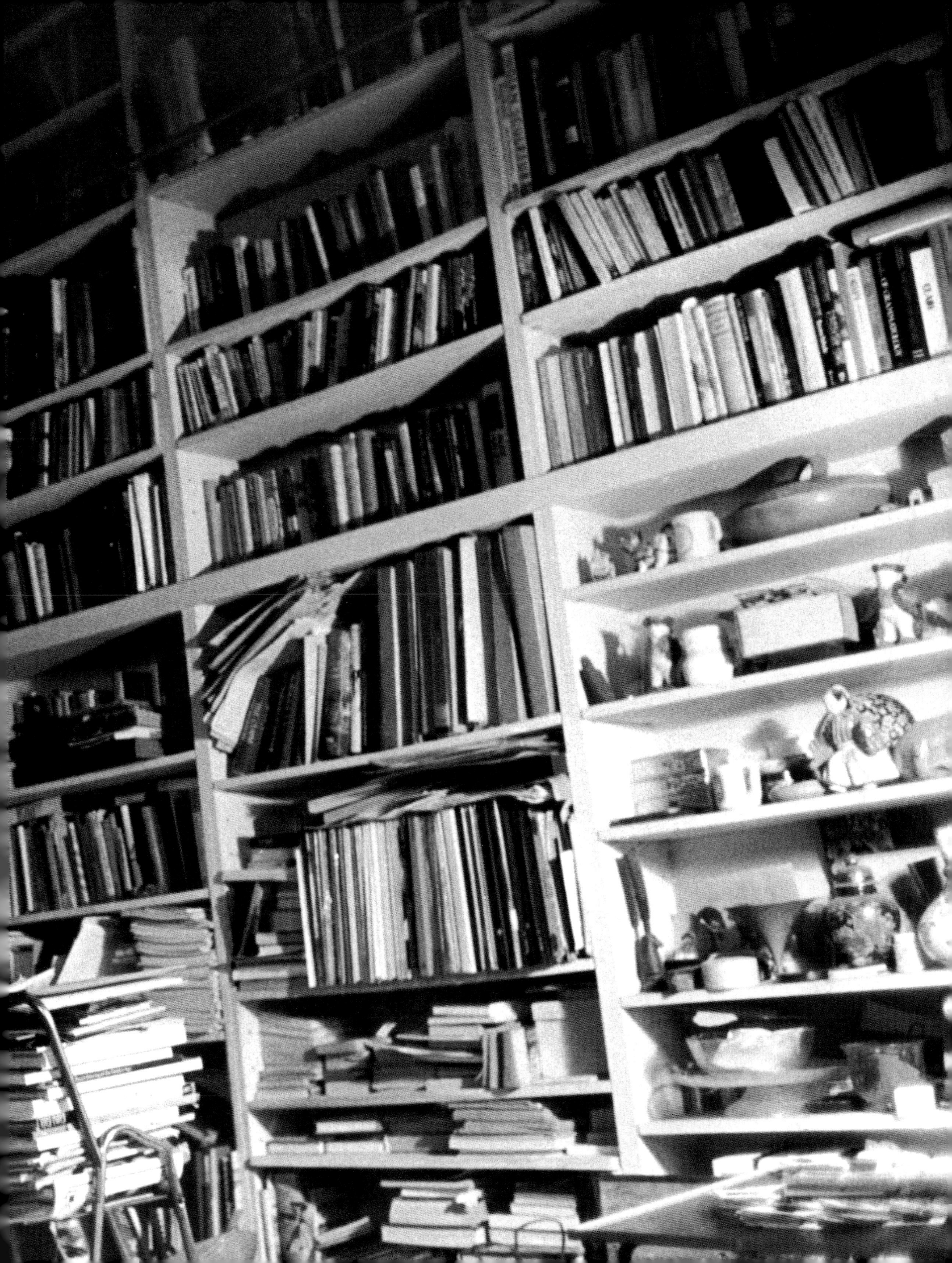

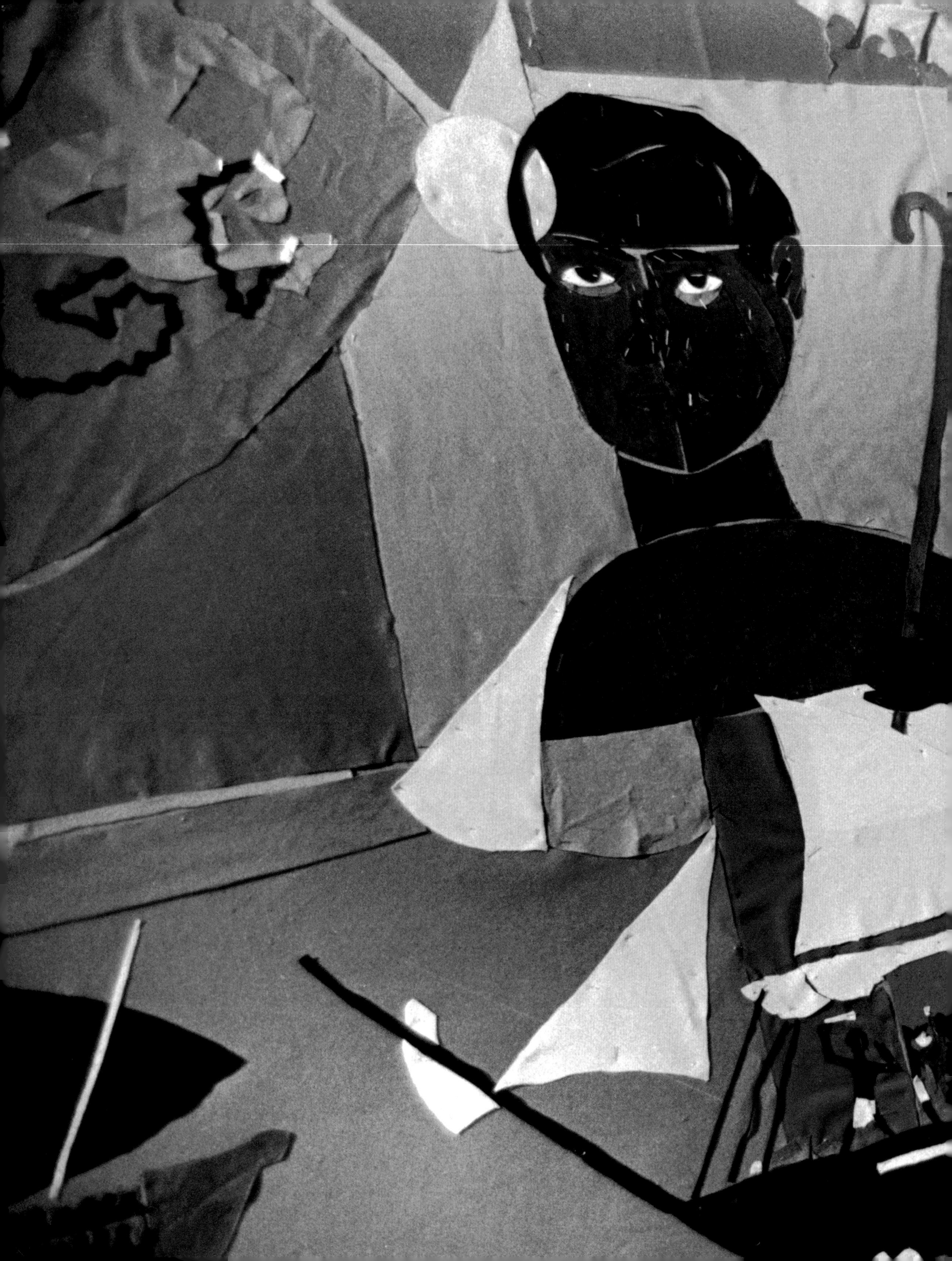

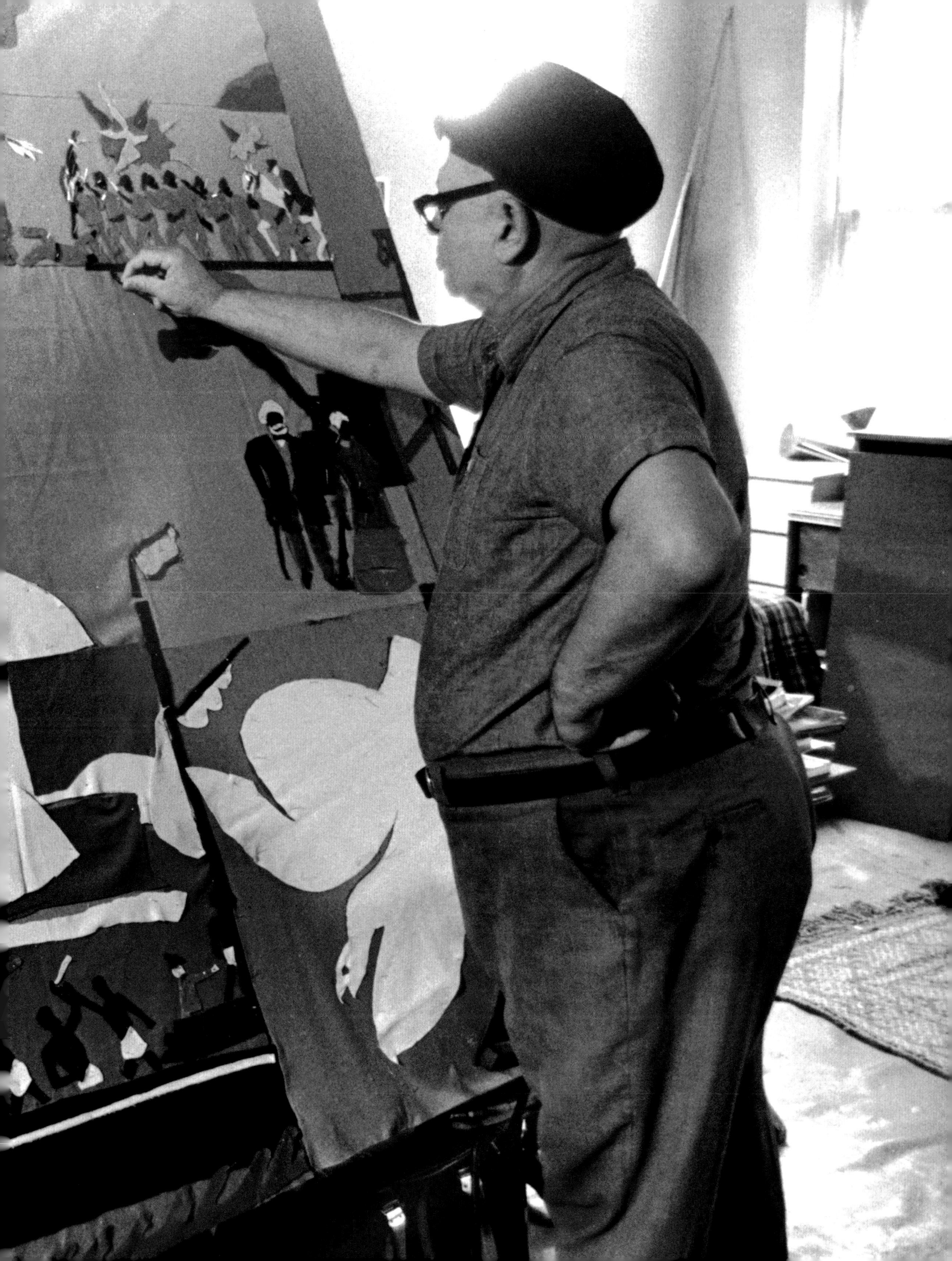

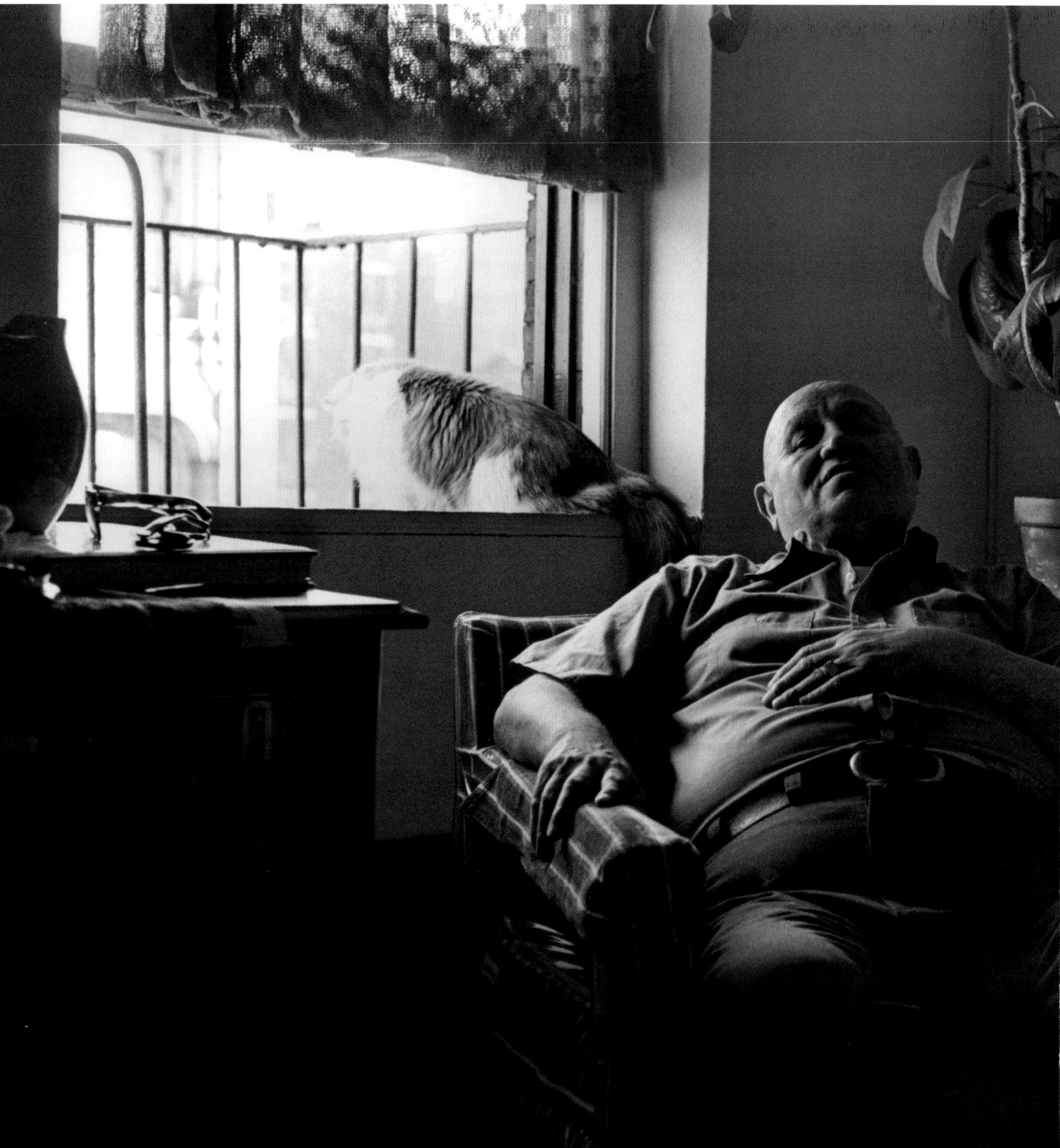

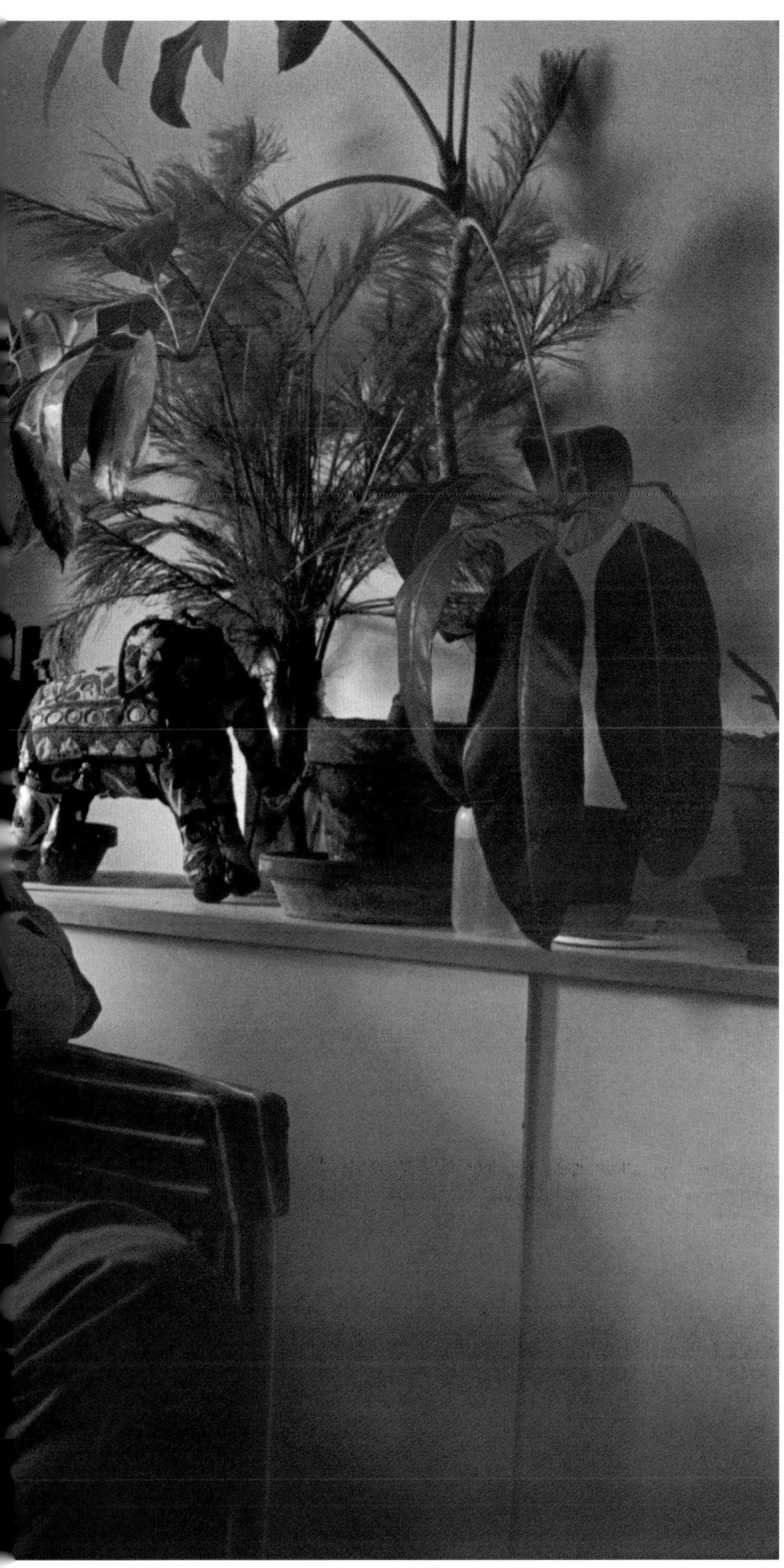

Count Rustikoff's on the windowsill. Romie's probably taking the role of someone else here. He was a great mimic. His whole face would go from one expression to the next. He'd get the voice, all the mannerisms. 1975

PRECEDING PAGES
Romie was a voracious reader. He read all the time, so he was up on everything. When he was young they called him "schoolboy" because he went to college. 1978

Romie's working on *Captivity and Resistance*. He would cut the fabric, place it, and pin it down. Then he took the piece somewhere for some woman to sew. It was a commission for the African American Museum in Philadelphia. 1975/76

LONG ISLAND CITY

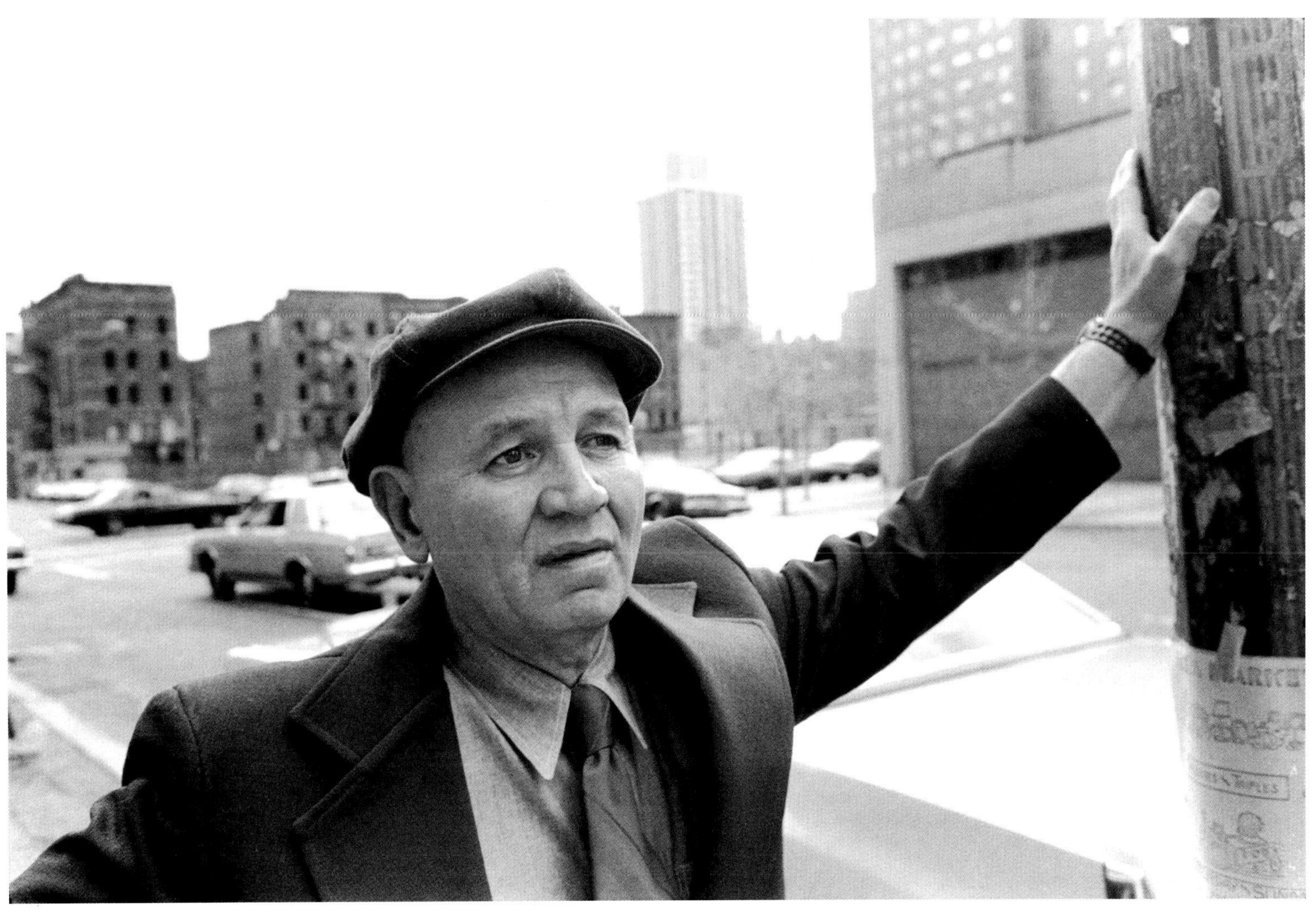

Romie's en route to his Long Island City studio. 1984

OVERLEAF
When Romie took the subway to the studio he would walk over to Broadway and catch the 4 or the 5 to Times Square and catch the 7 out to Long Island City. When he got there he would look back and see this landscape, the skyline of New York City. 1976/77

FOLLOWING PAGES
Henry and Rosa Kennedy, Romie's great-grandparents from Charlotte, North Carolina, are in the photograph that always hung on his studio wall. 1980

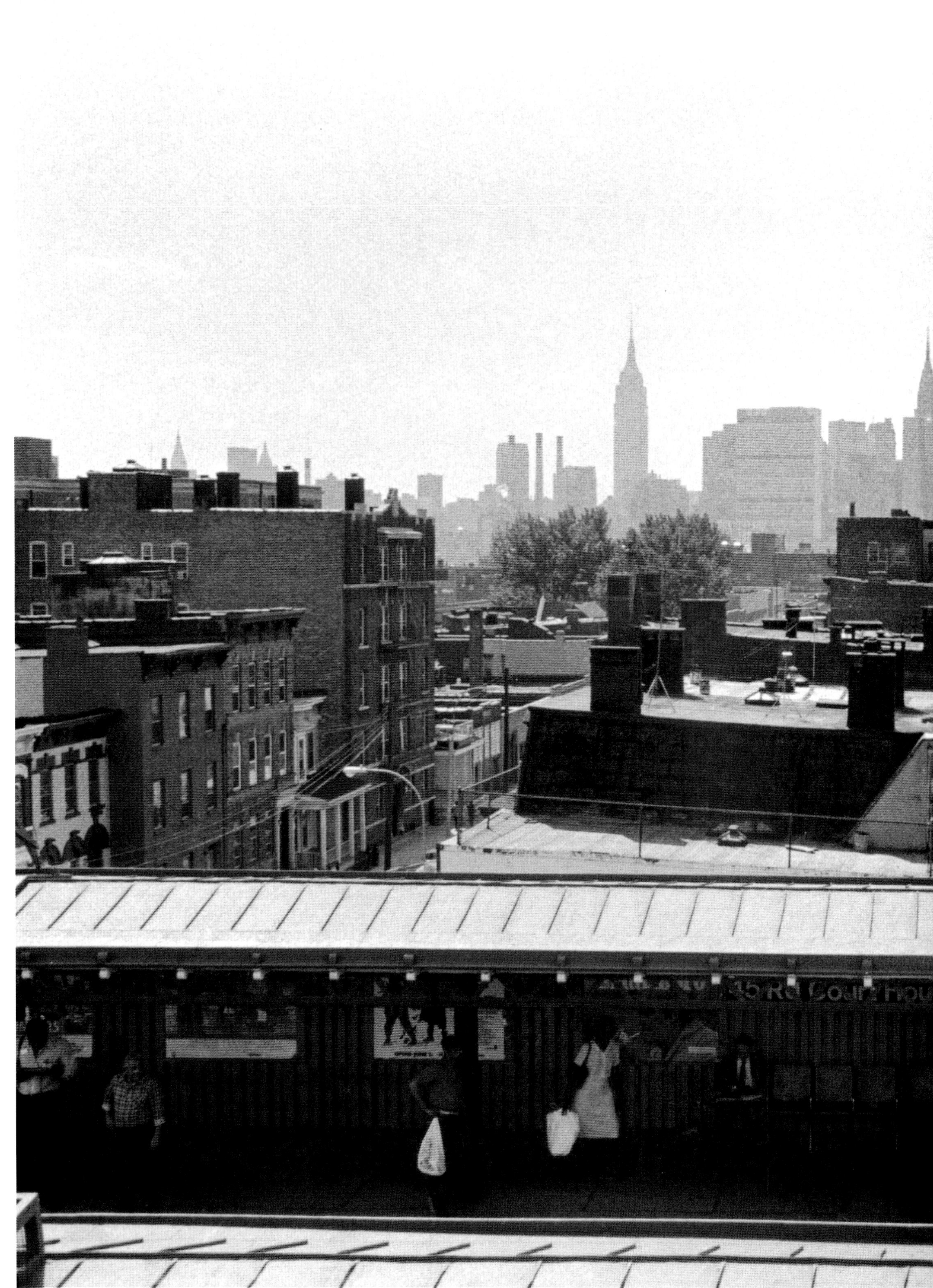

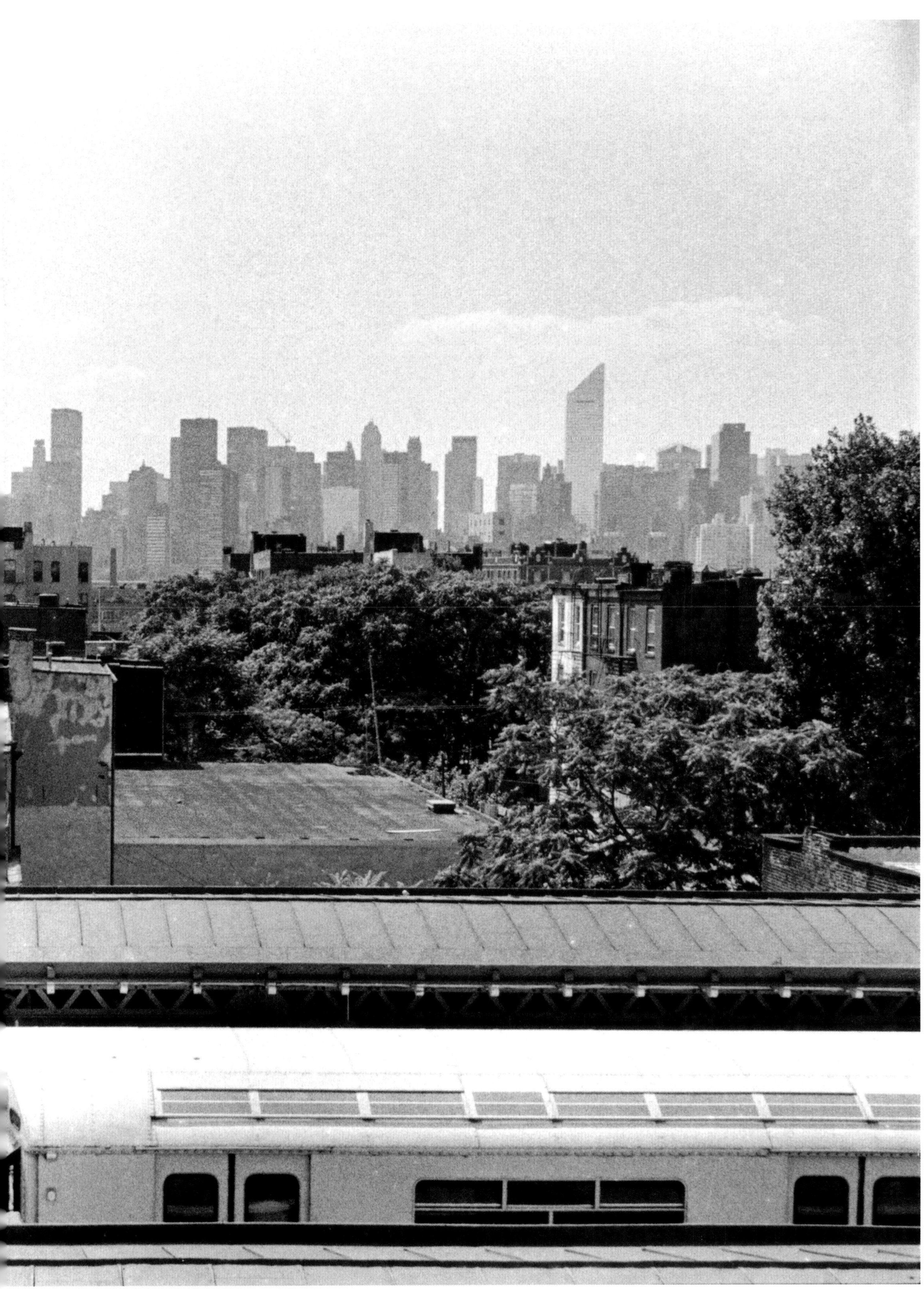

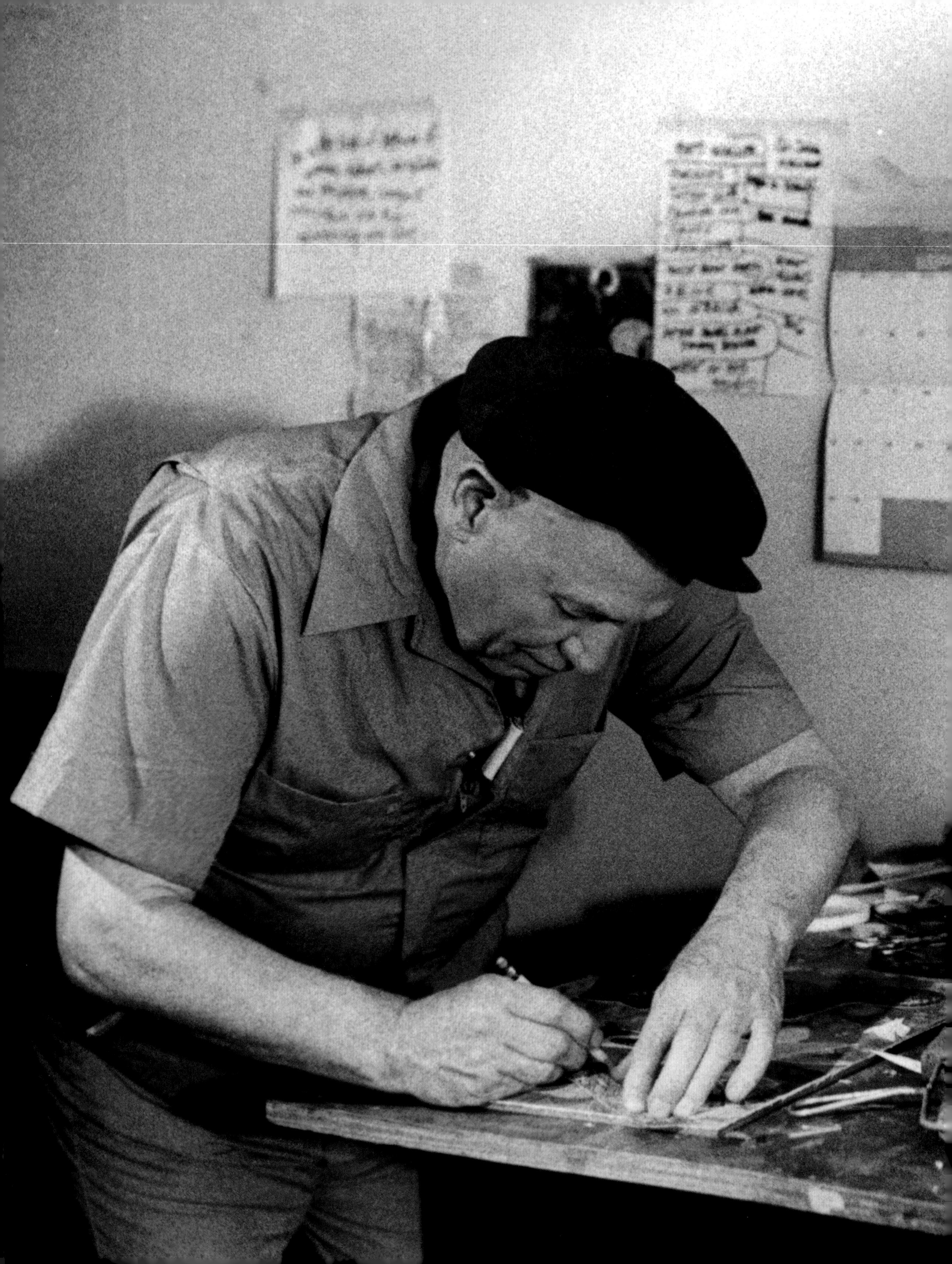

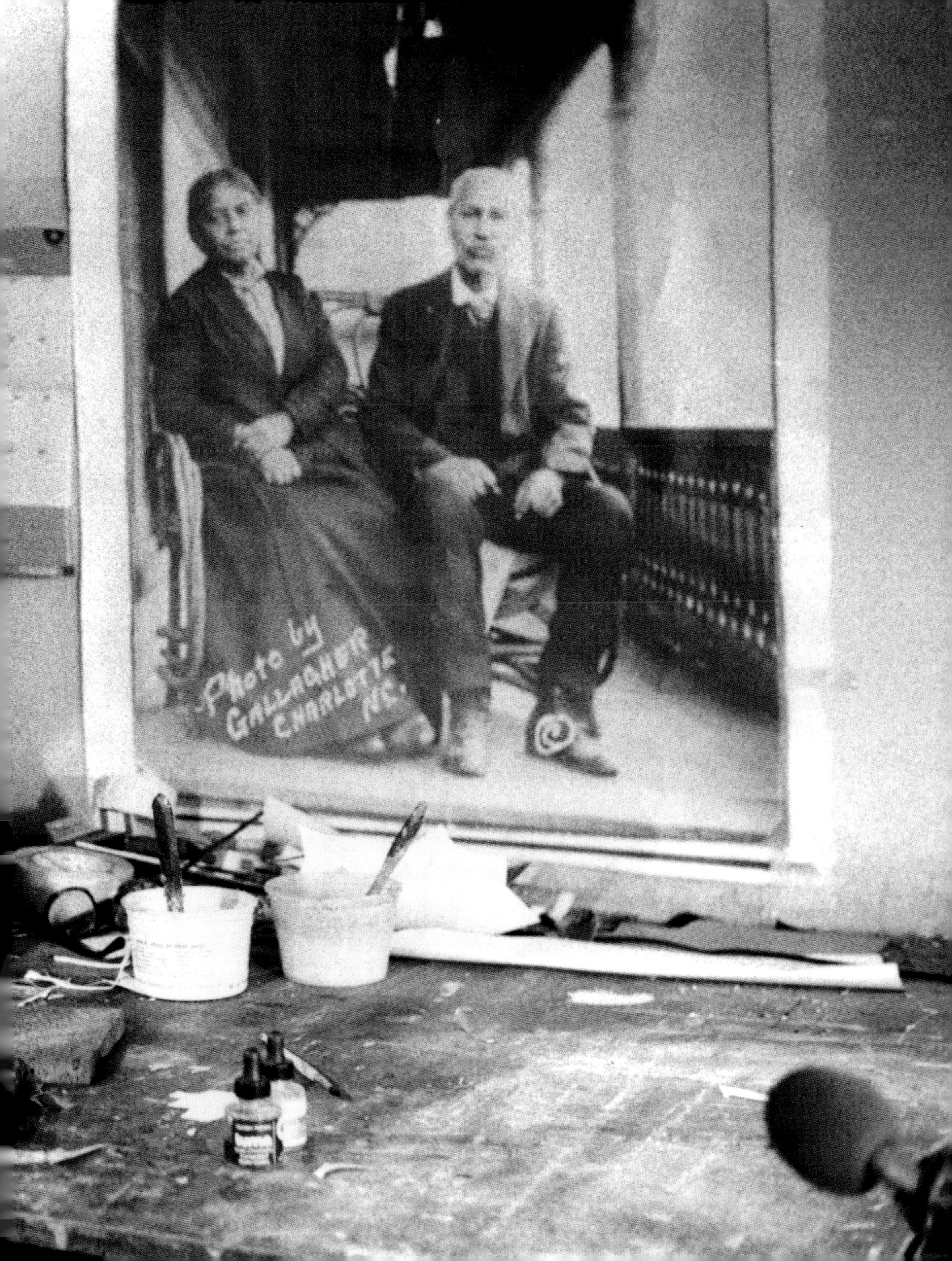
Photo by
GALLAGHER
CHARLOTTE
NC.

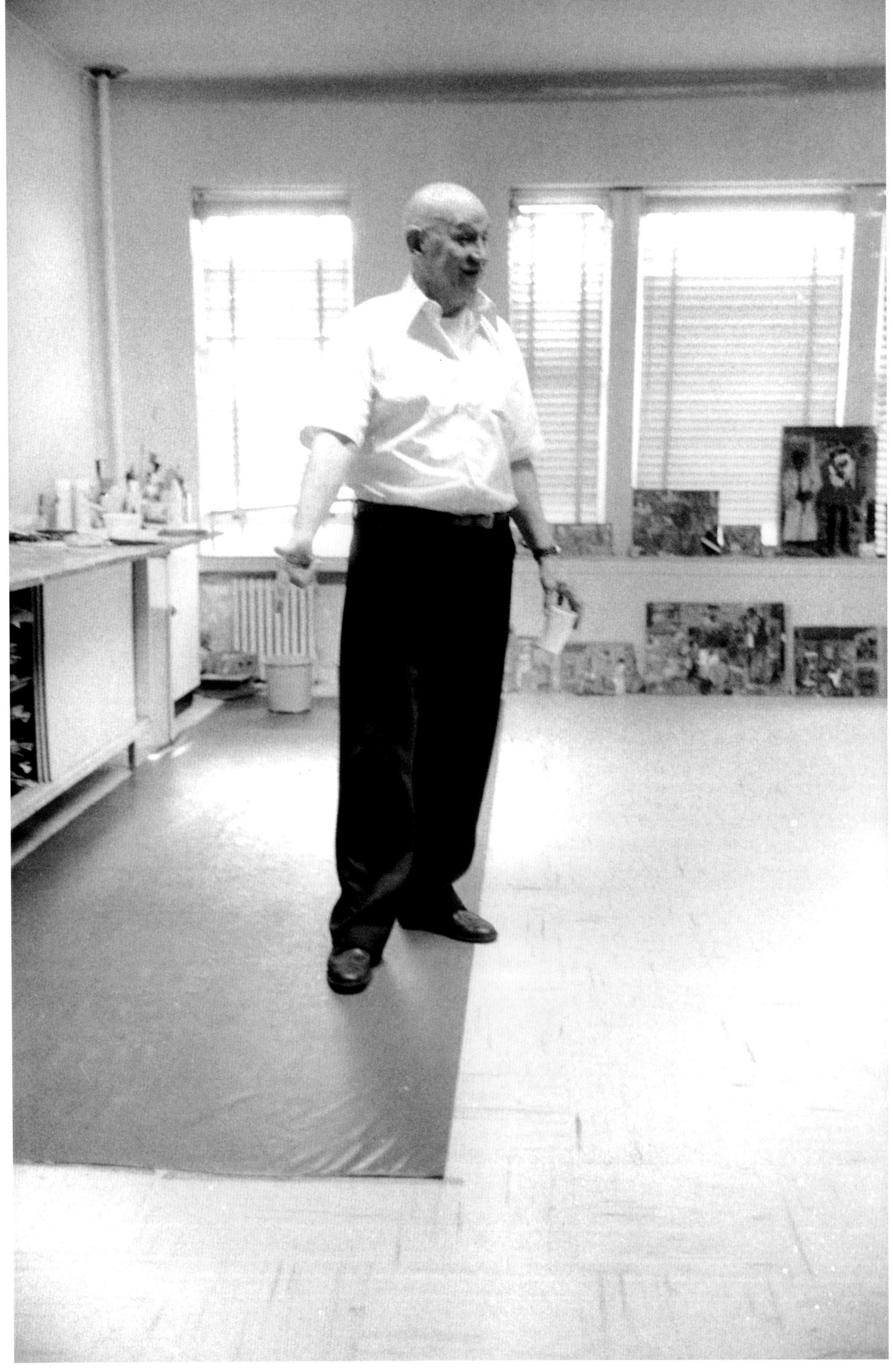

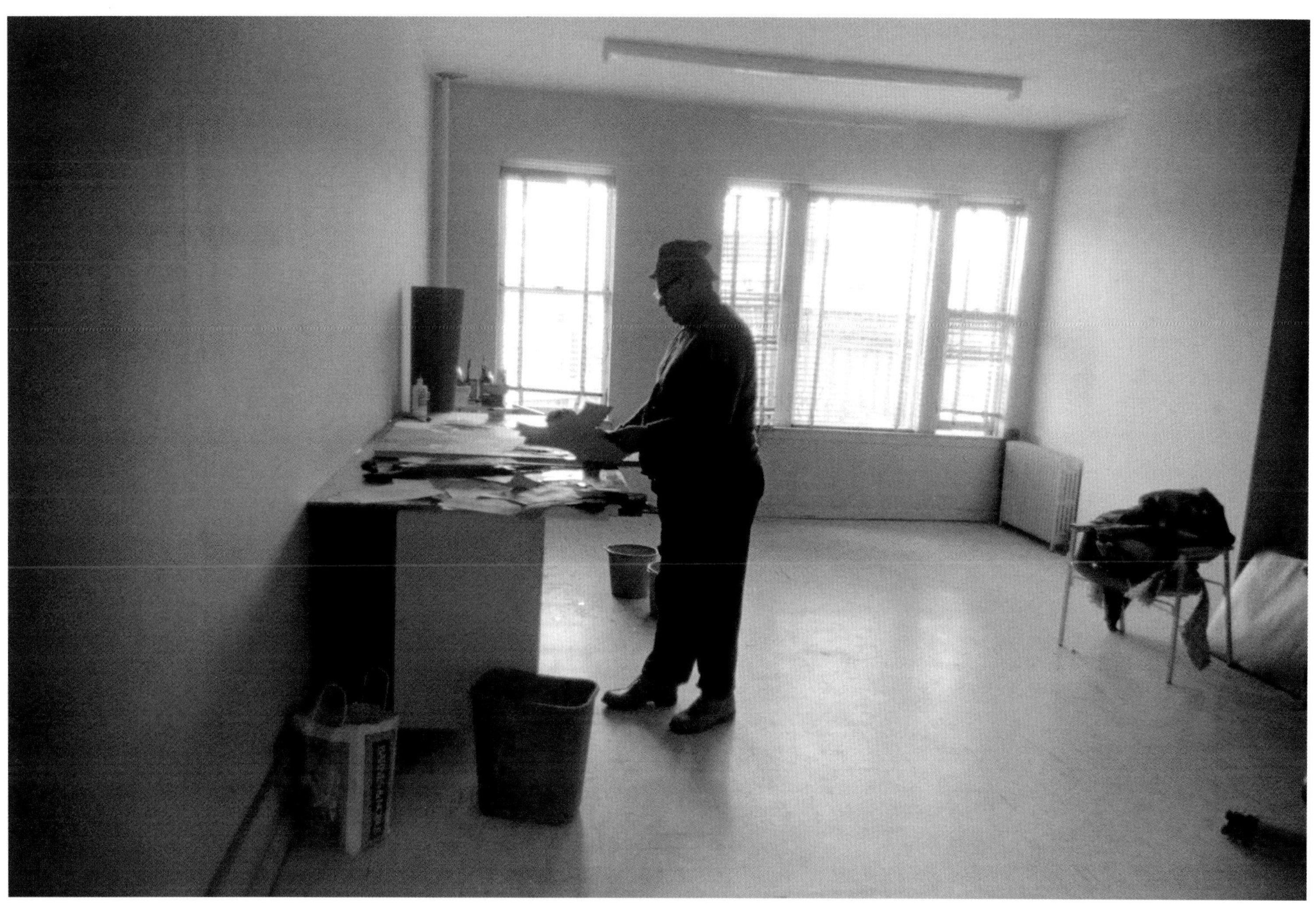

Romie worked in his studio just like it was a job. He'd take the subway out to Long Island City, do some work. Then he'd take his hour off for lunch. Sometimes he would have a lunch pail, just like he was working construction or something. He'd come back and then do some more work. 1976

FACING PAGE
Romie would finish a show, and I'd go to the studio and he'd have all these pieces sitting around. I'd ask, "Why don't you get them framed?" He'd say, "Oh no, they have to wait for Albert Murray. Al has to come and title these. They can't leave here until Al titles them." 1979

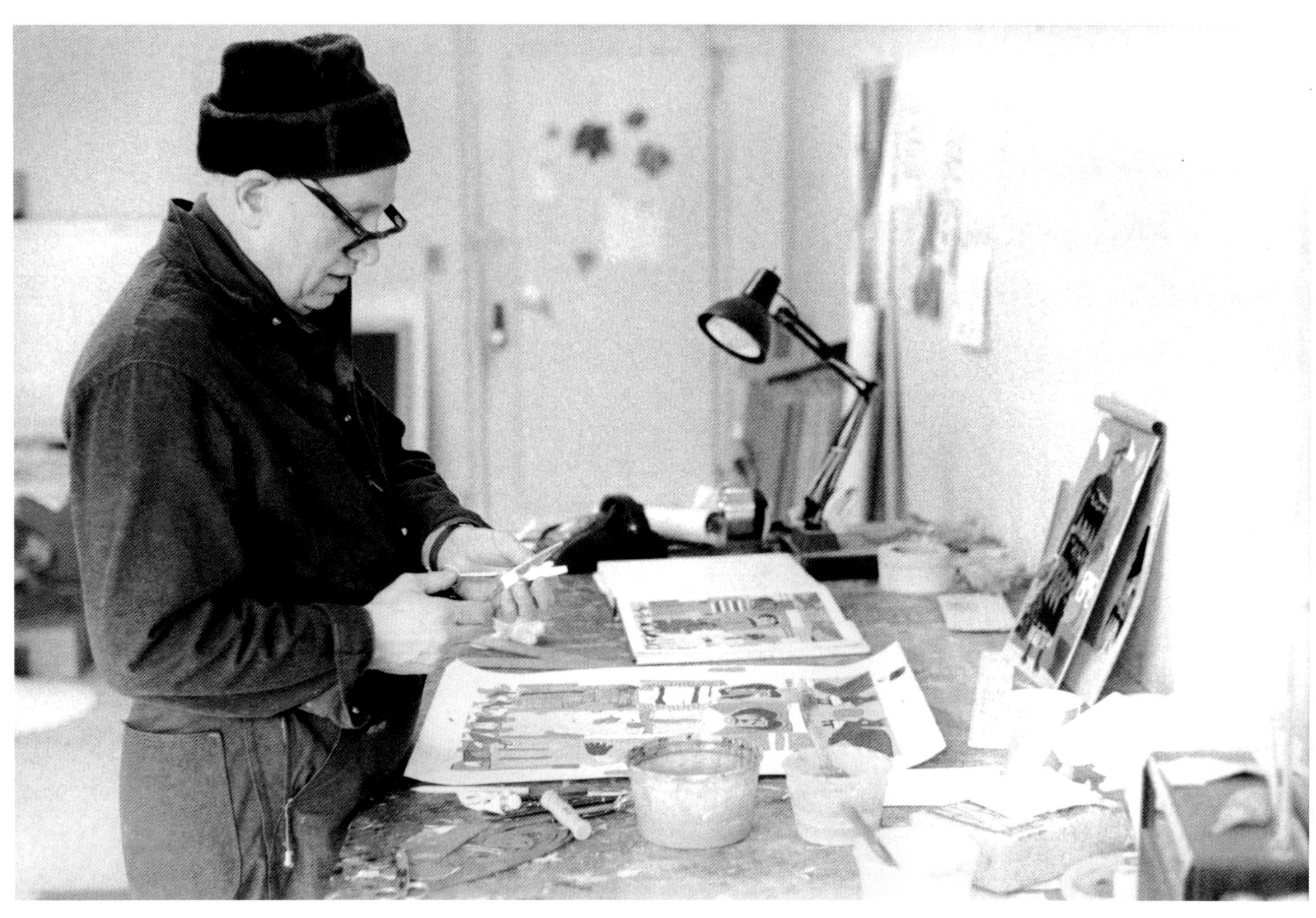

Romie didn't work on an easel; he worked flat. He was pasting down, so he needed that leverage. There was a logic to it, a necessity to it. Form follows function. Early 1980s

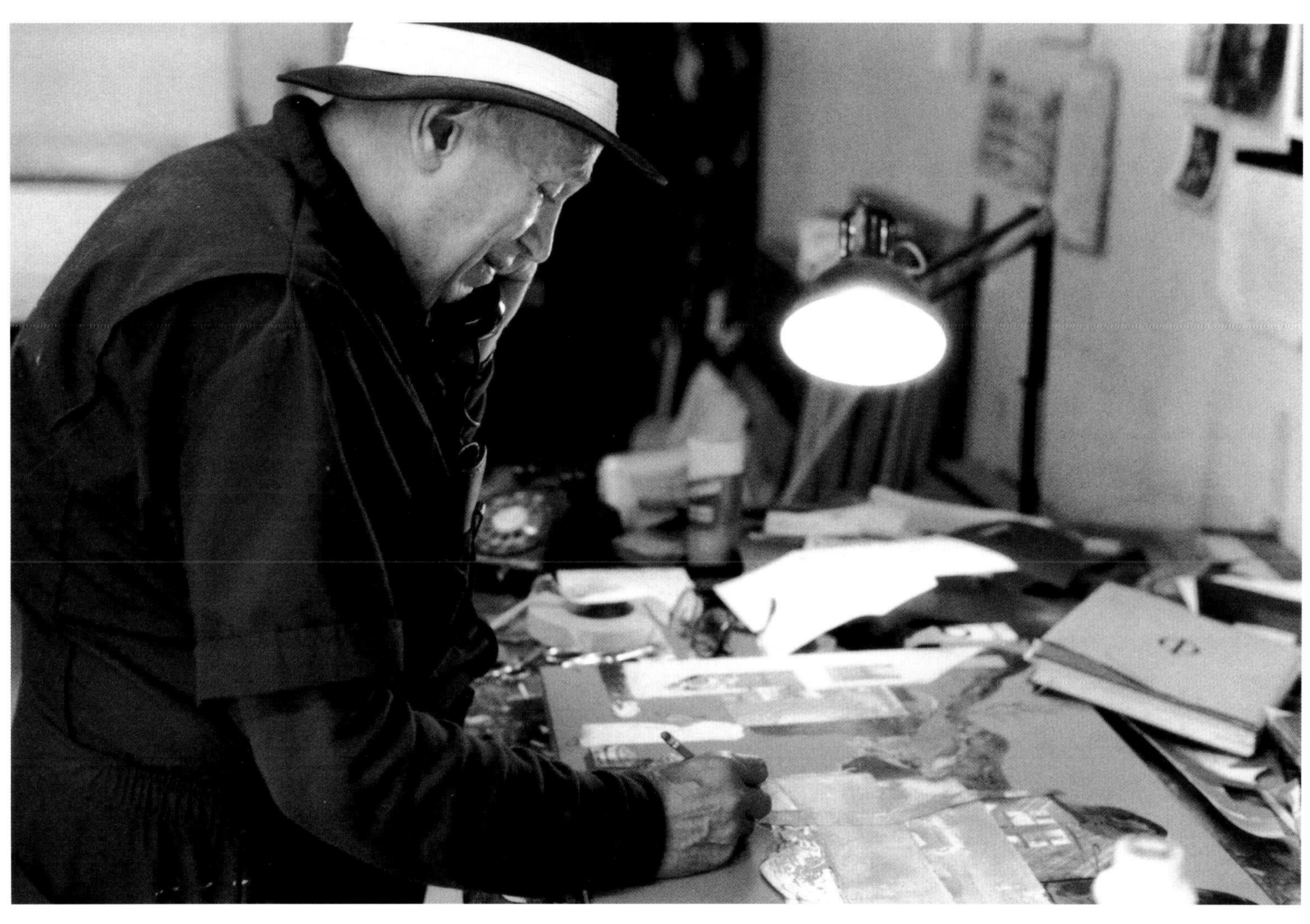

Romie loved the telephone. 1987

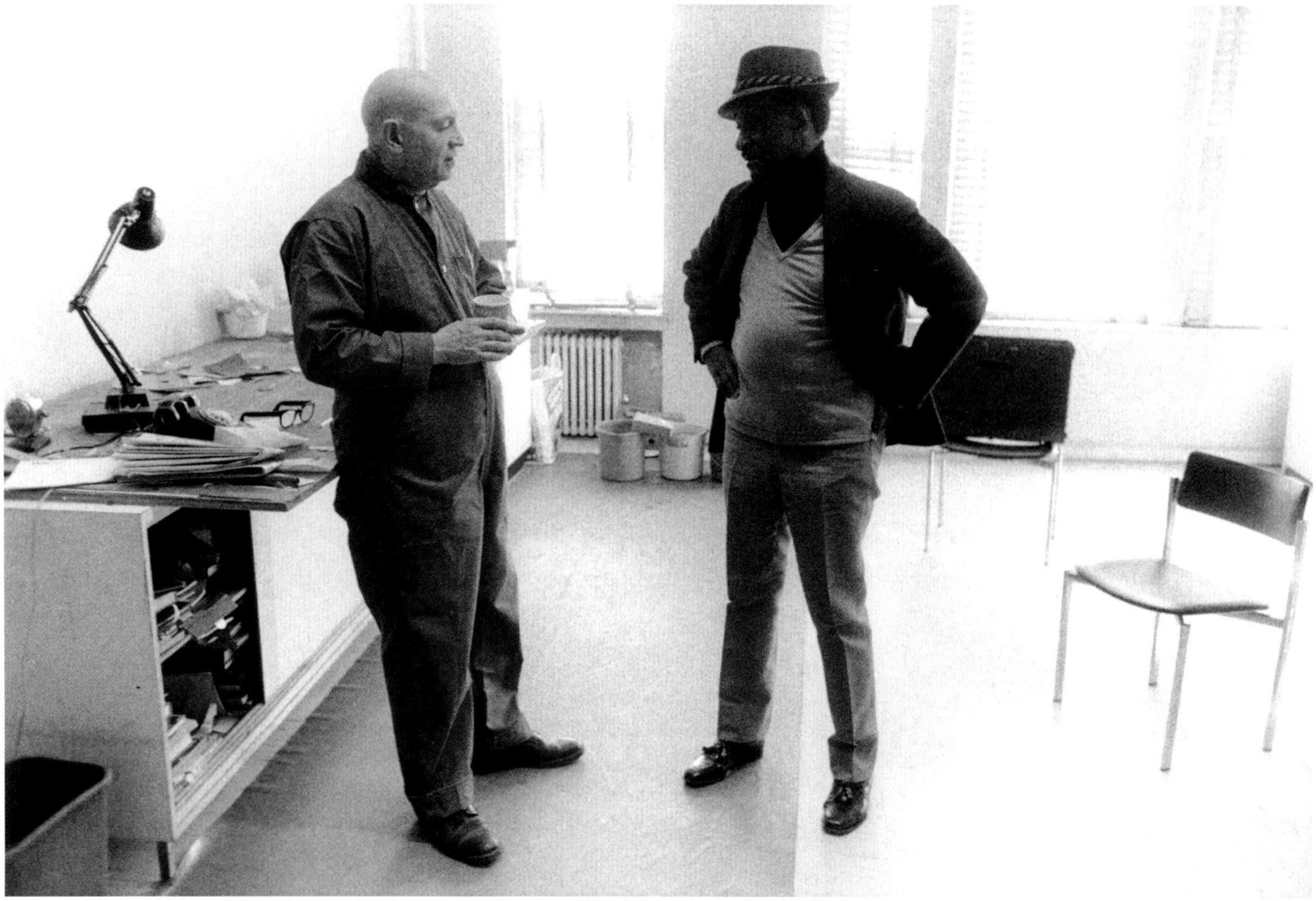

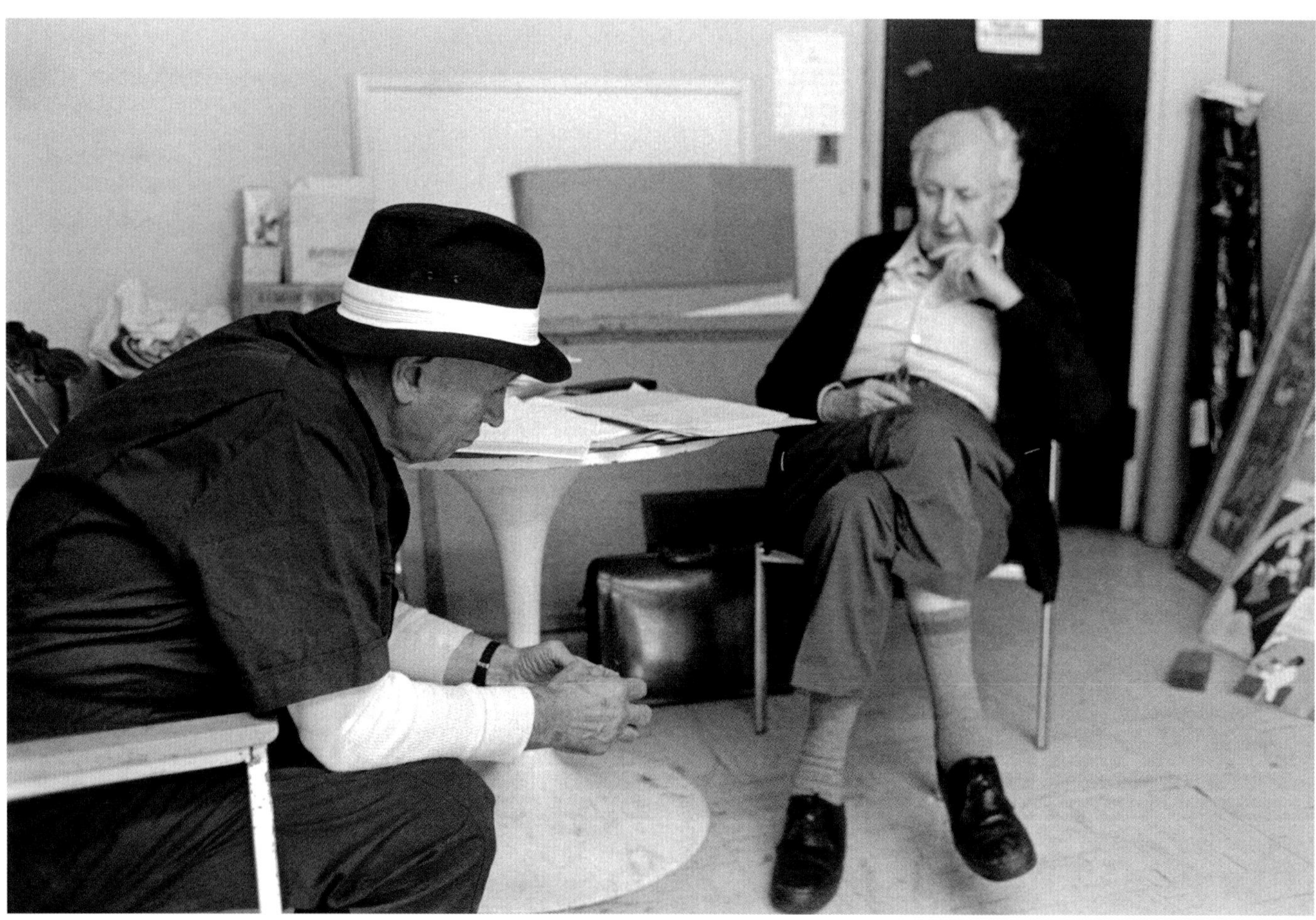

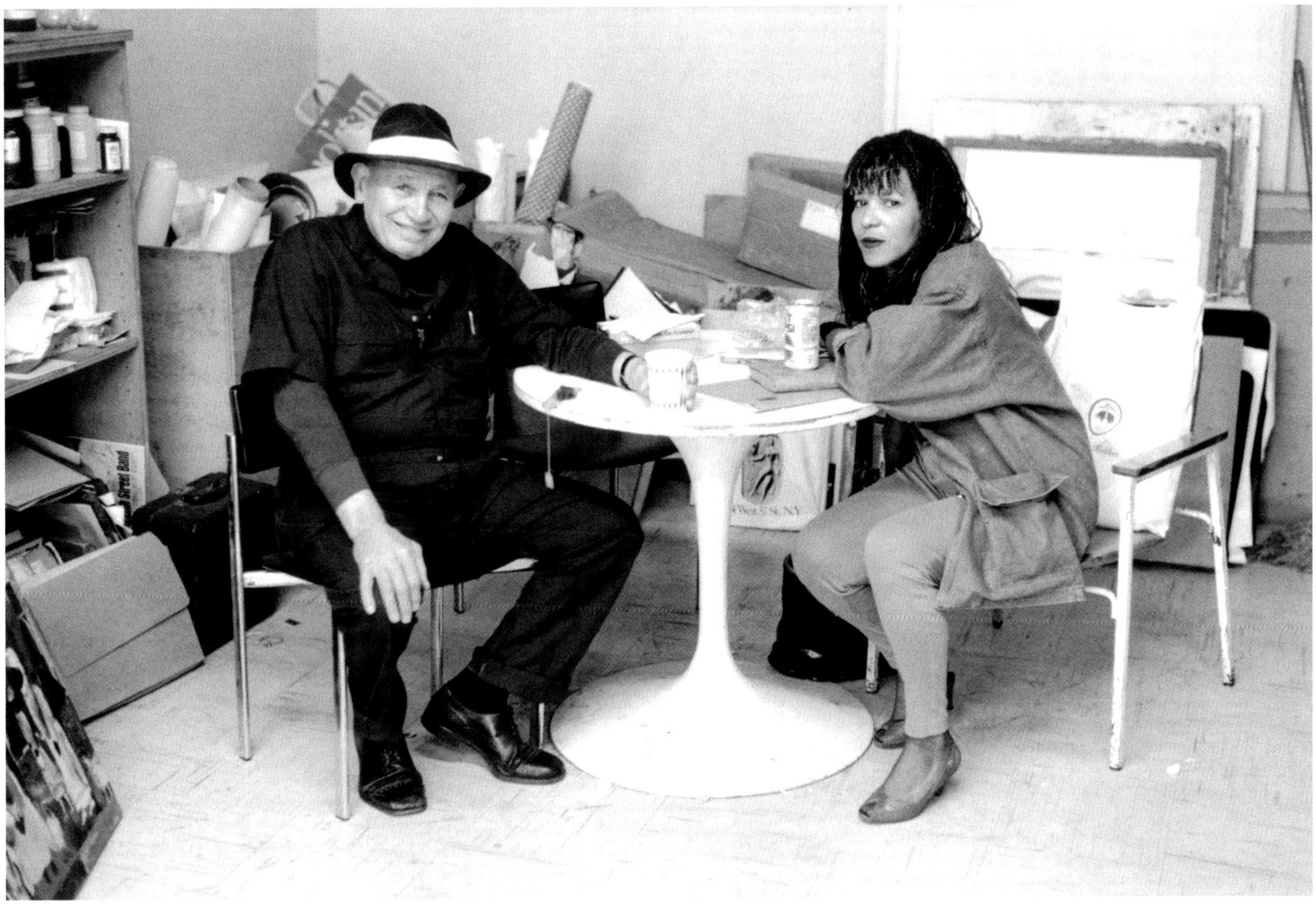

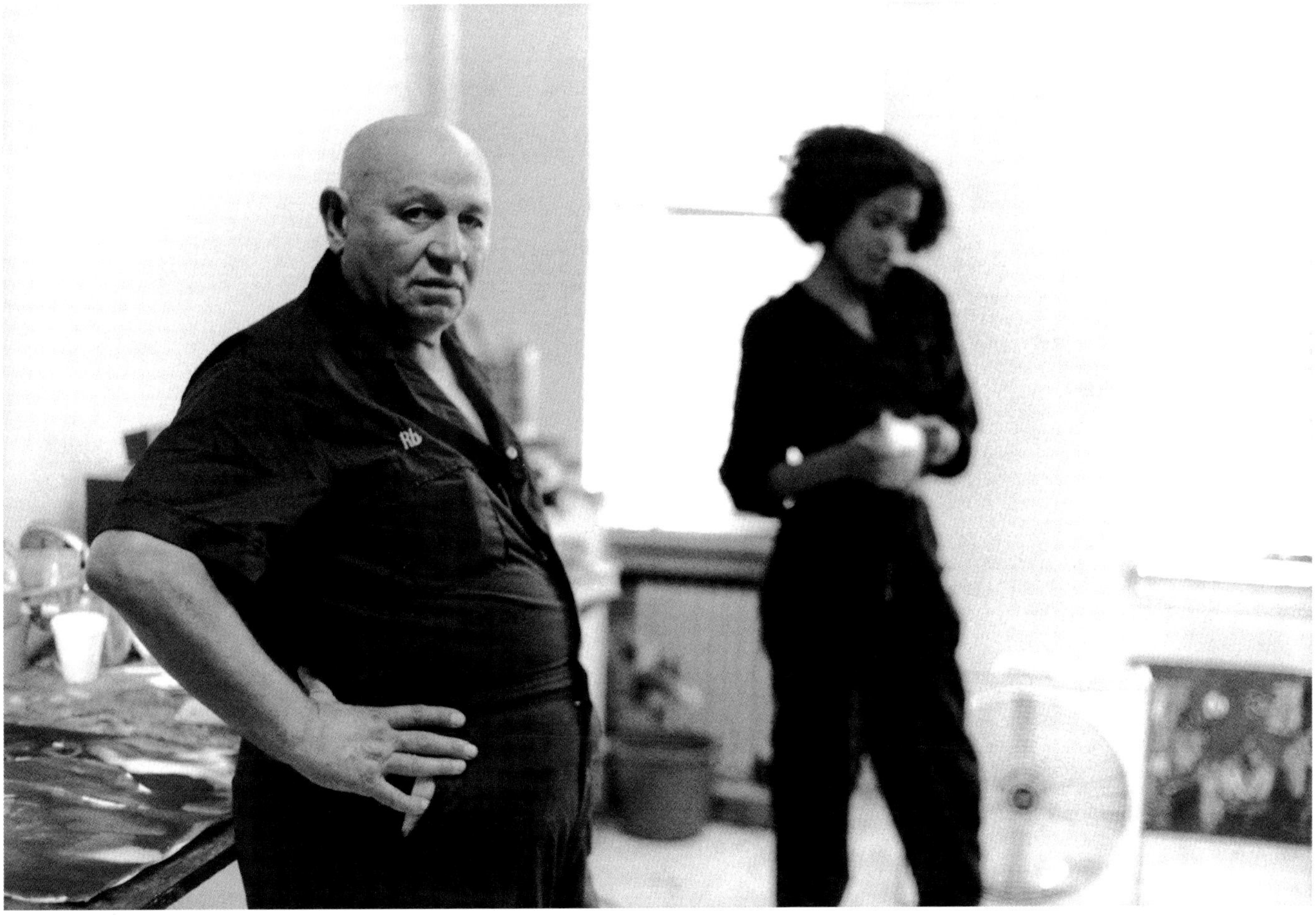

PRECEDING PAGE, TOP
Romie and Albert Murray. Al was from the South, too, and he would come up with these colorful titles, like *Prevalence of Ritual.* 1979

PRECEDING PAGE
I think Romie met Harry Henderson through Sam Shaw in the forties. Harry was a writer, and Sam was a photographer. Romie and Harry worked years on their book, *A History of African-American Artists: From 1792 to the Present.* Harry would be the one digging up the information. Then he would come with his findings so Romie could bring his expertise to the matter. 1987

PRECEDING PAGE, TOP
Ntozake Shange and Romie always talked about doing a book together. It didn't happen until after he died, when *I Live in Music* was published. 1987

PRECEDING PAGE
Romie told me that he did only about two or three hours of real work a day. The rest of the time somebody would come in, and he'd stop working and start engaging them, making up stories or something. Here he's with Halima Taha. 1984

FACING PAGE
Painter Herbert Gentry in Romie's studio. They met in Paris in 1950, and Gentry introduced Romie to a whole group of people there, so he had a real social life going. 1985

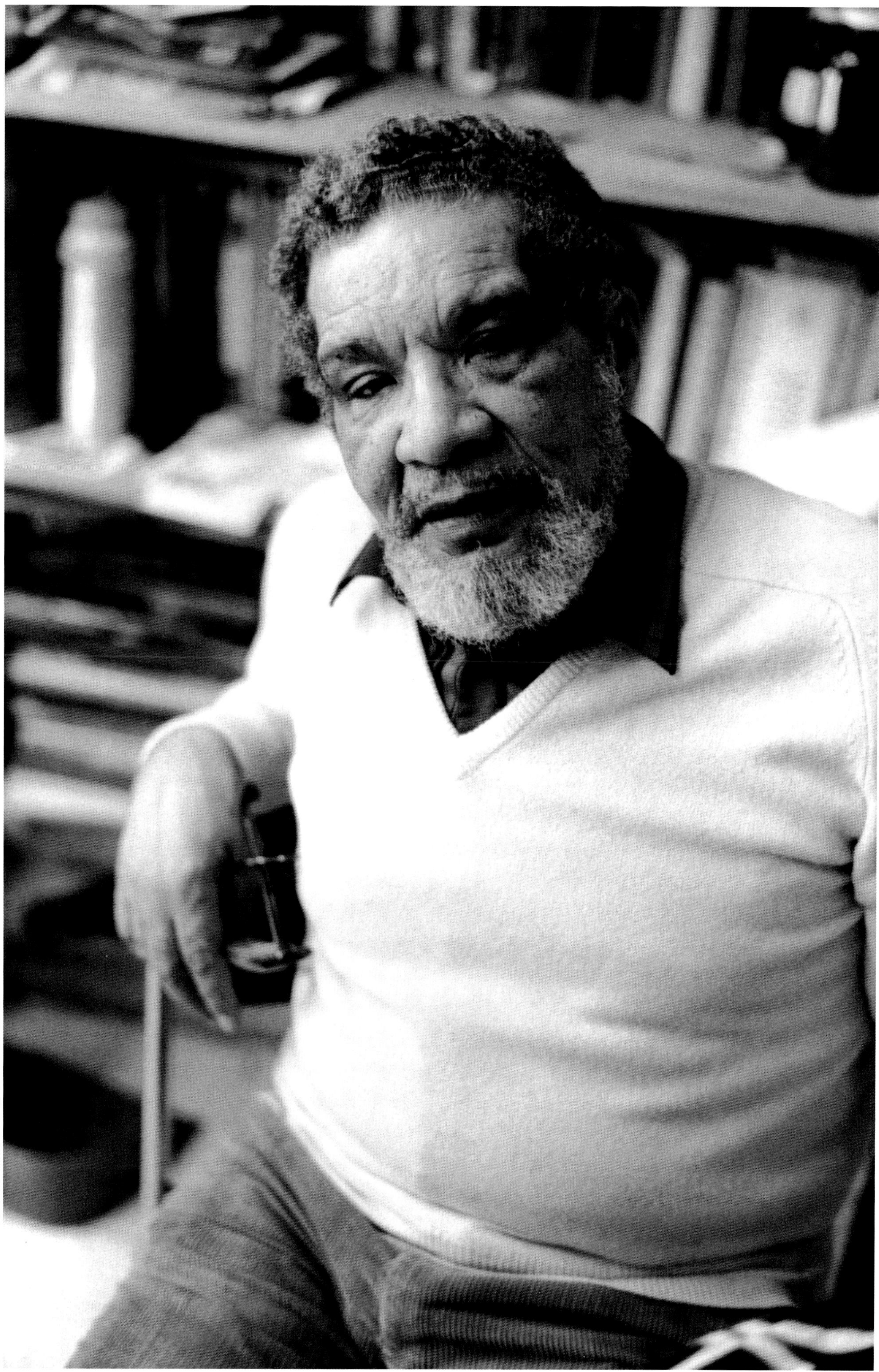

THE WORLD OF ART

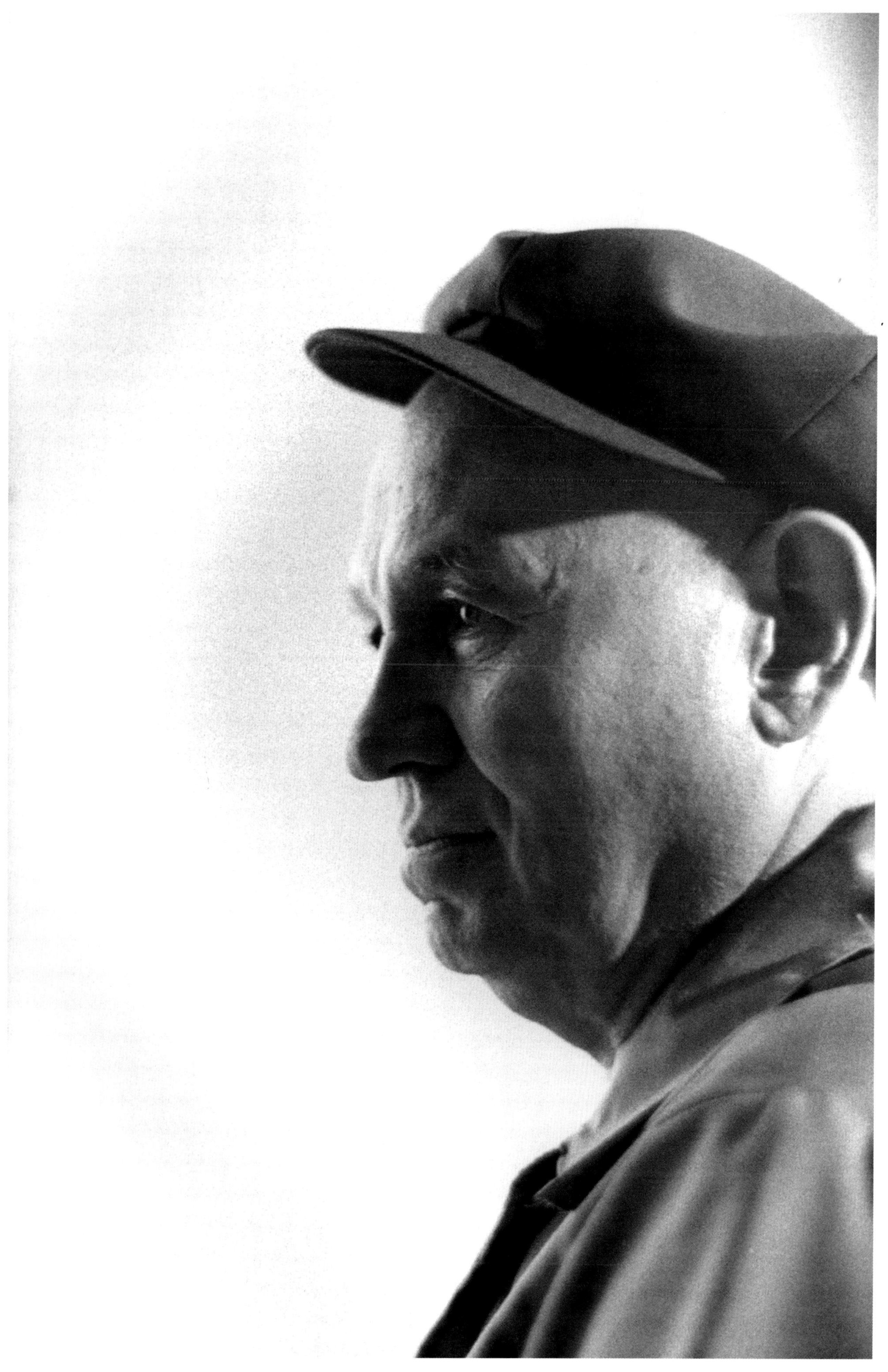

Romare Bearden. 1979

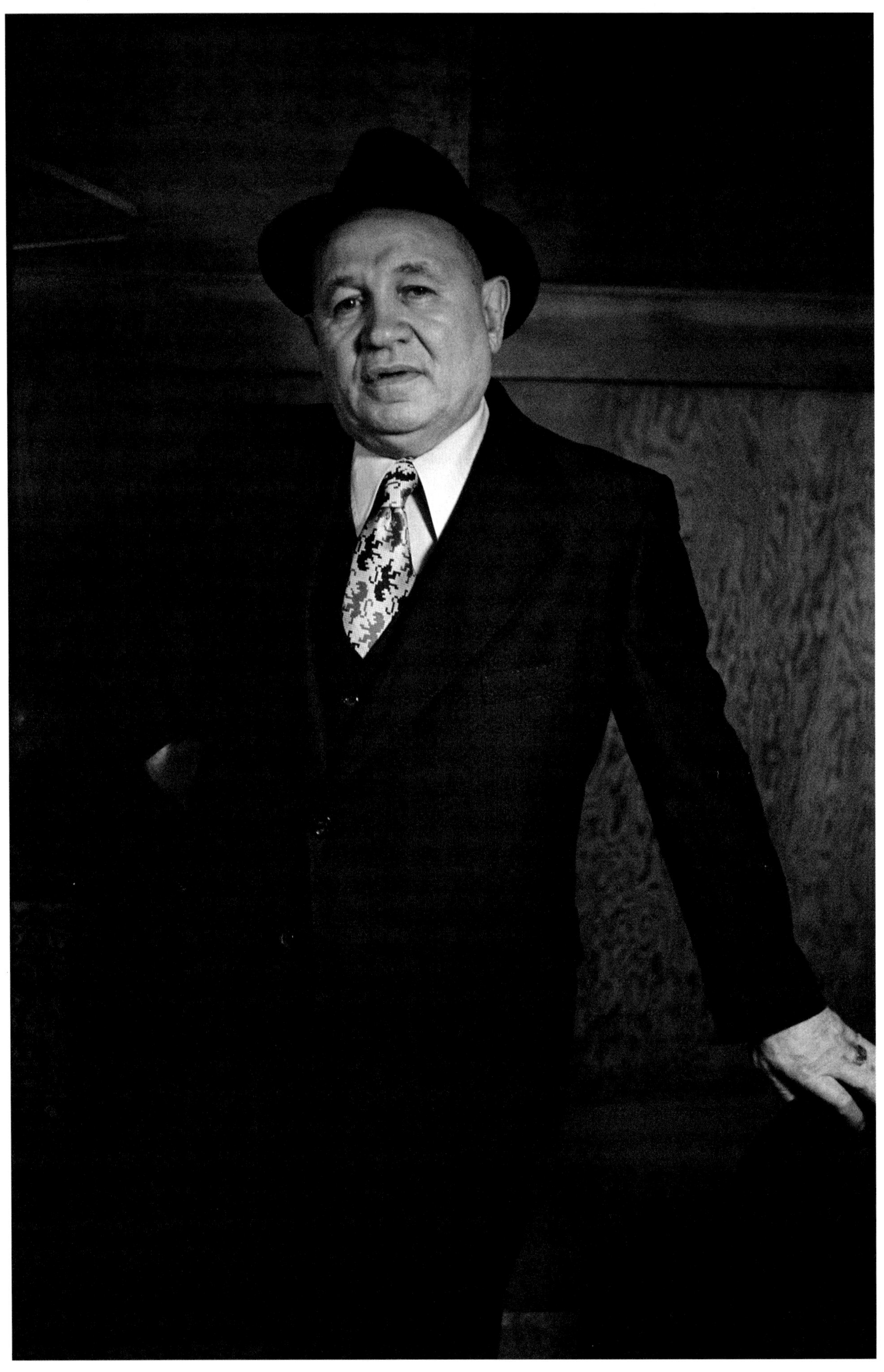

This was taken at the time of the "Romare Bearden: 1970–1980" exhibition, at the Mint Museum, Charlotte, North Carolina. 1980

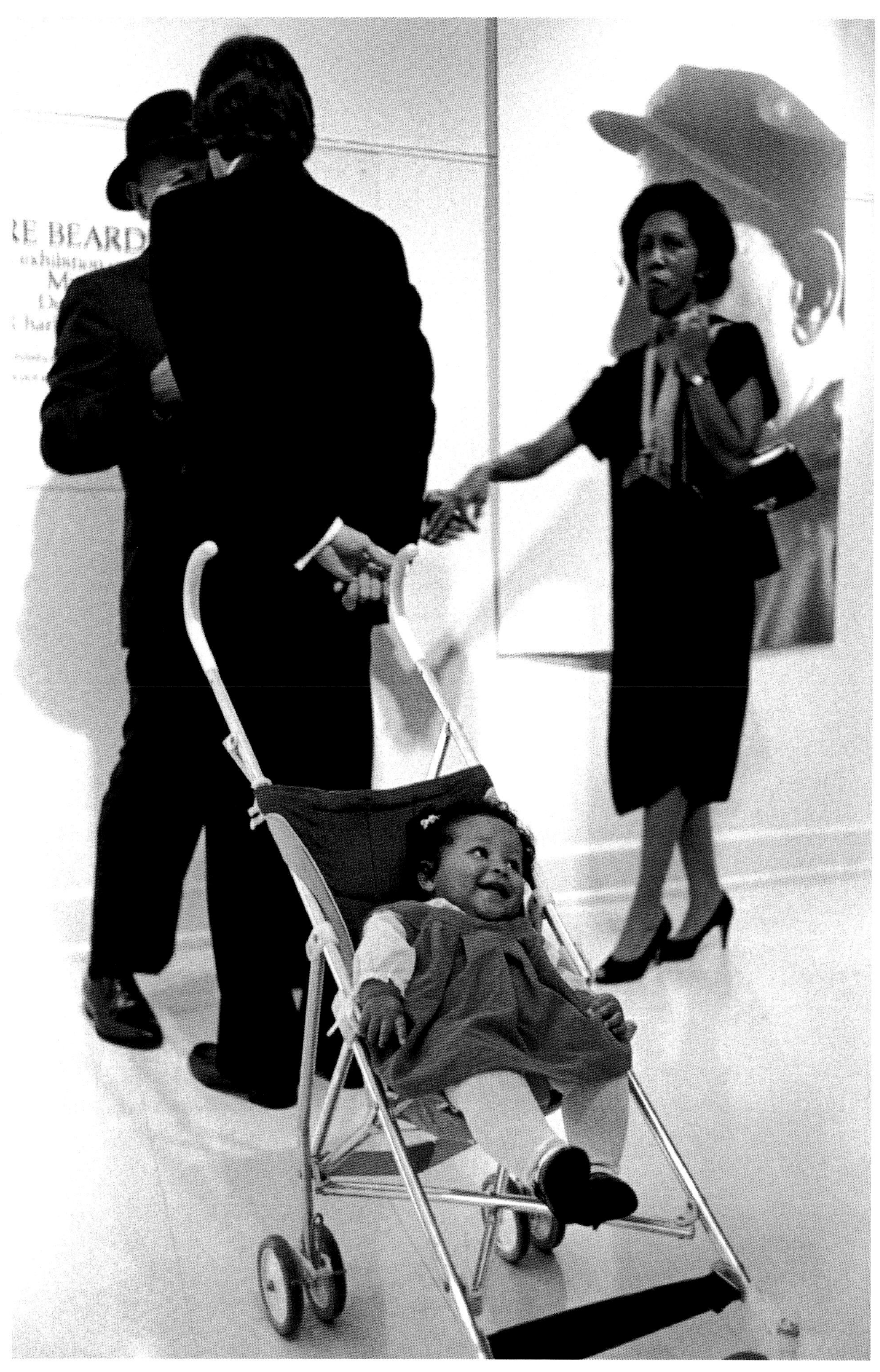

Romie's holding June Kelly's hand and talking with Nelsen Breen at the opening of his retrospective at the Mint Museum in Charlotte. The baby is my daughter Sing Stewart. 1980

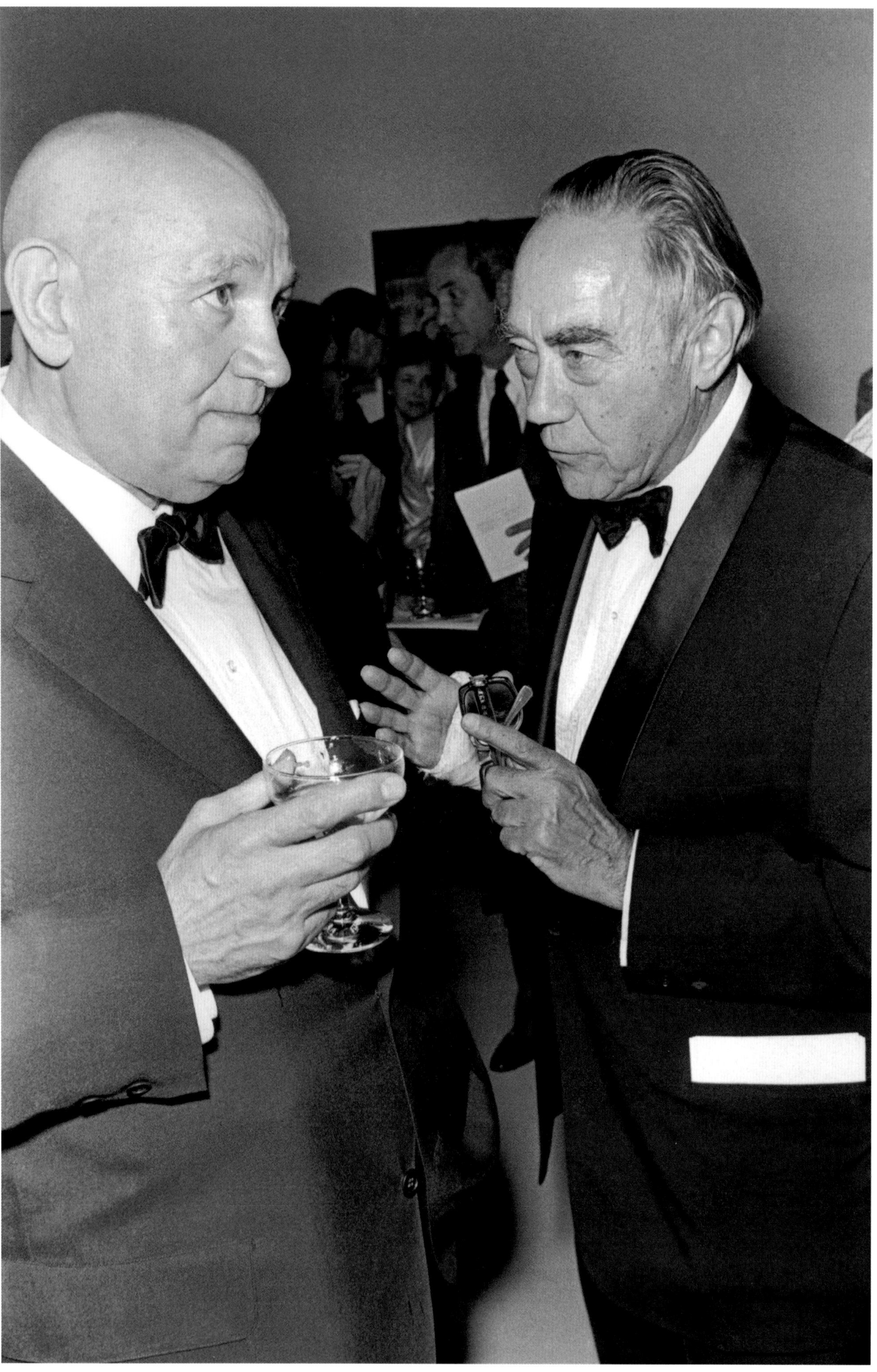

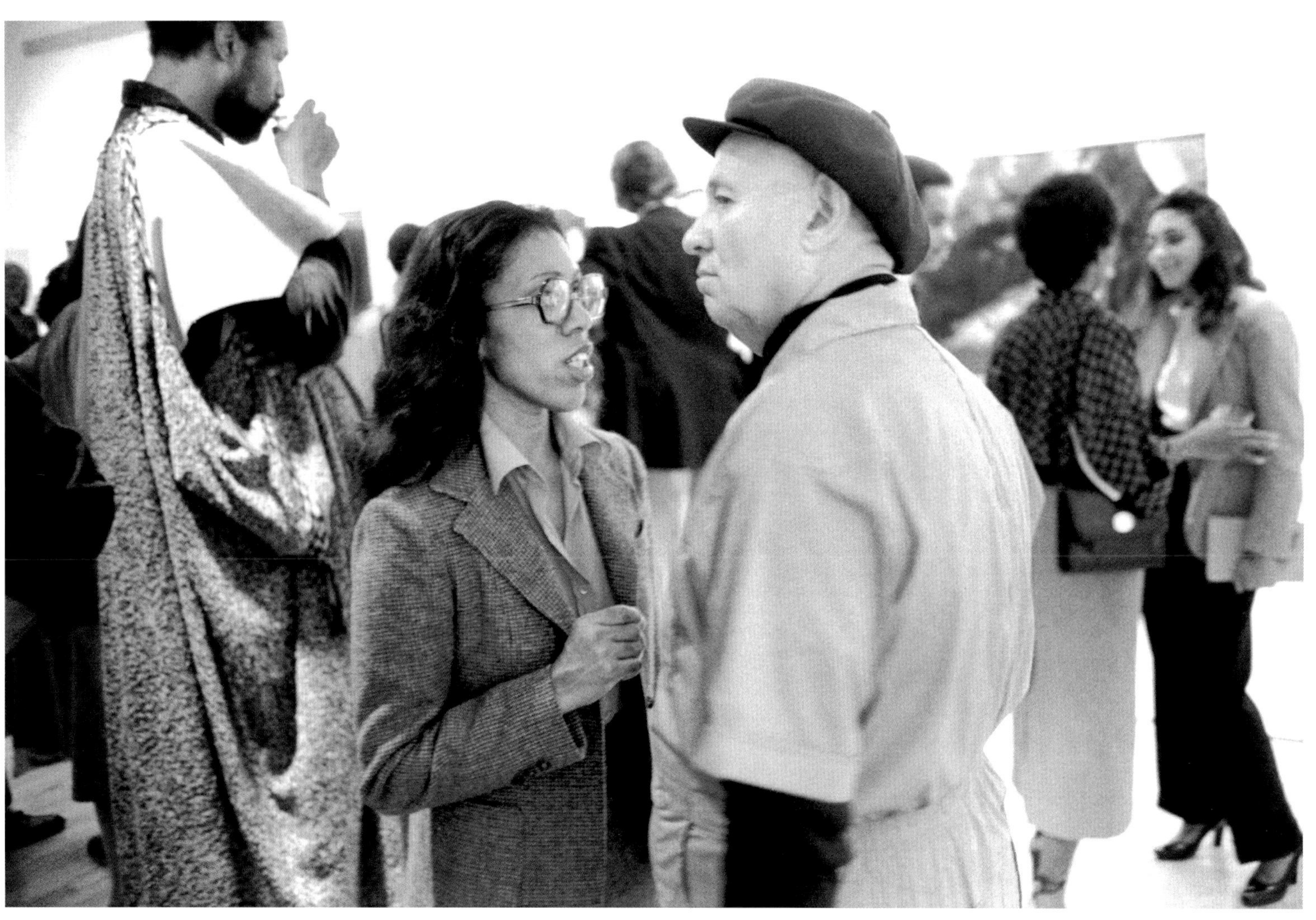

Romie's with June Kelly, his manager. She set shows up and did the advance work. She'd get the commissions and do the follow-up. She smoothed the road out, so to speak, for this boy. She was there from the time I started working with Romie in 1975. She really did a conscientious job. 1980

FACING PAGE
Romie's talking to his old friend, writer Barrie Stavis, at the Mint Museum opening. I don't know how much they saw each other in these years, but Barrie wrote about Romie's paintings for a Kootz Gallery catalog back in 1947. 1980

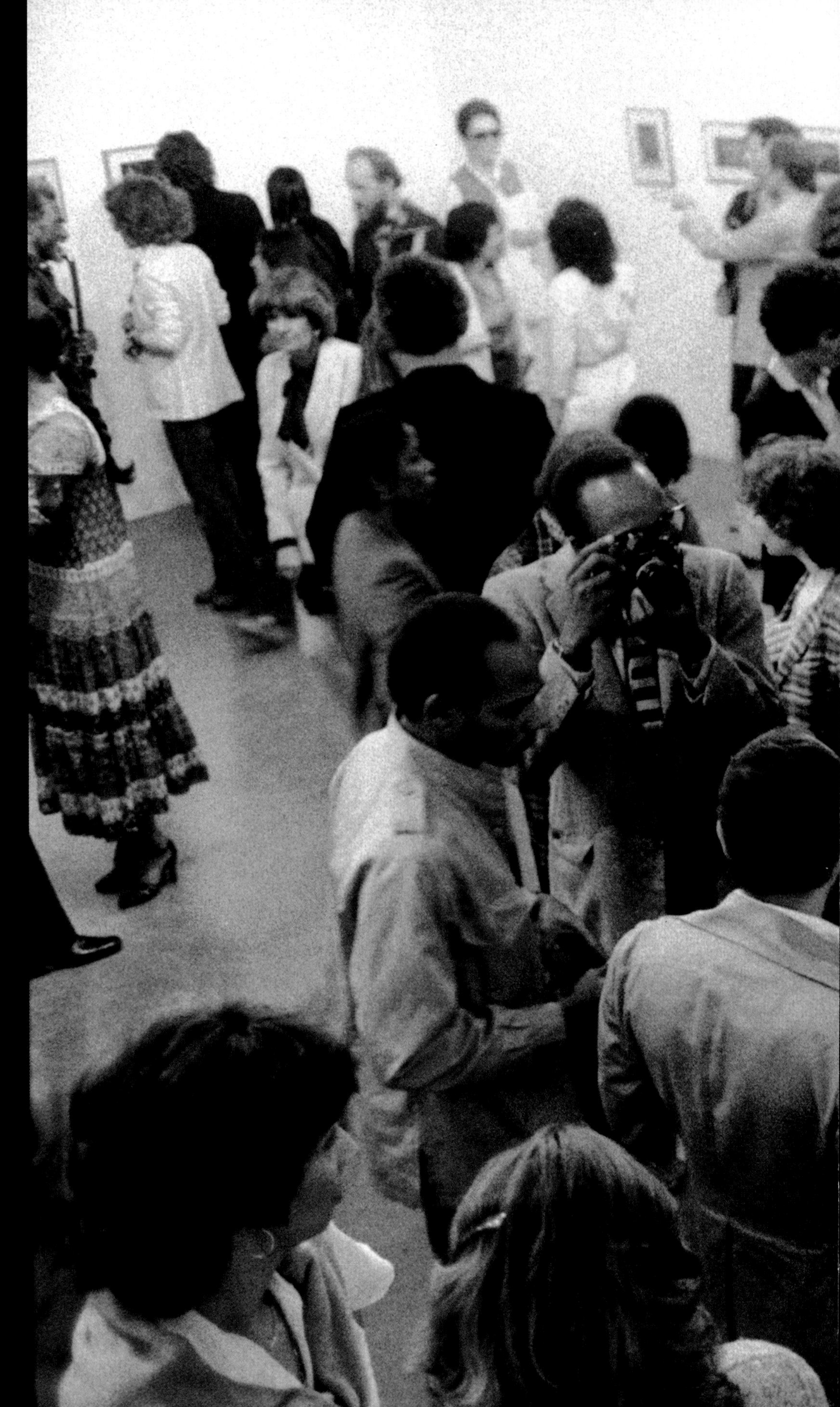

One of those few times we actually had to travel on a plane was out to Venice, California, where Romie had a show at a place called the

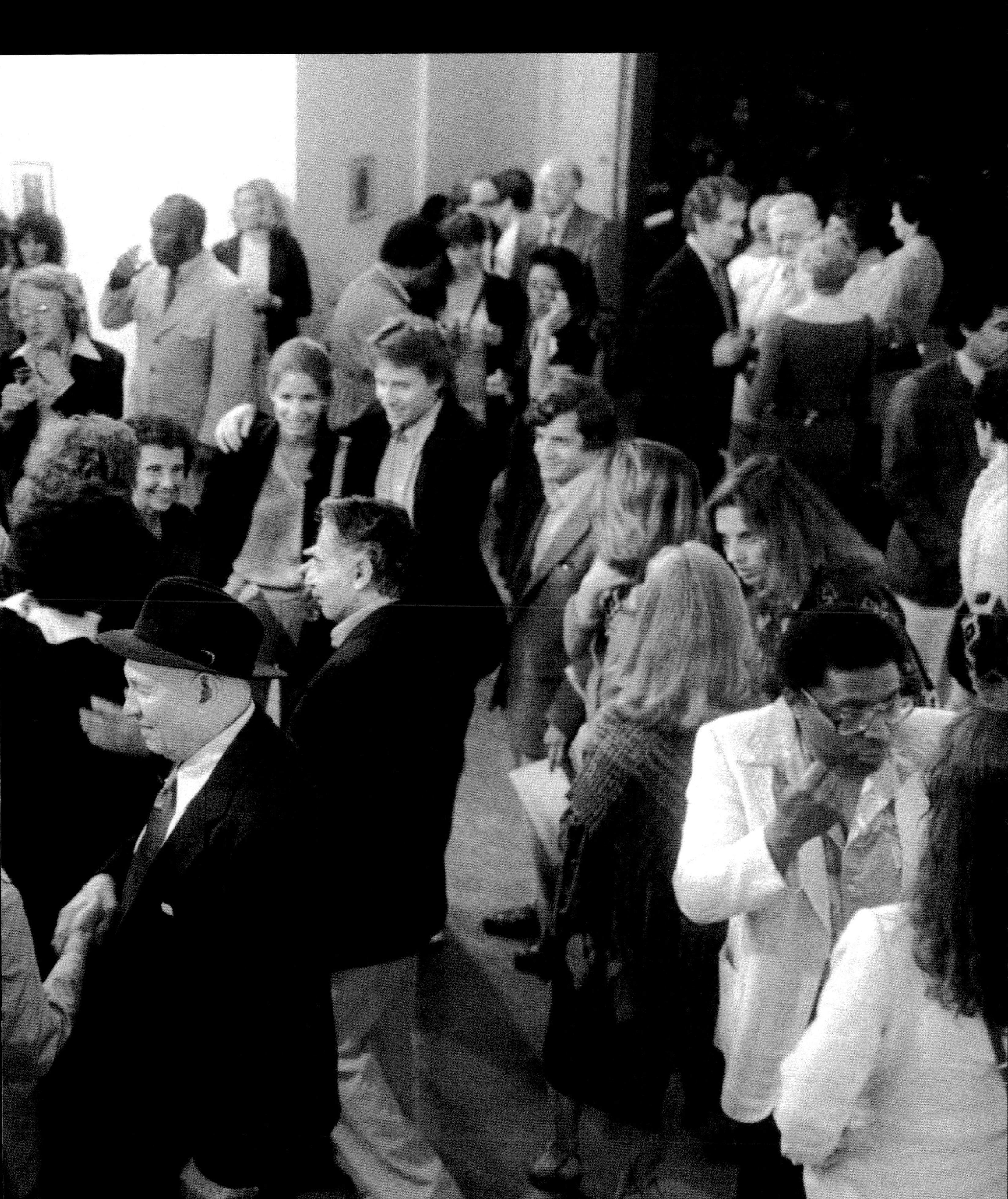

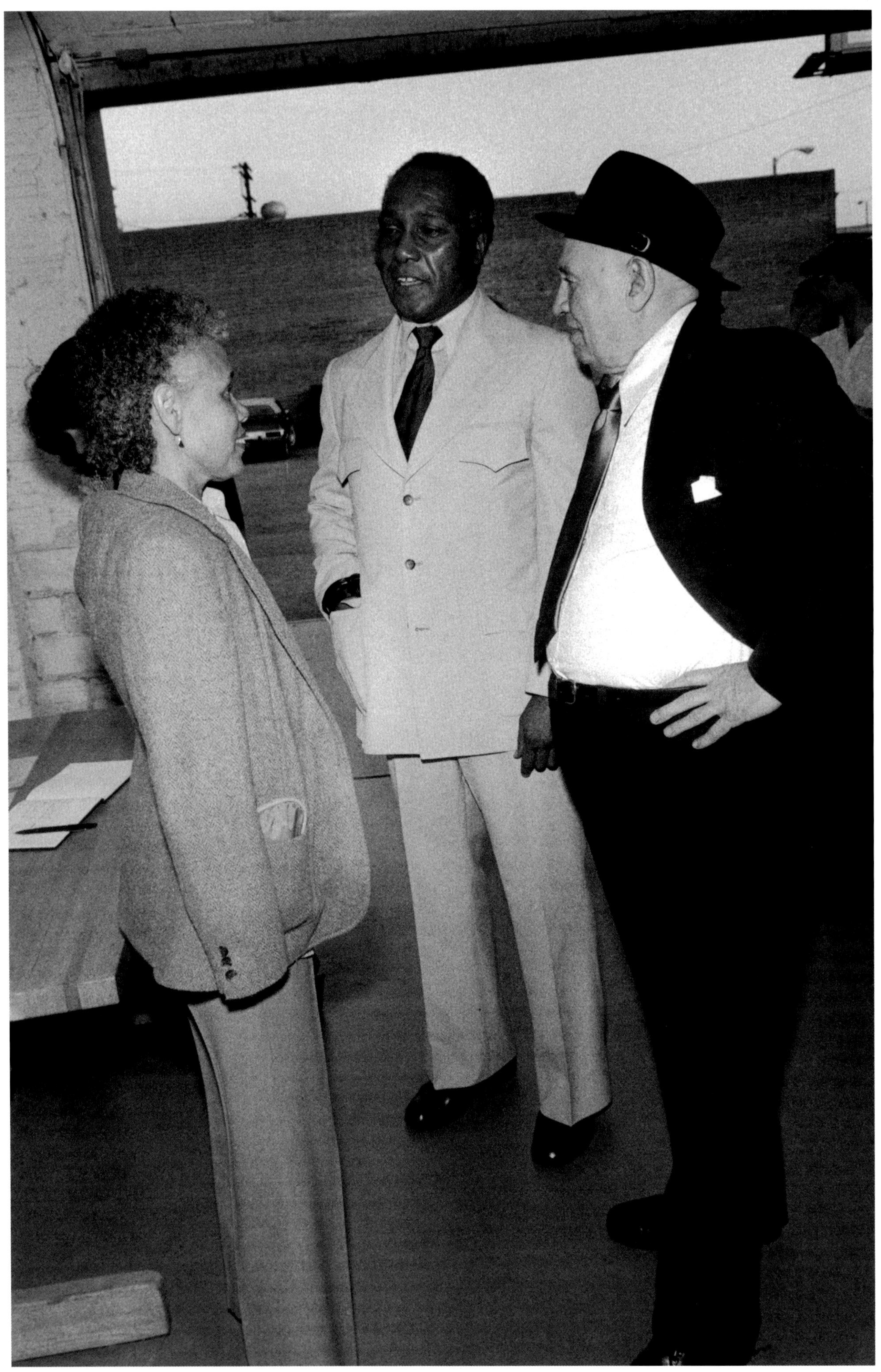

Betye Saar, an unidentified man, and Romie at the Art Garden. 1980

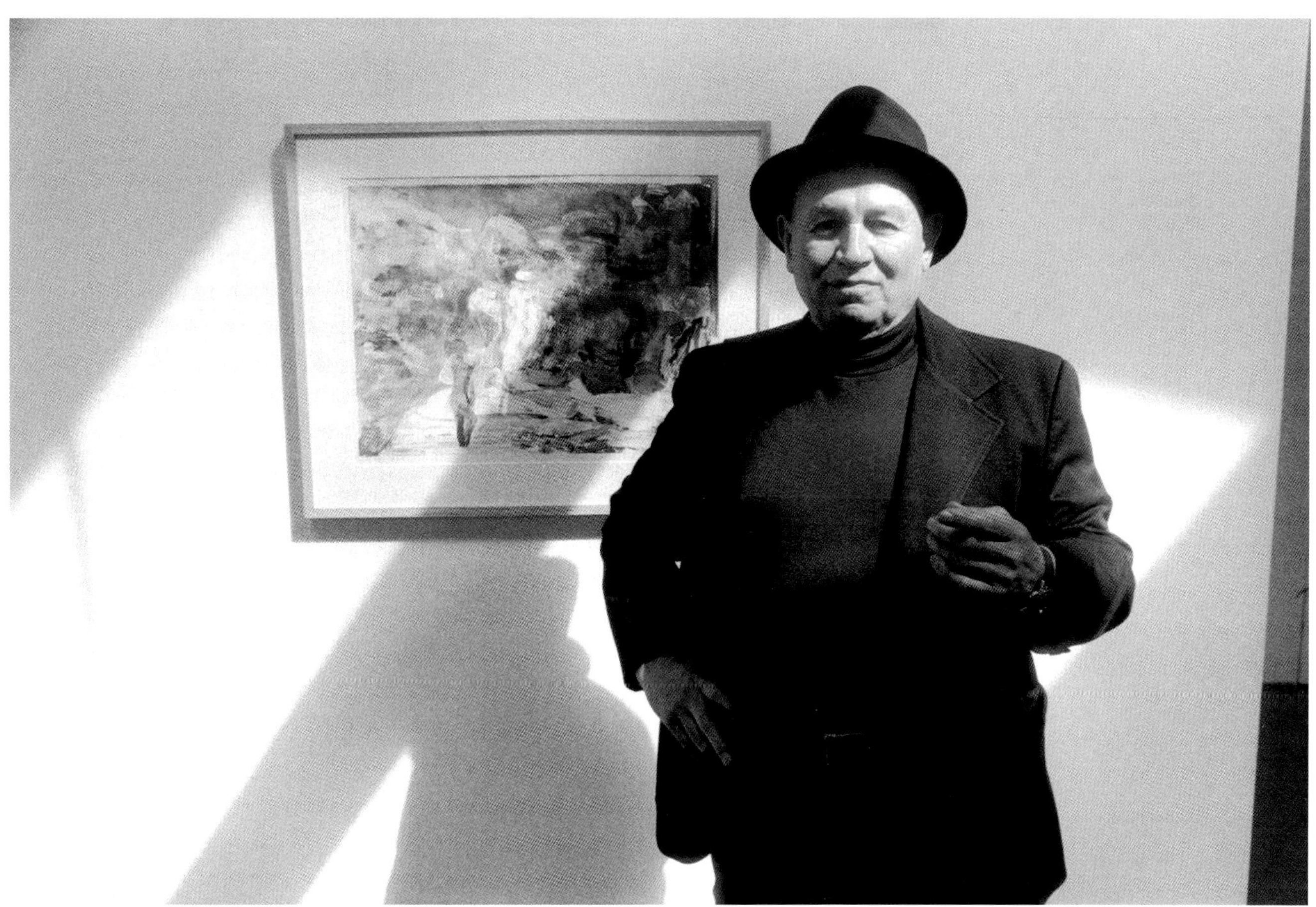

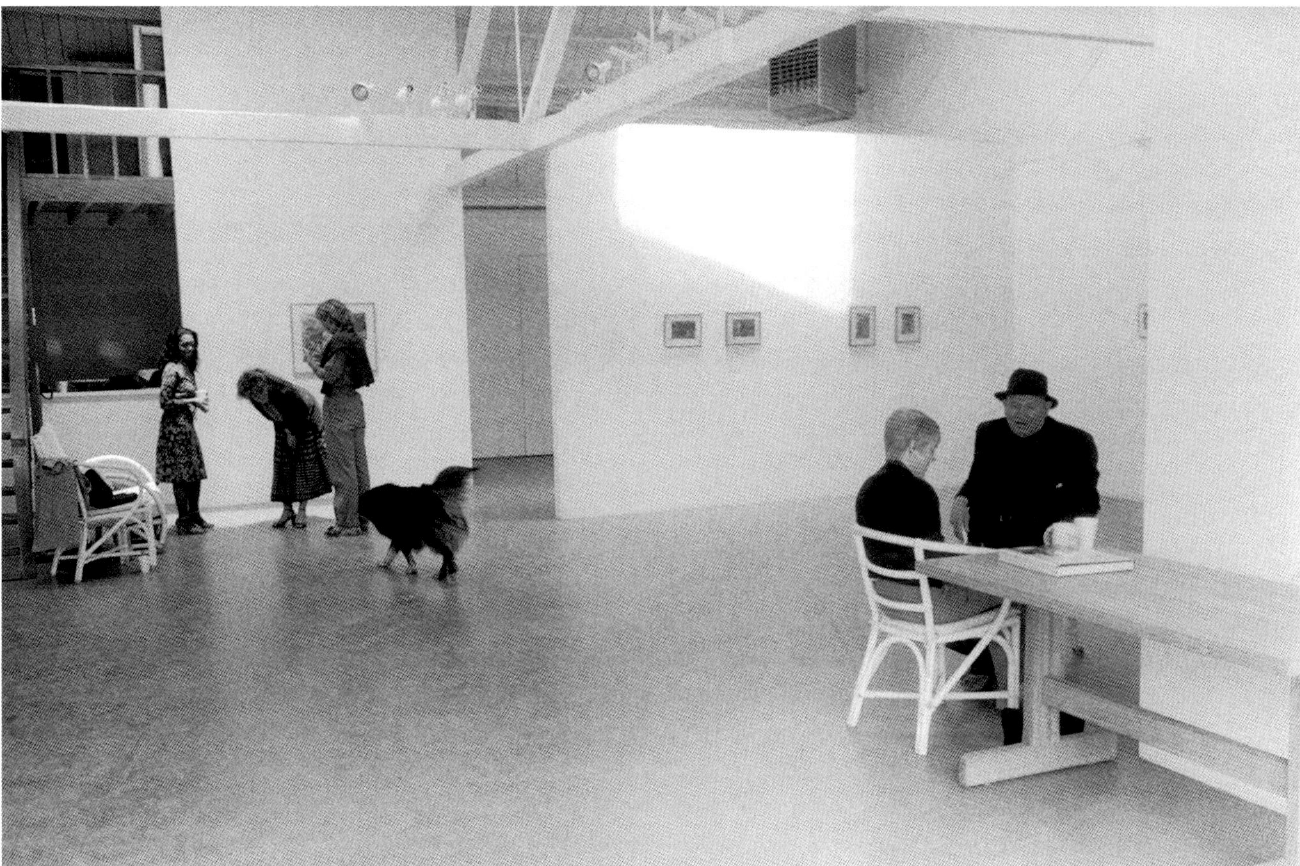

Romie's at the Art Garden in Venice, California. He was in his element when he had a show because people would come around and he could tell everybody what he knew and what he was doing and what the pieces were about. He loved all of that. 1980

Romie's being interviewed by a local reporter on the morning of his Art Garden opening in Venice. June Kelly is in the back, at the left, with the gallery people. 1980

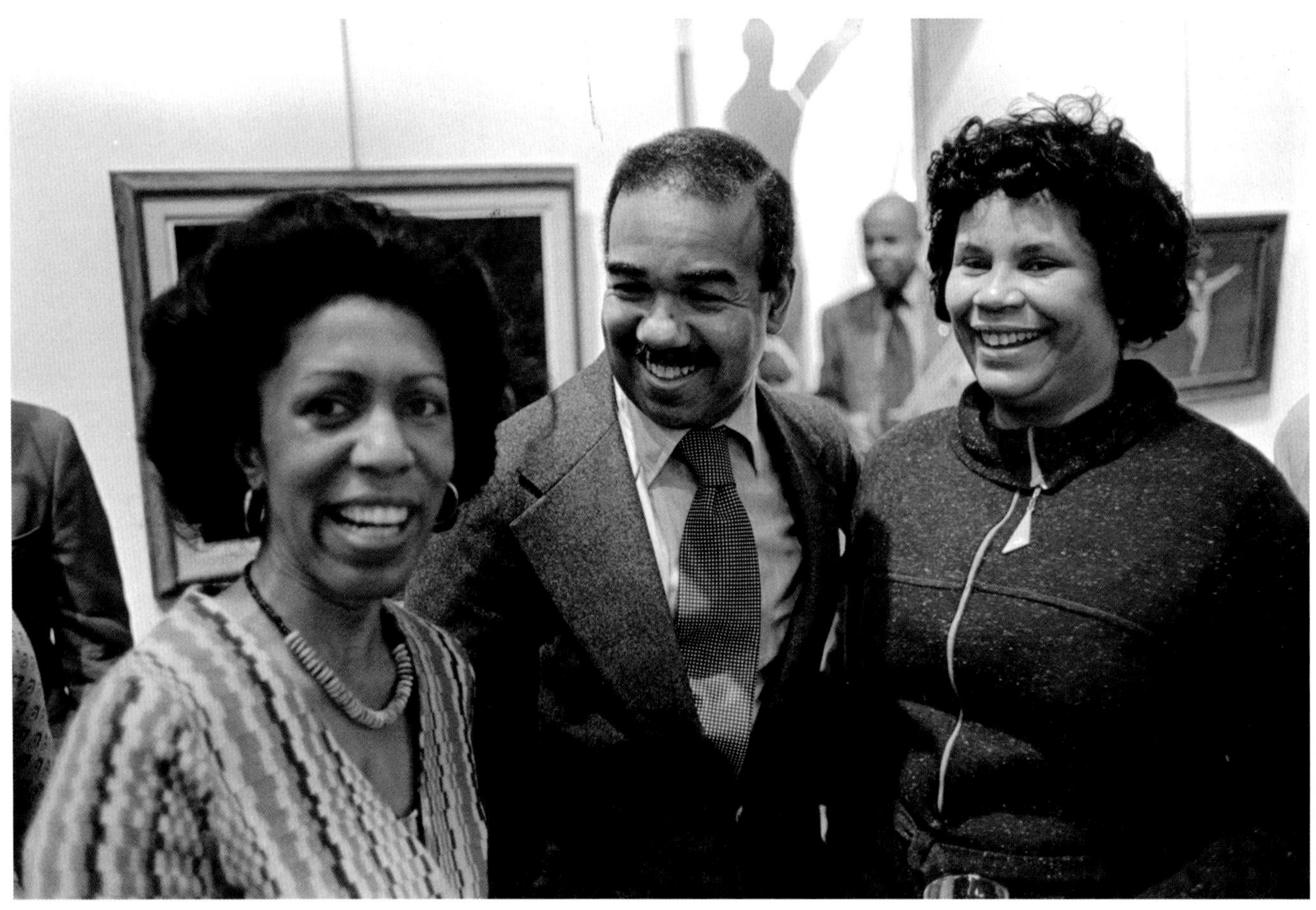

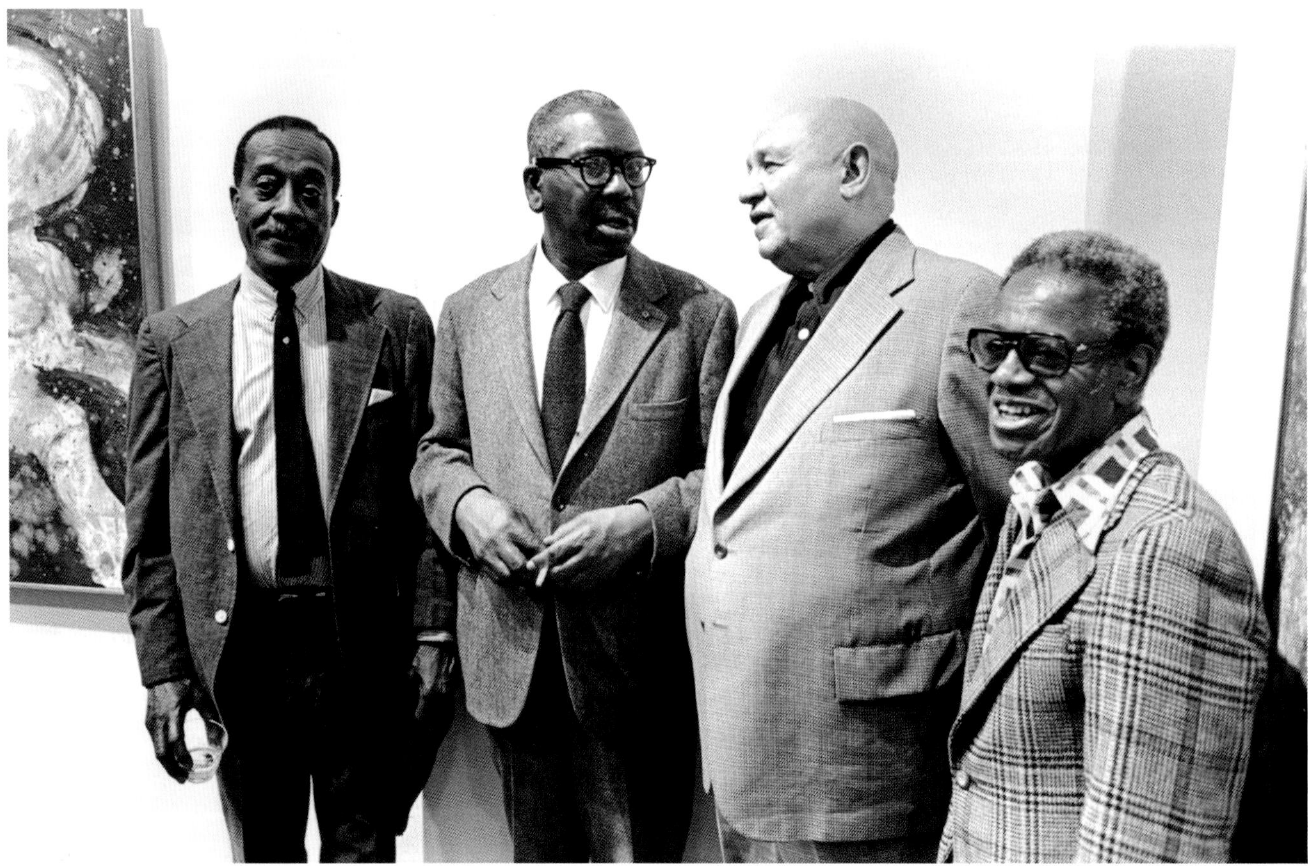

June Kelly, Bobby Short, and Nanette at a Horace Pippin exhibition at the Terry Dintenfass Gallery. If Romie was there, Nanette was going to be there, too. Most couples aren't that glued together. c. 1977

Norman Lewis, Jacob Lawrence, Romare Bearden, and Ernie Critchlow. Norman, Romie, and Ernie started Cinque Gallery. Romie was a race man, as they say. He loved African American culture; he loved African American art and artists. He loved the whole history of it. c. 1977

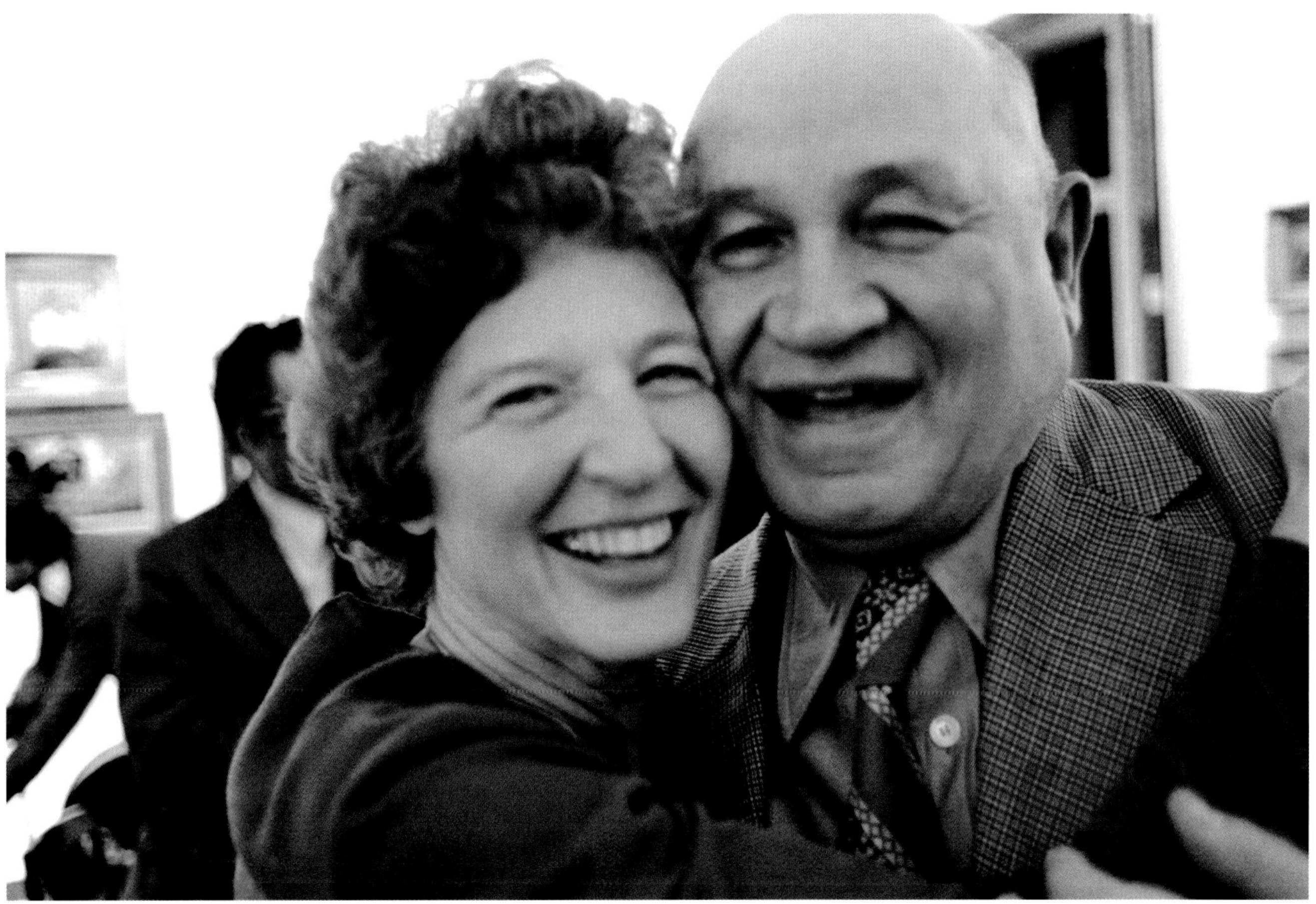

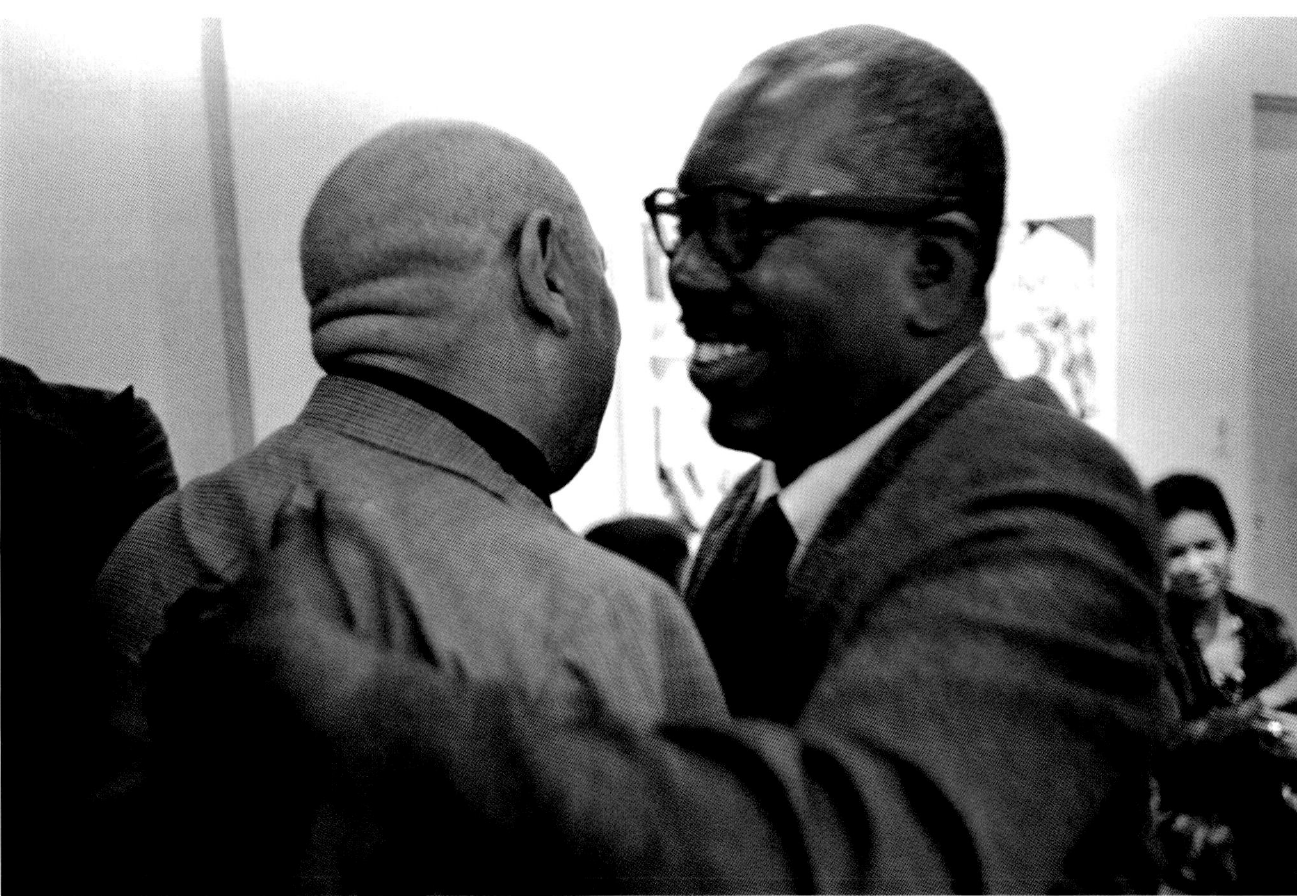

Romie liked people. I didn't ever meet too many people he didn't like. Here he's with Terry Dintenfass at her gallery. c. 1977

Romie's with Jacob Lawrence at an opening of Jake's show at the Terry Dintenfass Gallery. Back in the forties they both had studios in a building on 125th Street. Romie told how he was intimidated by going into Jake's studio because Jake would have thirty paintings all lined up. Romie would go back to his place, and he would have this one canvas that had been there for months without him putting anything on it. c. 1977

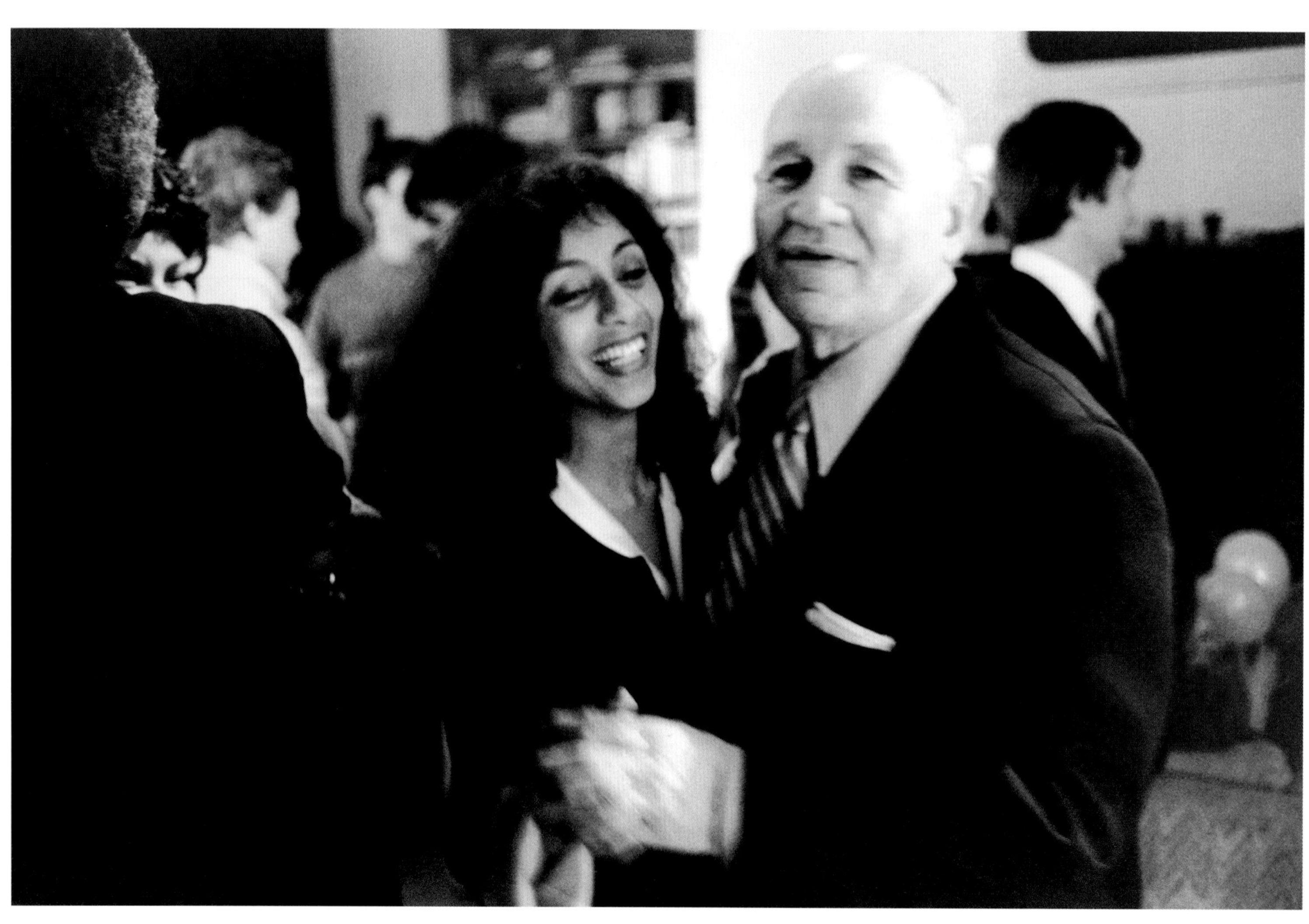

At Hugh McKay's soirees there was a lot of dancing going on. Romie's dancing with Tei Sing Smith, an artist who worked with Bob Blackburn. At the left, Nanette's dancing with Hugh. 1979

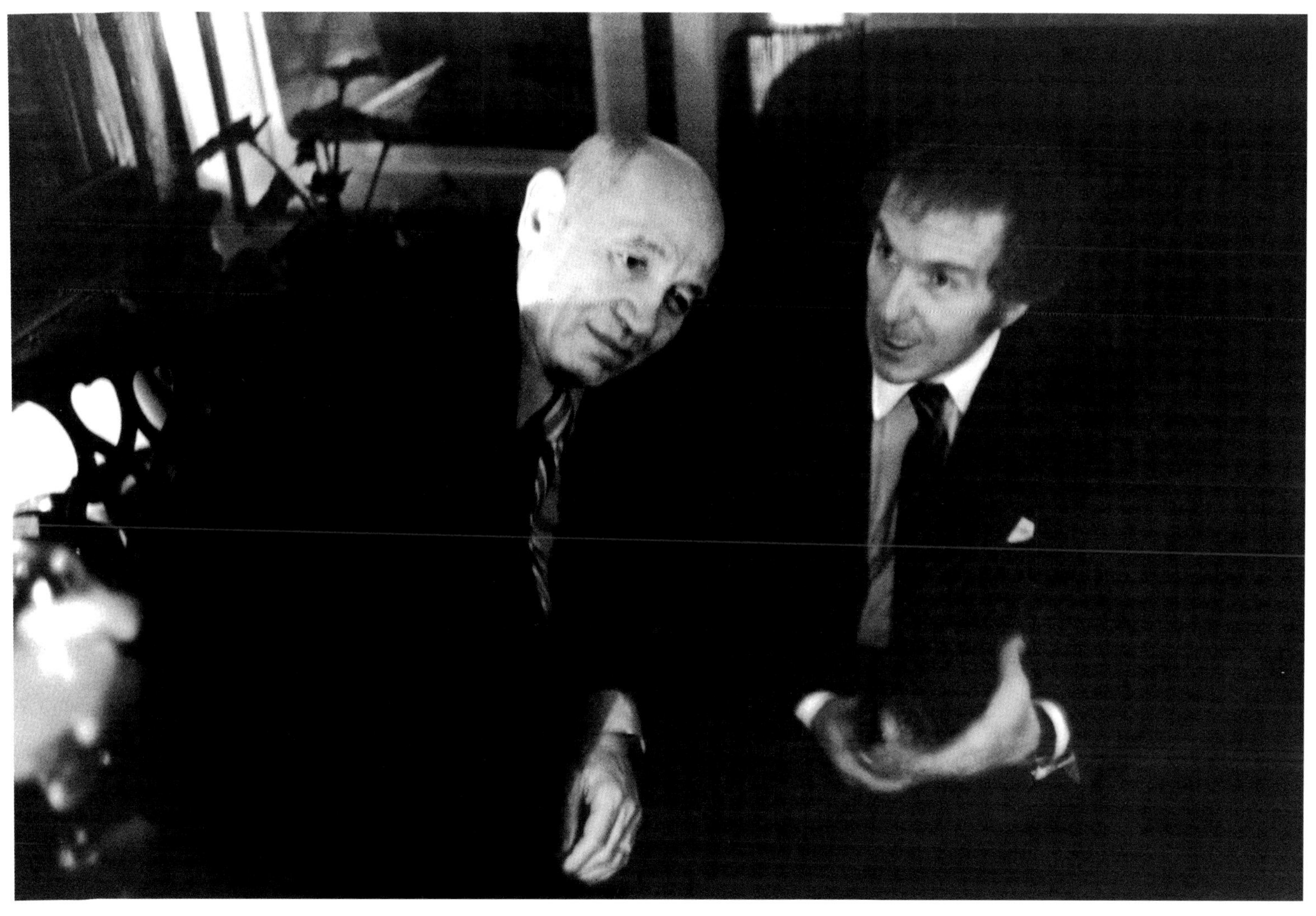

Romie's with Hugh McKay, who had a big, lavish, duplex apartment on Gramercy Park, in the National Arts Club Building. The top two floors. Hugh was an art dealer, and he published a lot of prints, including Romie's *Odysseus* series. 1979

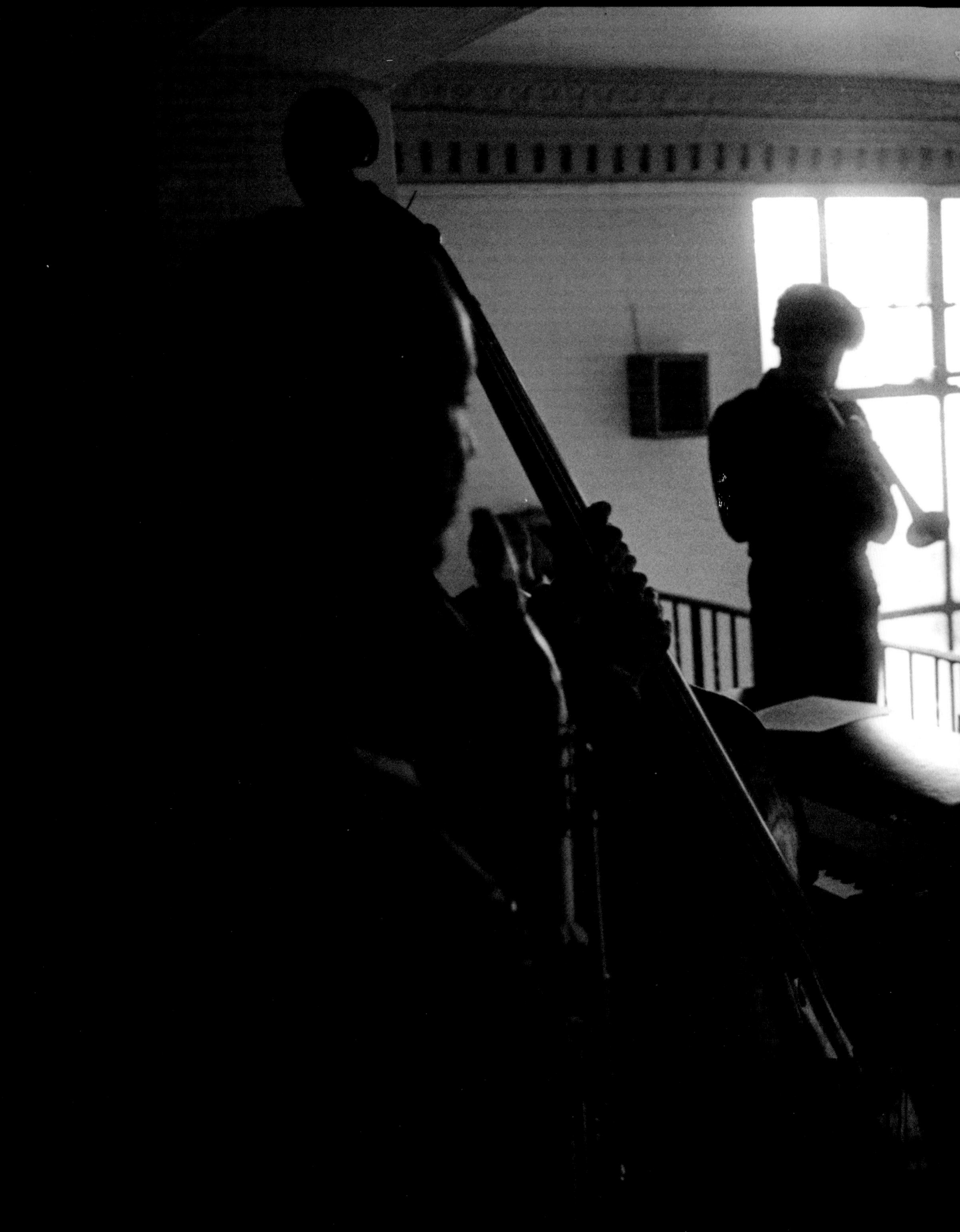

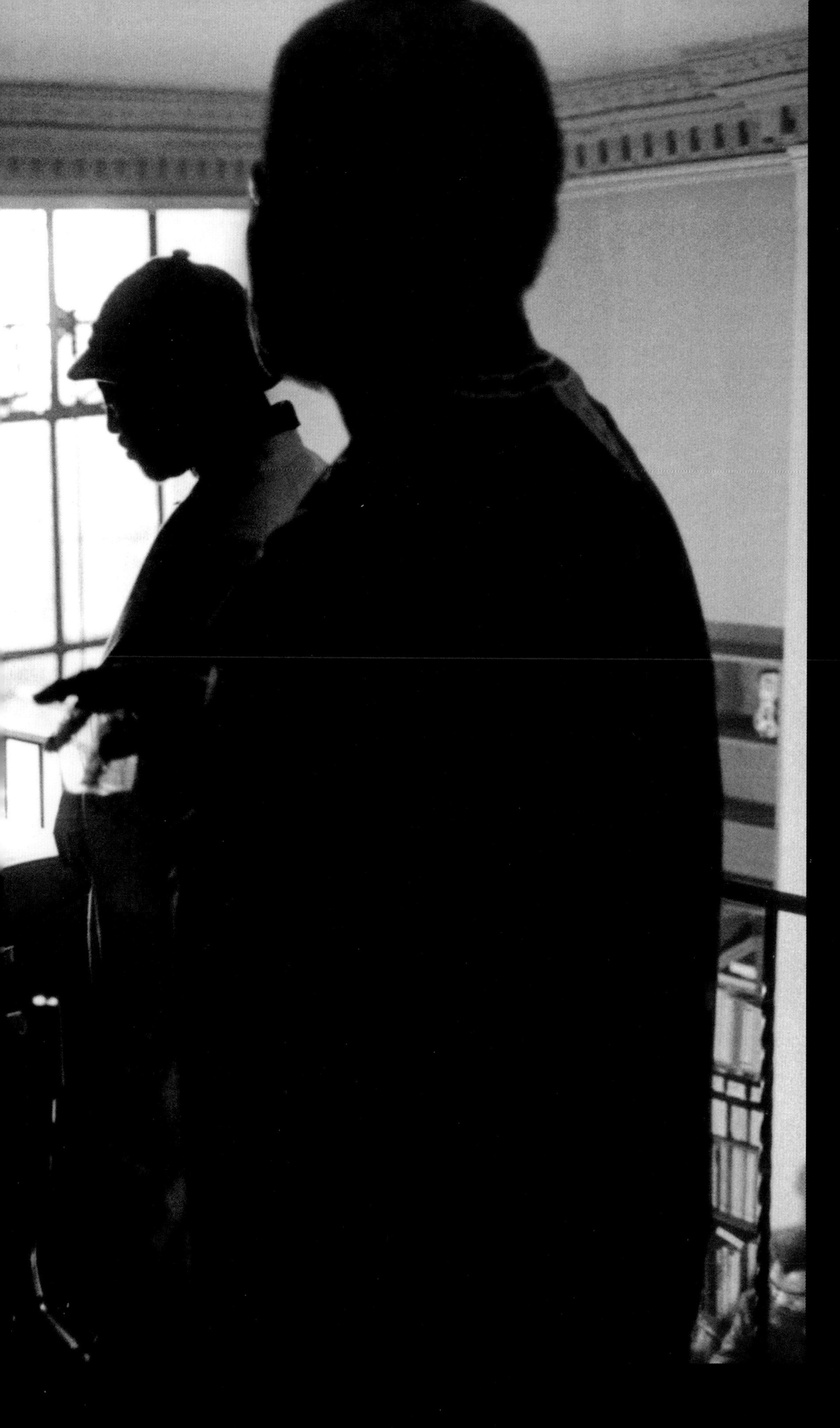

Hugh McKay's soirees would have jazz. Merton Simpson would play, and he would contract the musicians, and they'd come and play for the whole afternoon. It was the place to be if you were invited. 1979

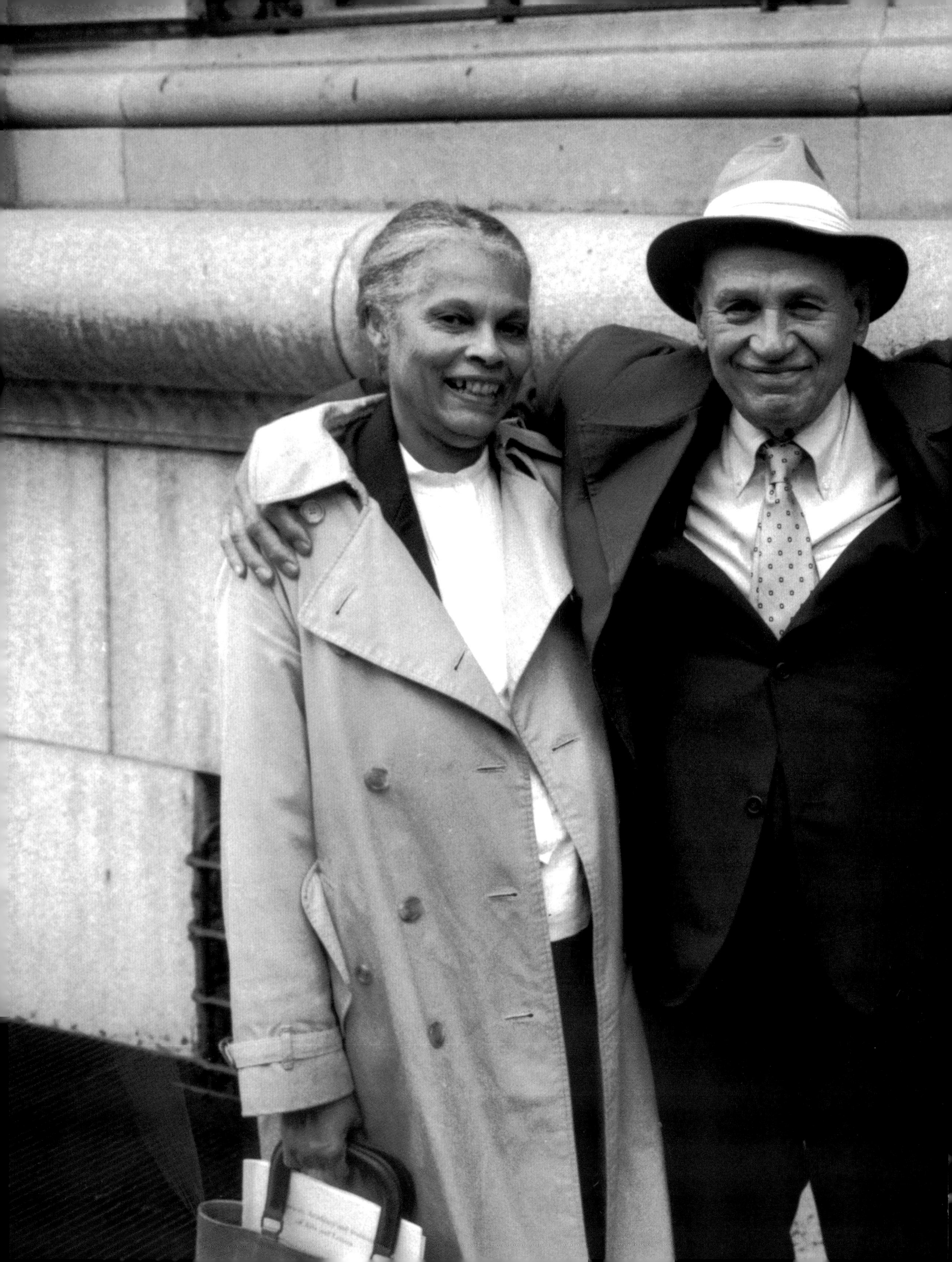

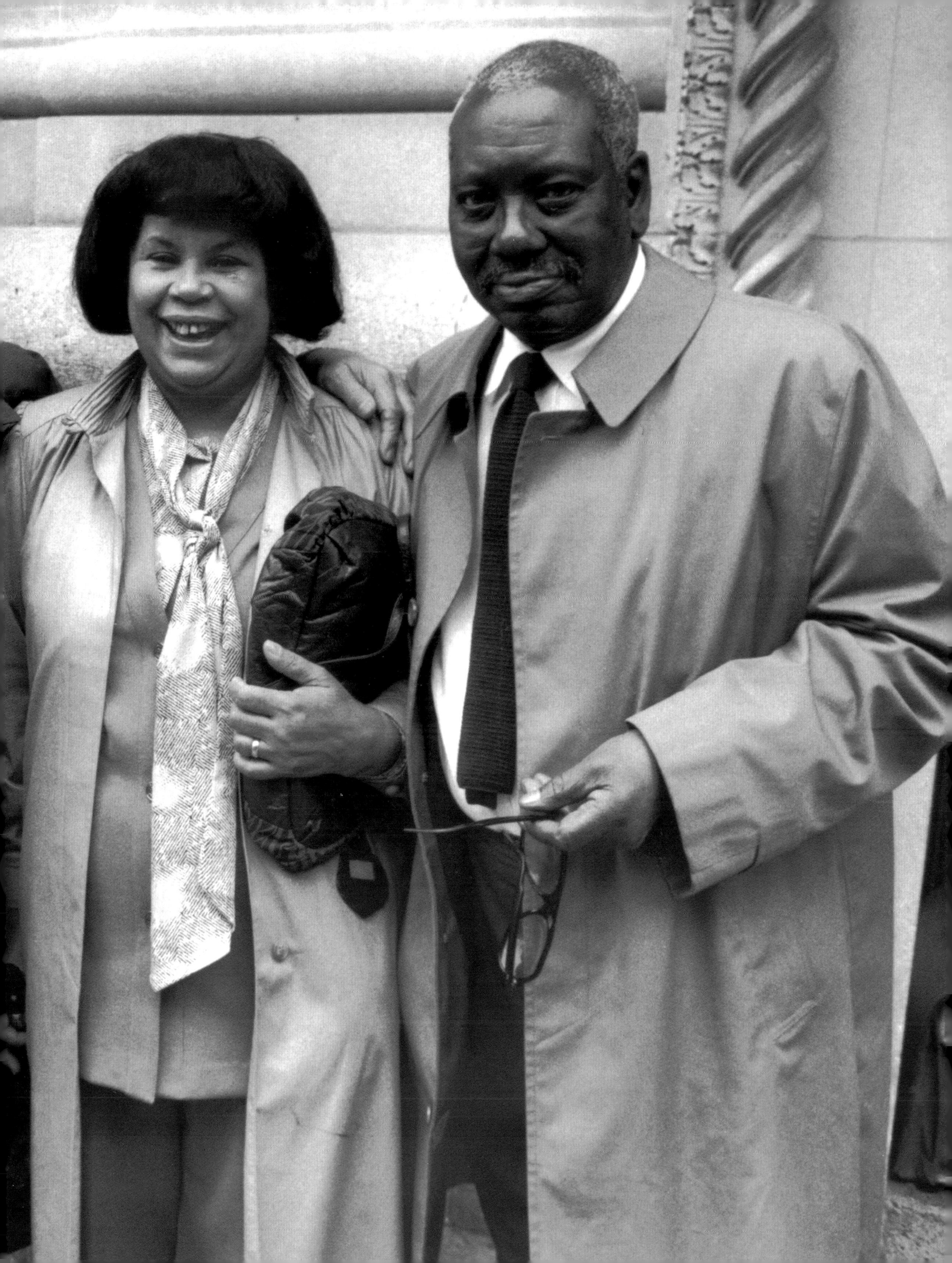

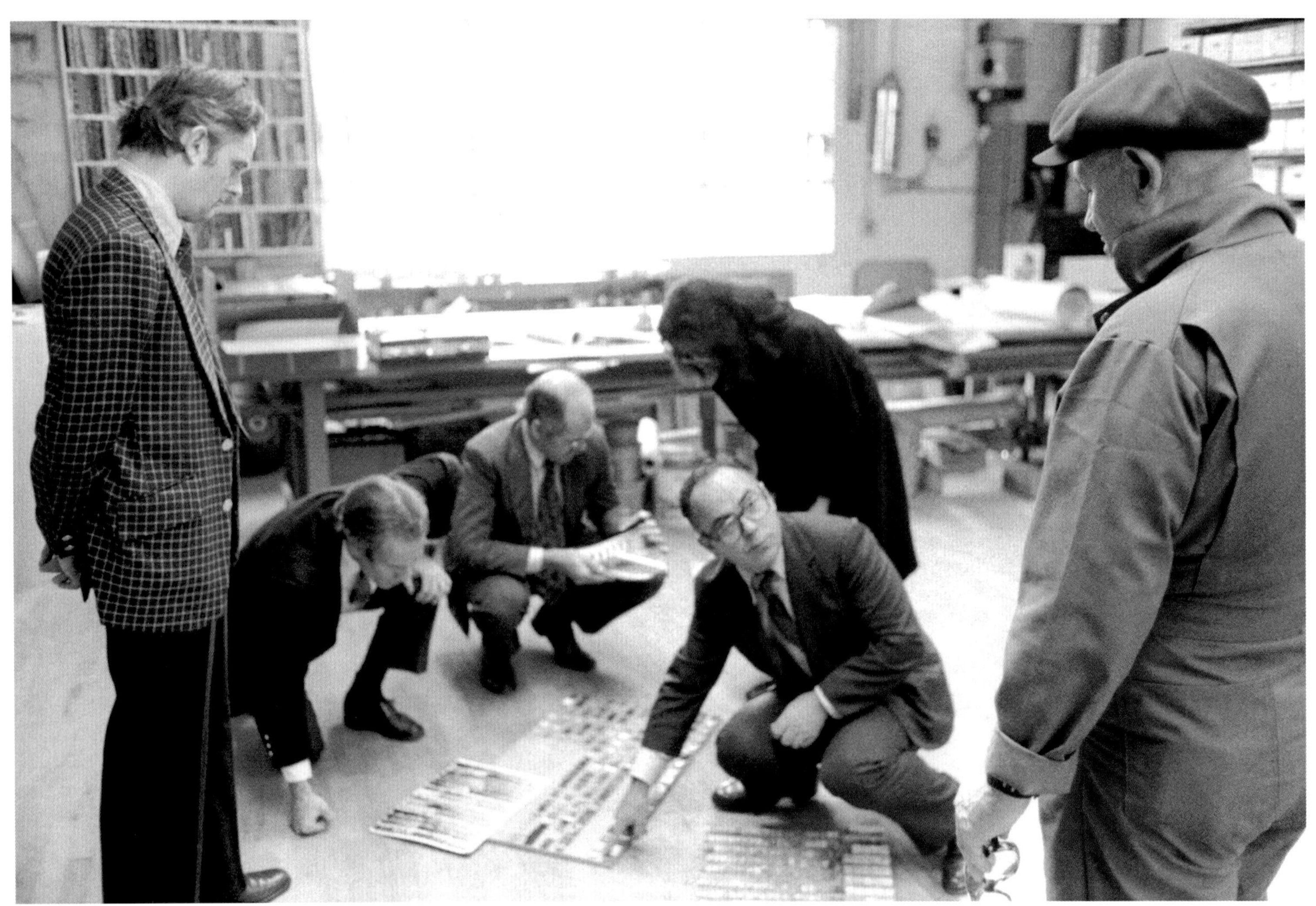

These are the people from Cravatto Mosaics in Yonkers at the time of a Baltimore commission. They actually executed Romie's murals. They're probably talking about the type of color he wanted, what he thinks should go where. 1982/83

PRECEDING PAGES
Romie, Jacob Lawrence, Gwendolyn Knight Lawrence, and Nanette are outside the American Academy of Arts and Letters. It wasn't like they hung out a whole lot in these later years, but when they saw each other they were glad to see each other. Driving them around Harlem I was all nervous, thinking, "I have half the culture in my car; if I have an accident . . ." 1986

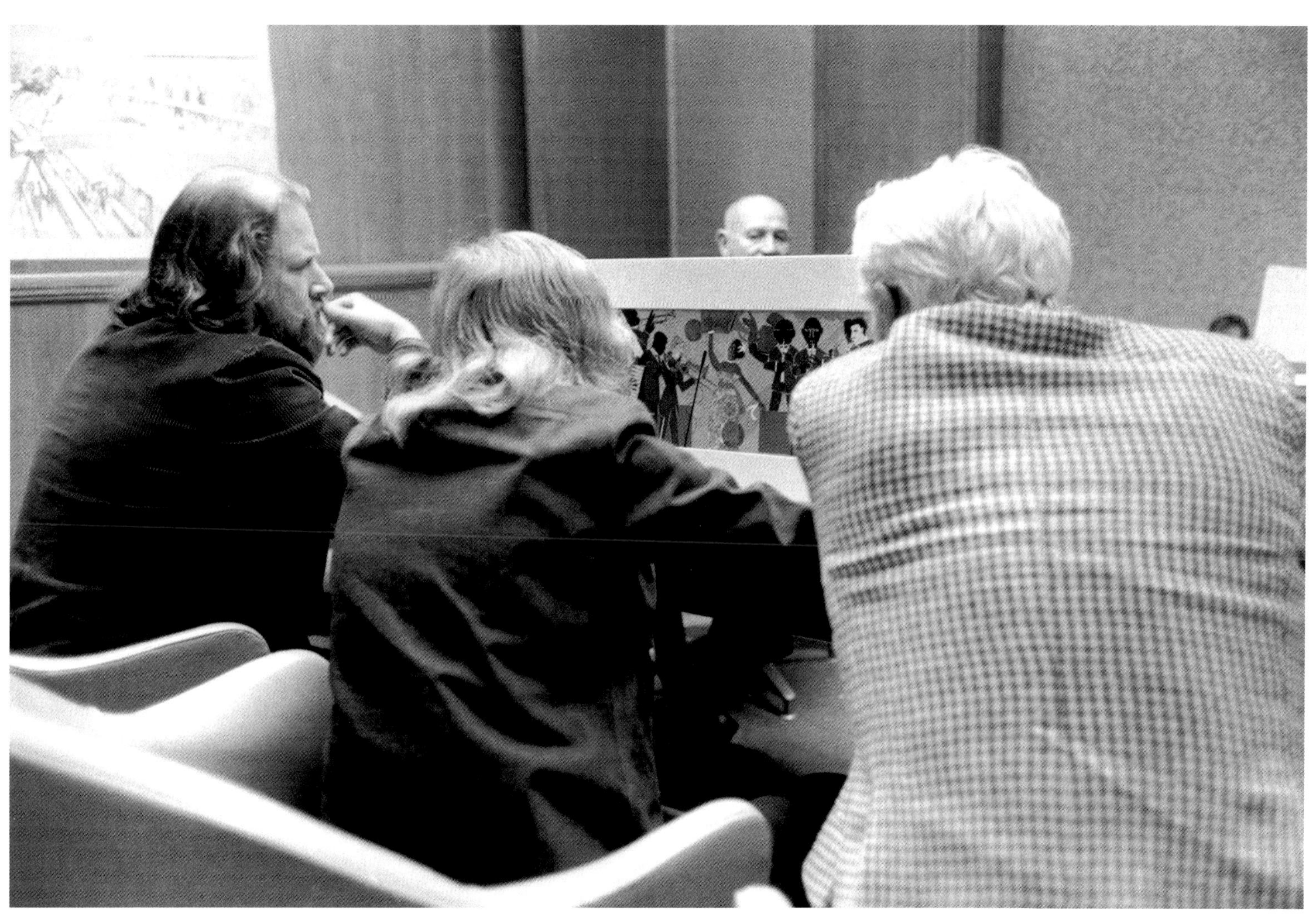

Romie's showing a committee his maquette for a Baltimore subway mural. June Kelly, Romie's manager, was the spokesperson, but they'd ask Romie a question or two and then he'd say something. It has that air to it of a courtroom, like he was defending his idea. 1982/83

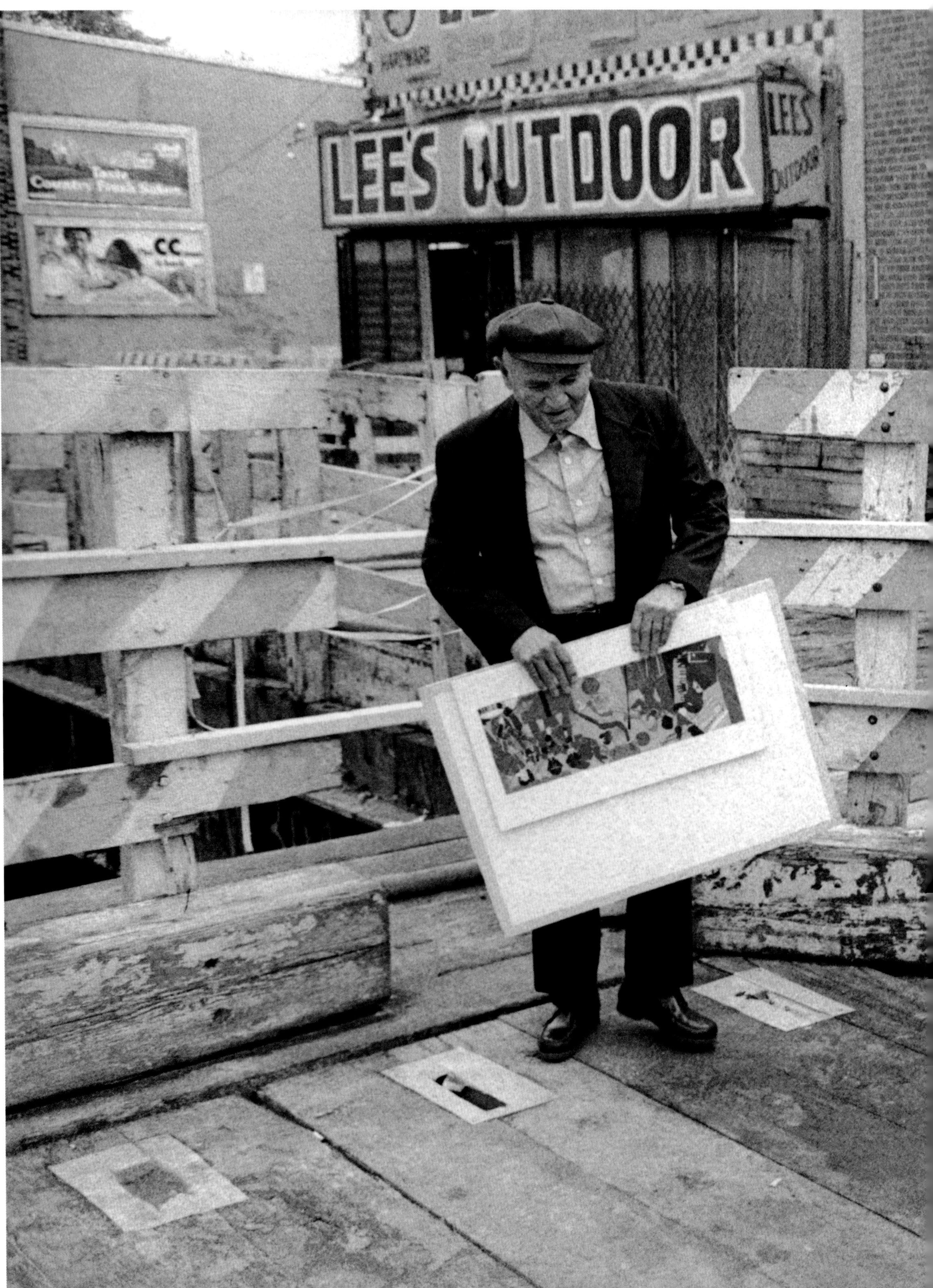
LEE'S OUTDOOR
LEE'S

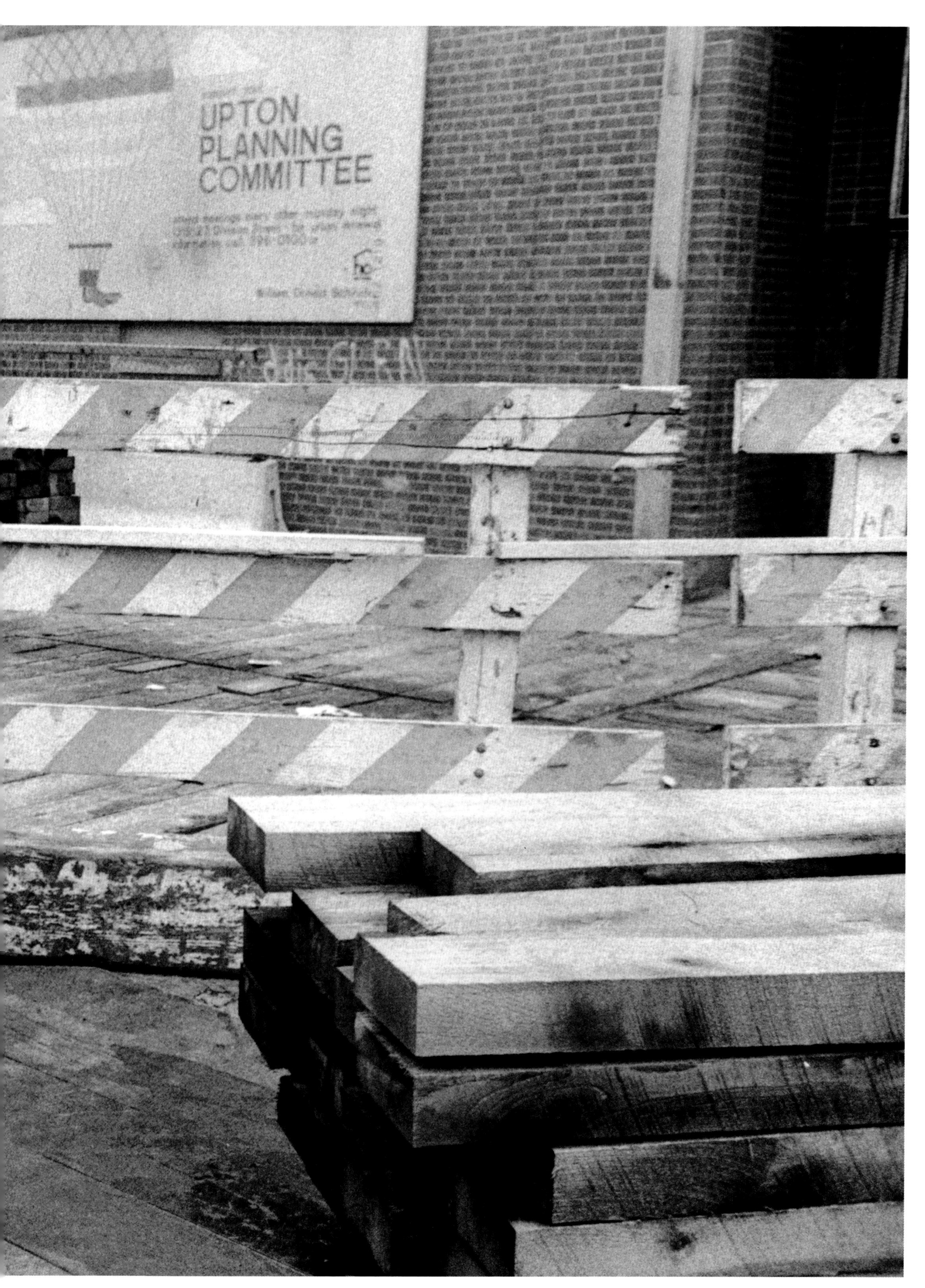
UPTON
PLANNING
COMMITTEE

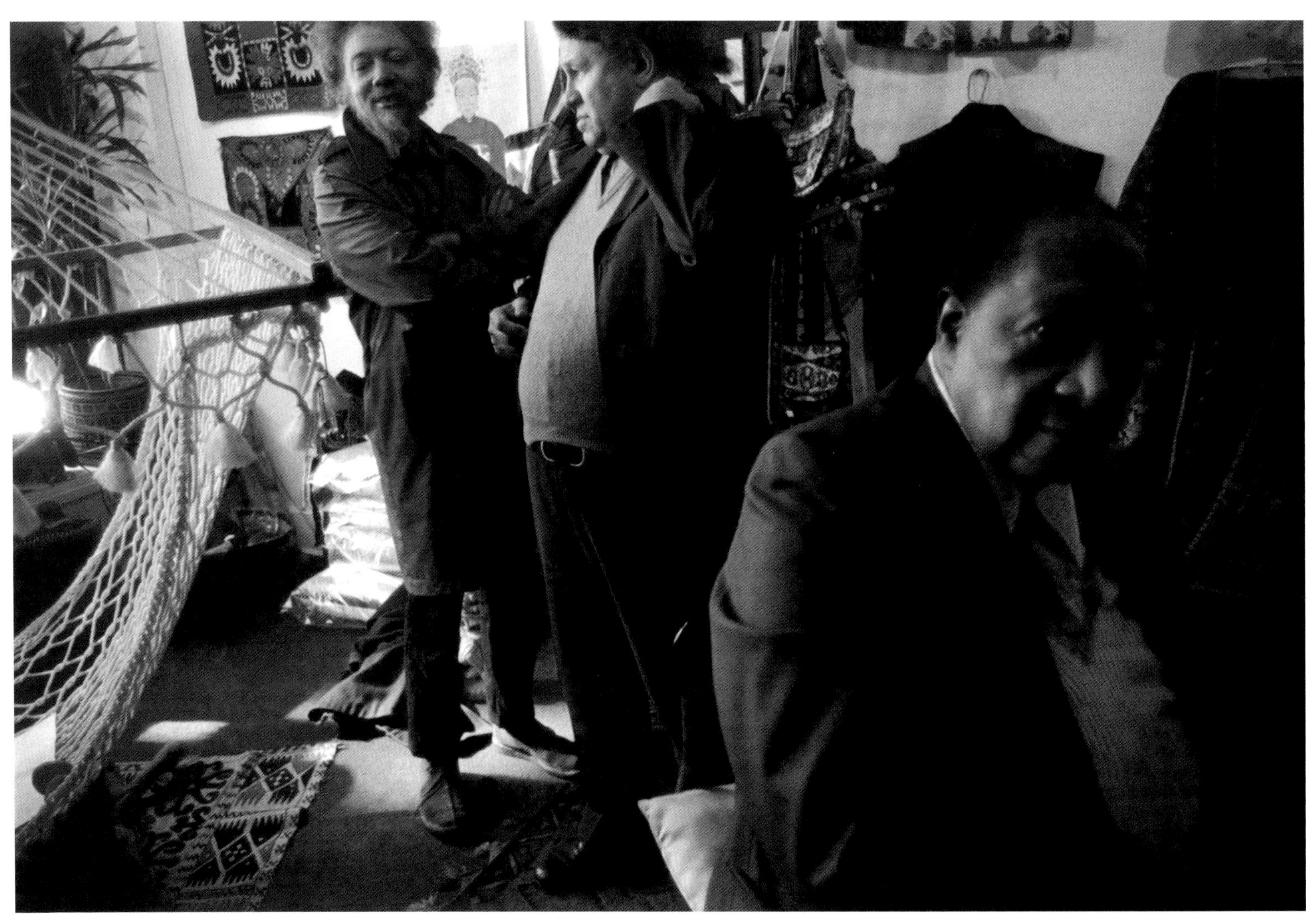

Benny Andrews, Romie, and James VanDerZee at the Knobkerry Store in New York. 1975

PRECEDING PAGES
Romie's out near the Baltimore site where a mural was going to be installed, Upton subway station. I think the central figure in this maquette is Billie Holiday, who came from Baltimore. 1982/83

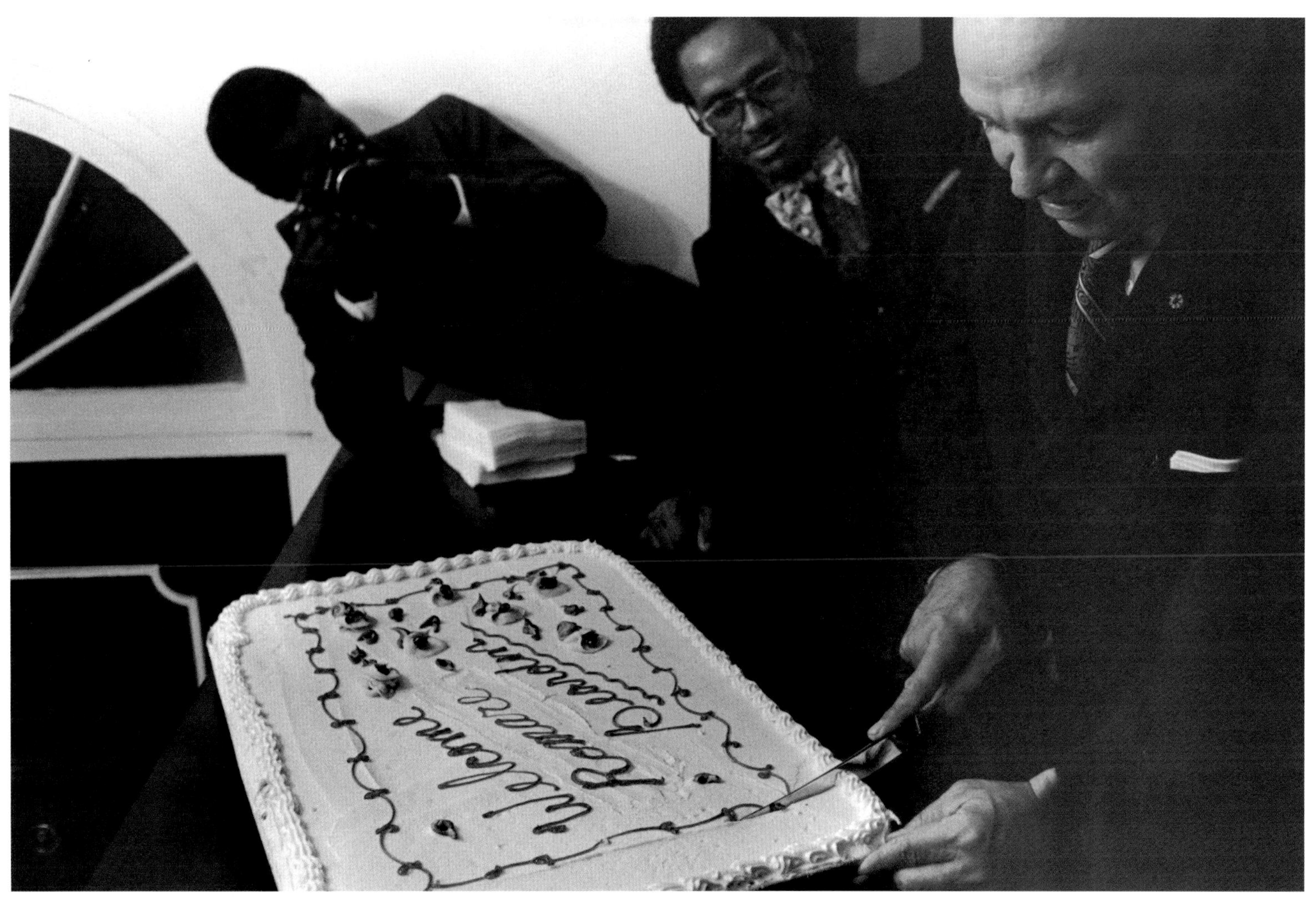

Bill Perrineau, Alan Edmunds, and Romie at the Brandywine Graphic Workshop in Philadelphia. 1977

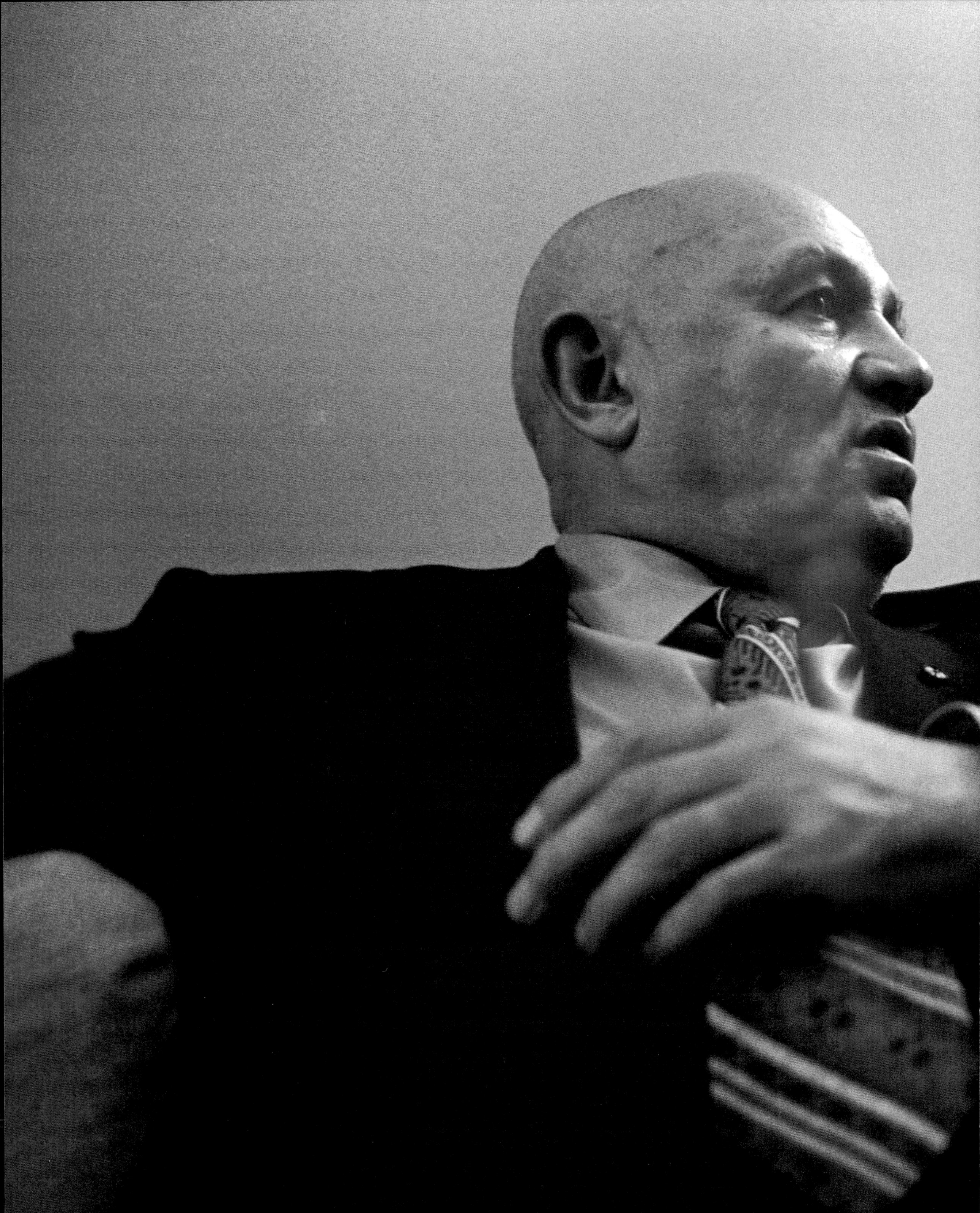

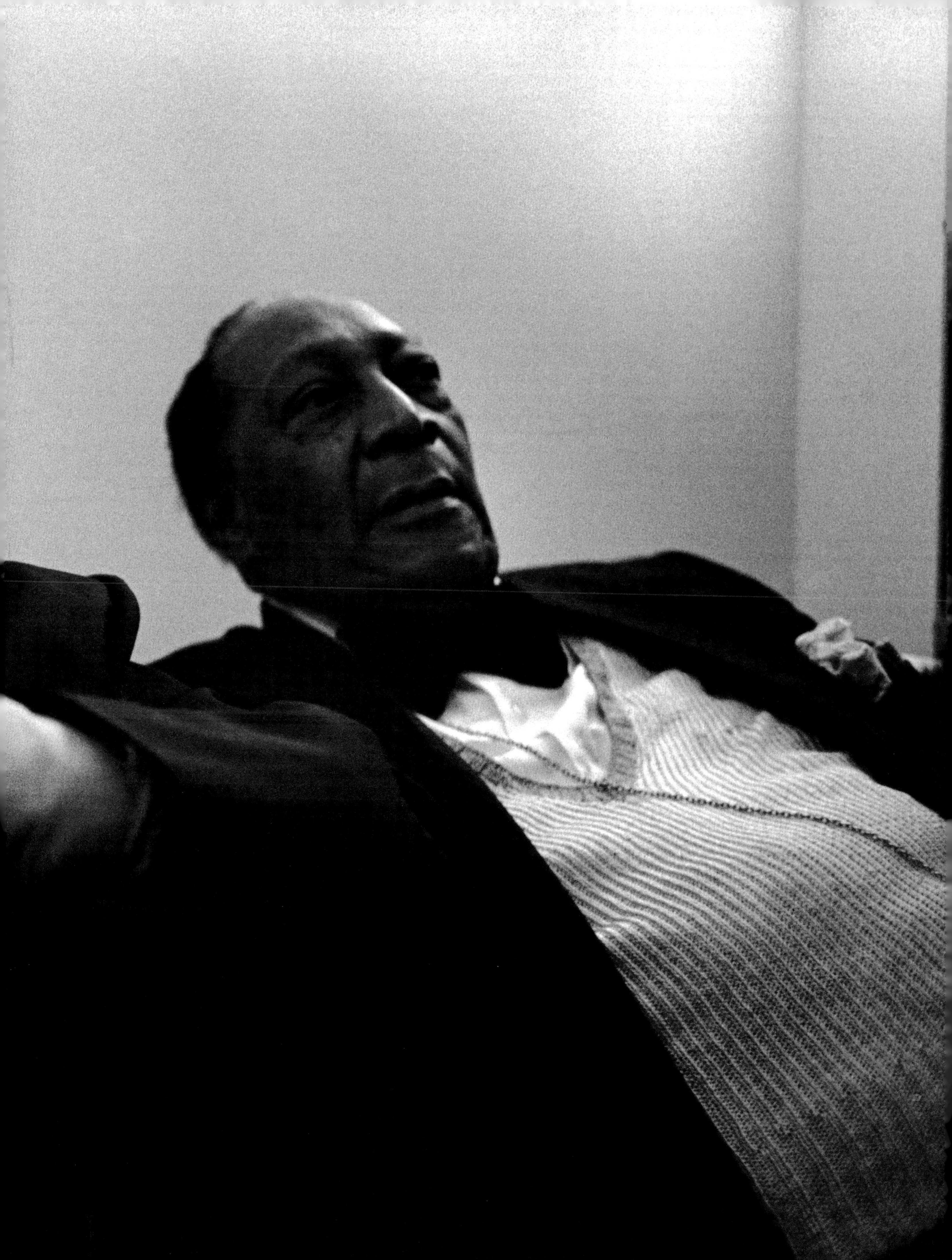

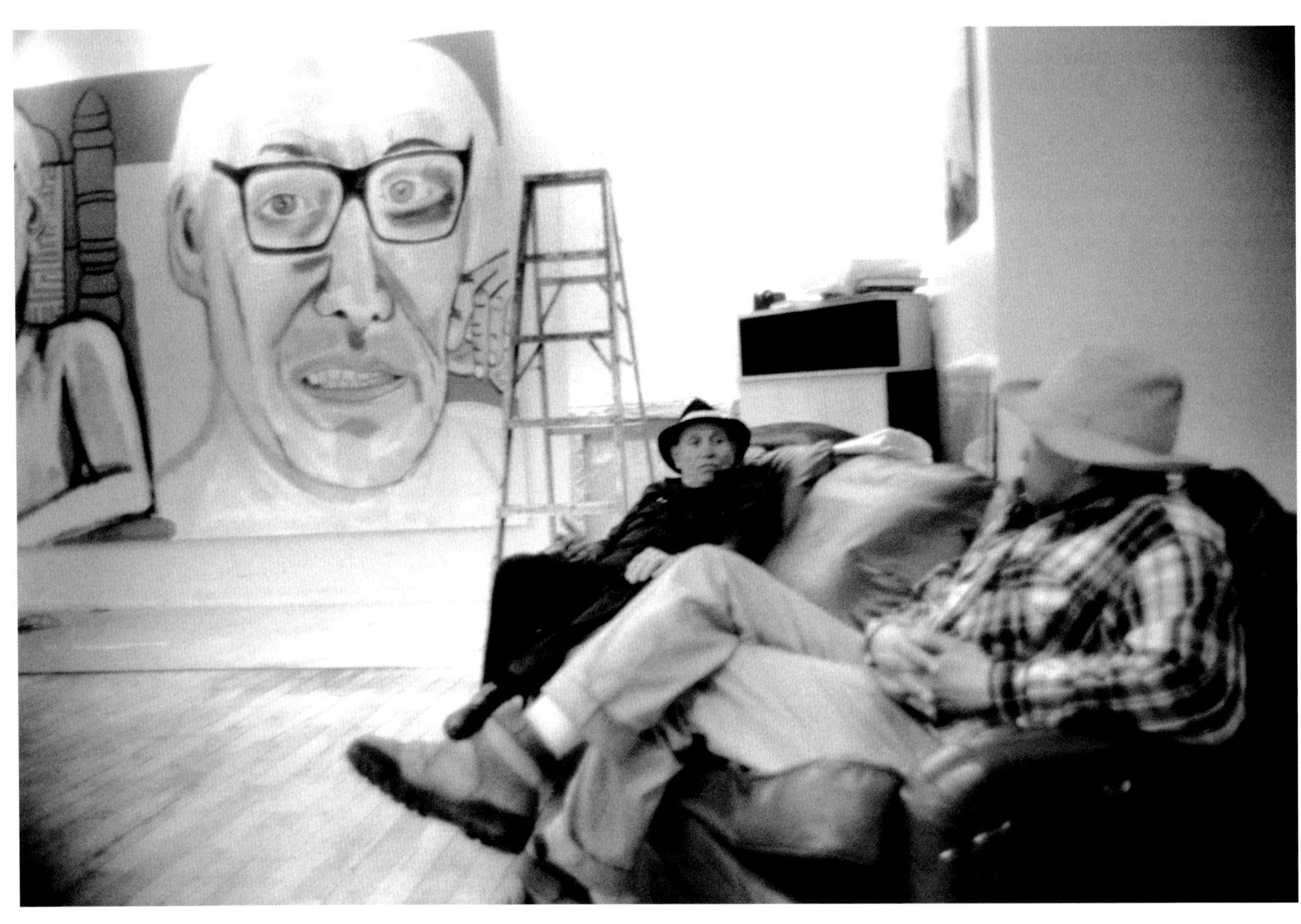

Romie's in Frederick J. Brown's studio, with Brown's painting *de Kooning* in progress. c. 1985.

PRECEDING PAGES
Romie and James VanDerZee, the day Romie received the first annual James VanDerZee Award from the Brandywine Graphic Workshop. 1977

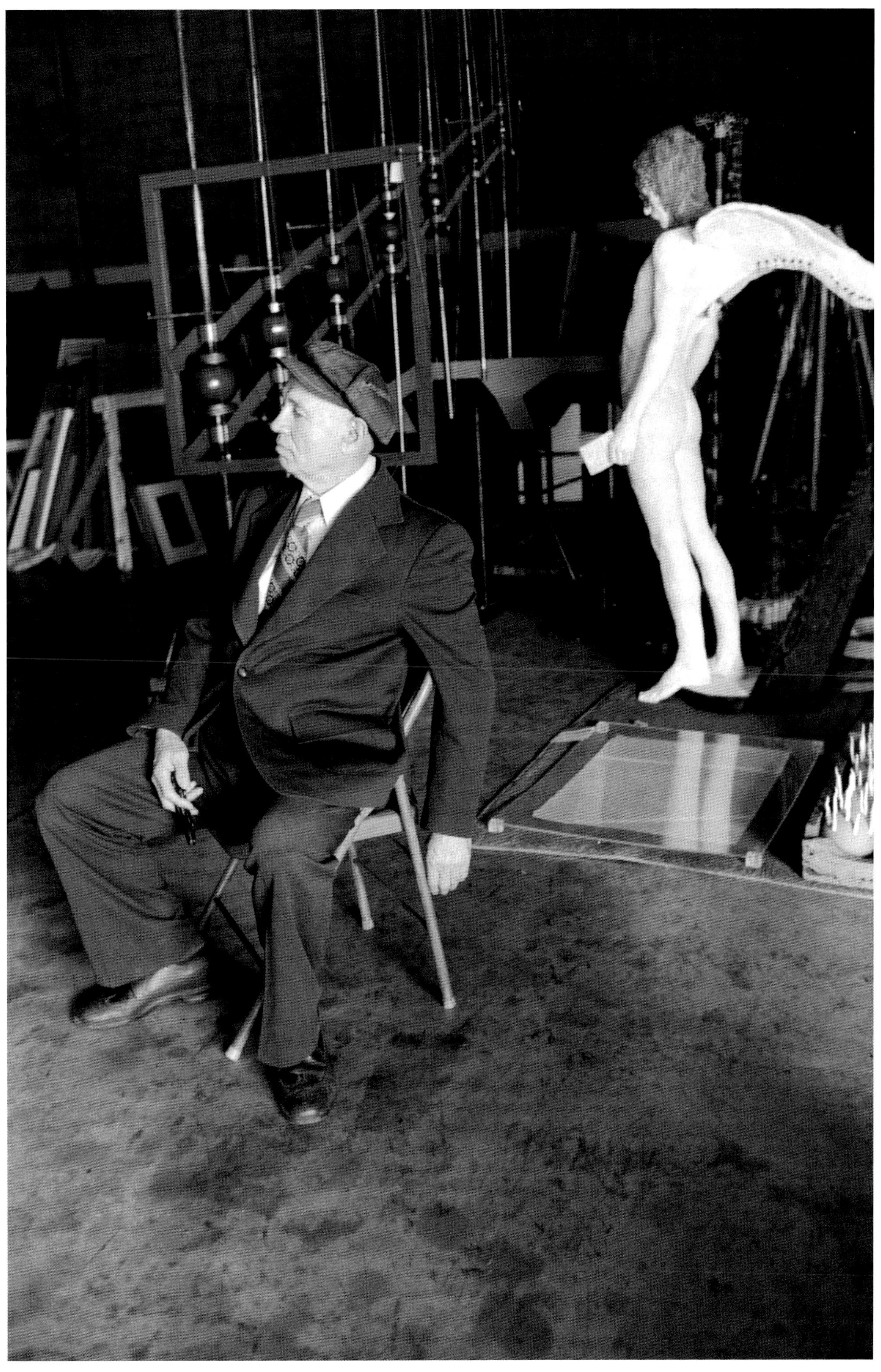

Romie's at Morgan and Morgan Storage Warehouse, with an unidentified sculpture behind him. 1982

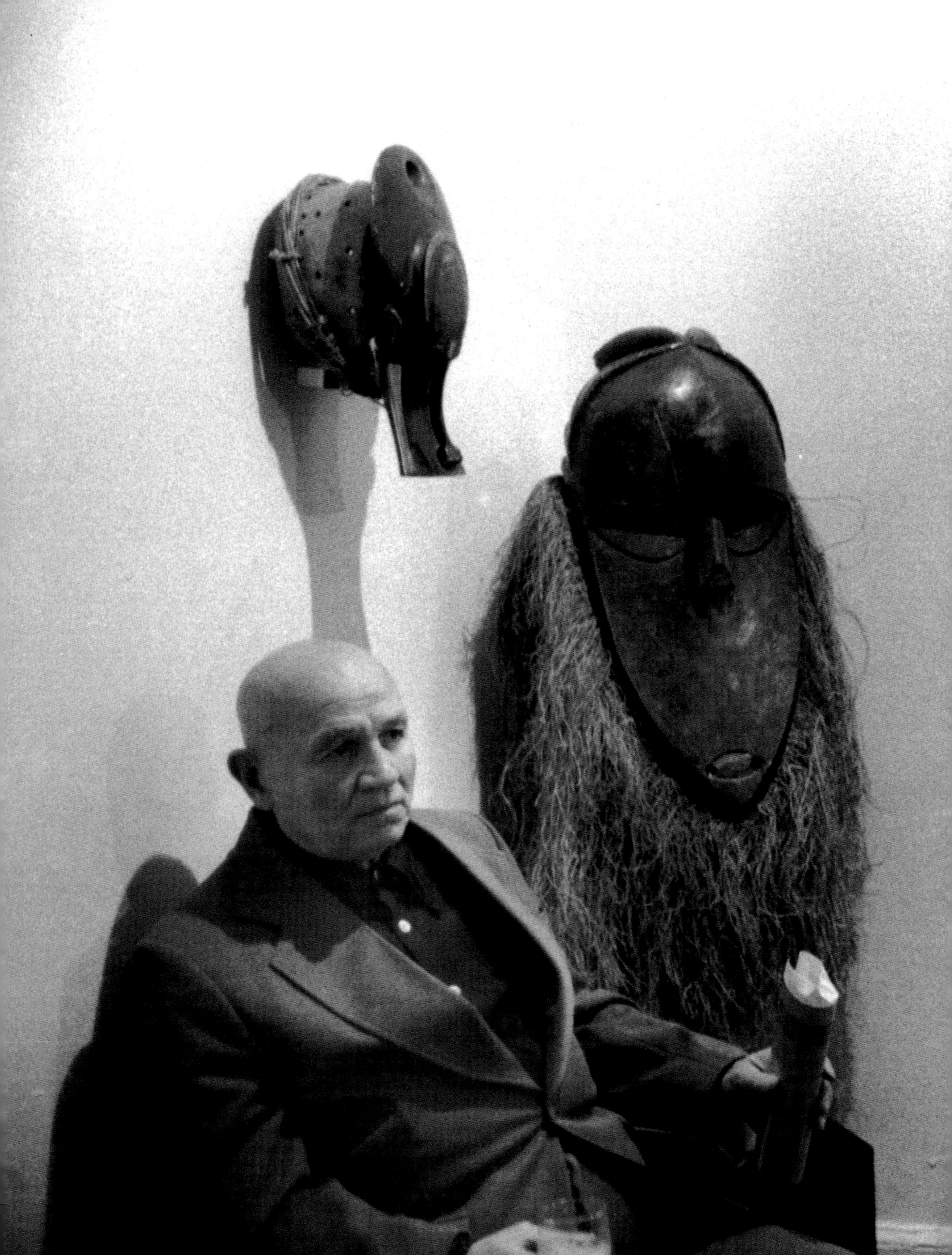

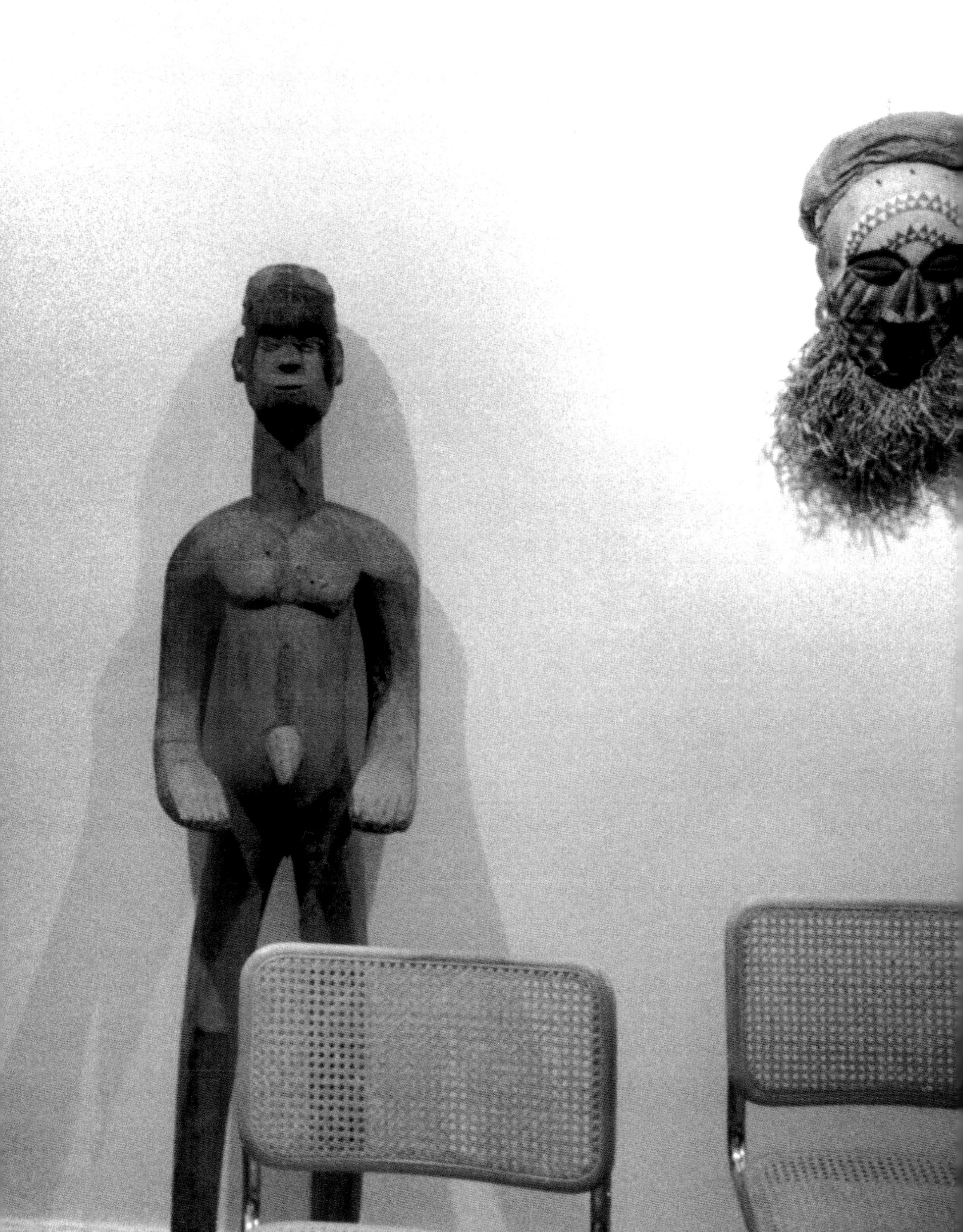

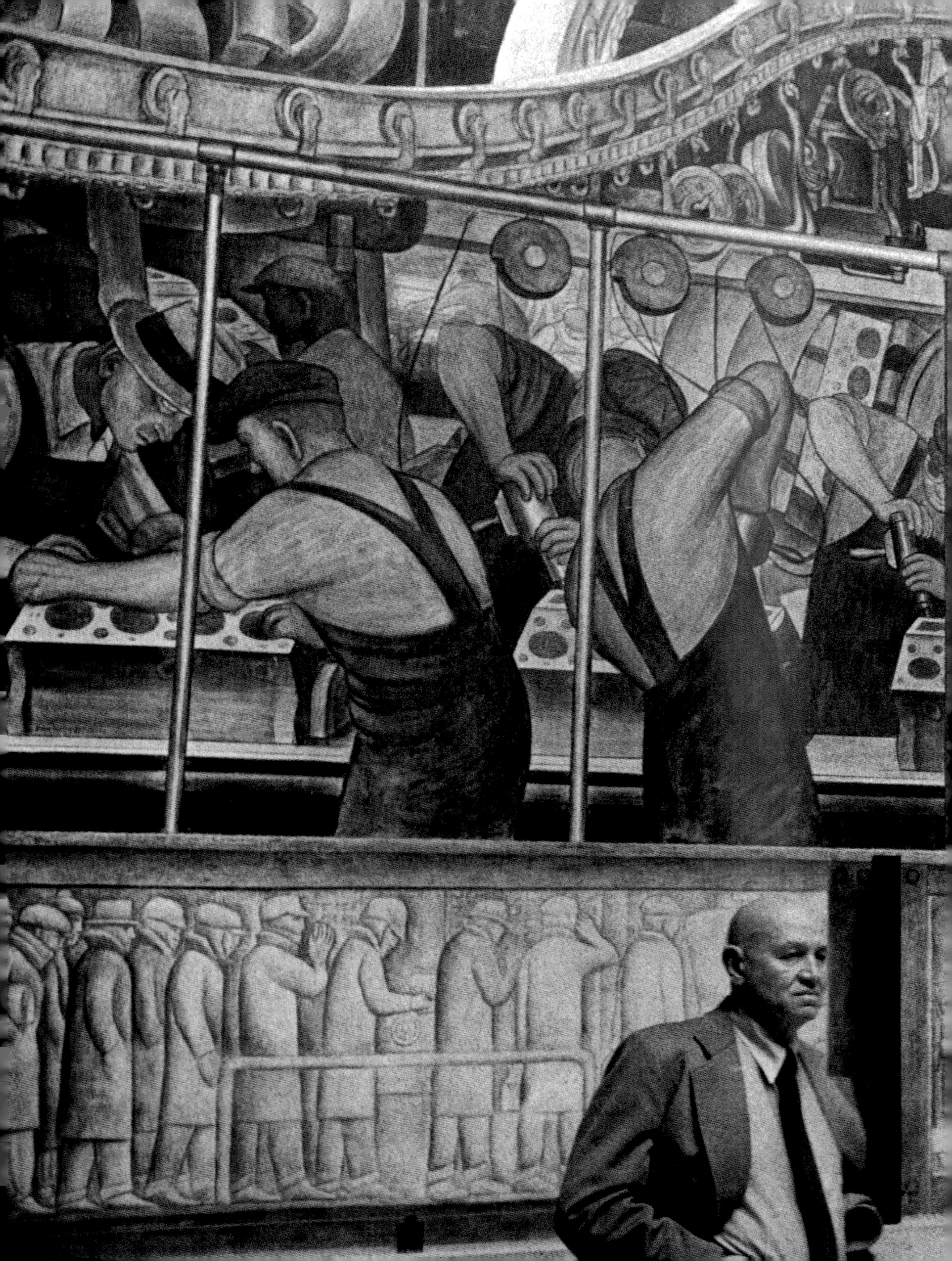

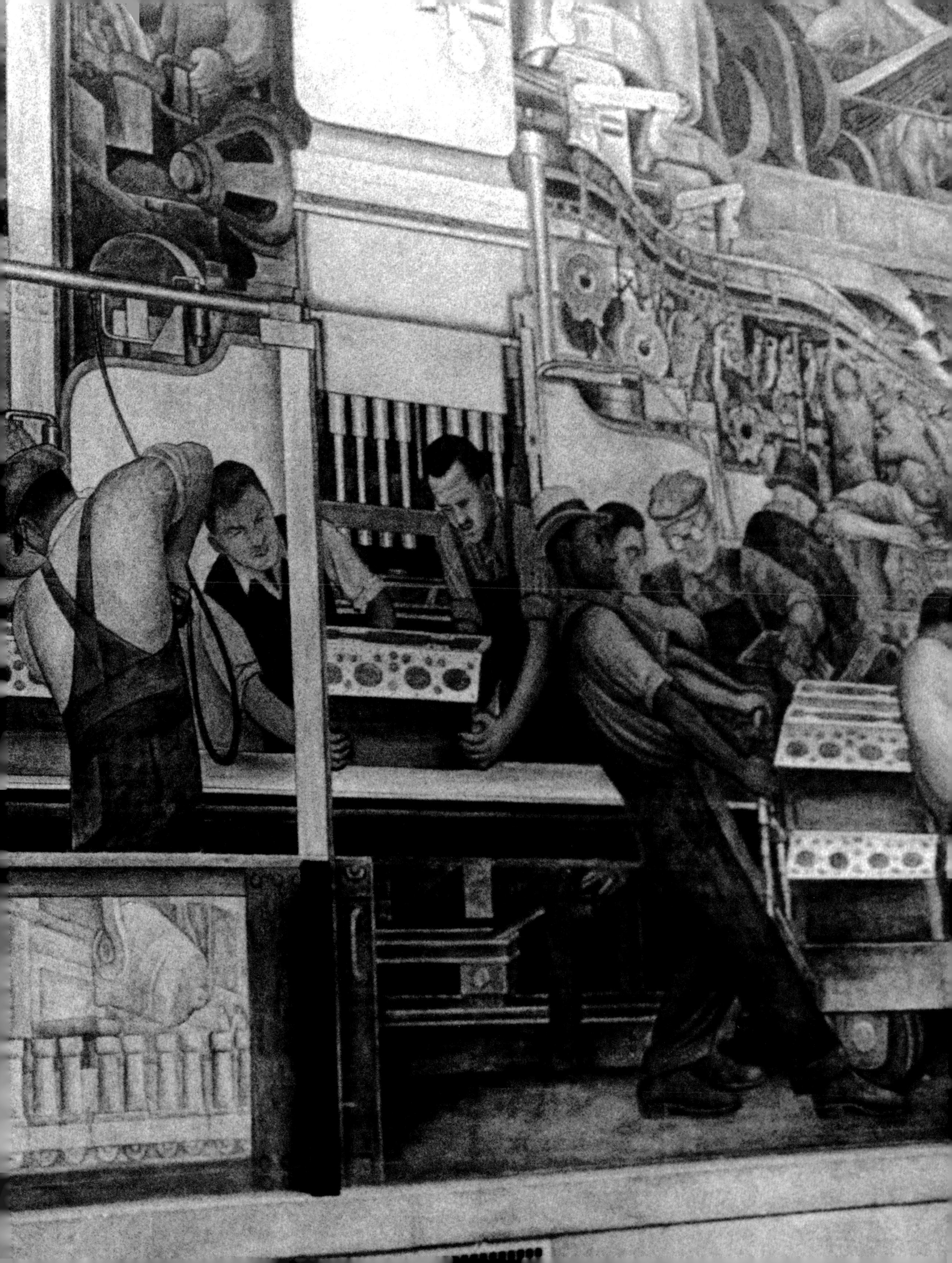

PRECEDING PAGES
Romie was very interested in African art. Here he's at Izaka Zango Gallery, New York. Late 1970s

Romie was influenced by the Mexican muralists. One of his favorites was Diego Rivera. When we went to visit the collector Walter O. Evans, we also went to the Detroit Institute of Arts and saw Rivera's *Detroit Industry* murals. c. 1978

LECTURES AND TEACHING

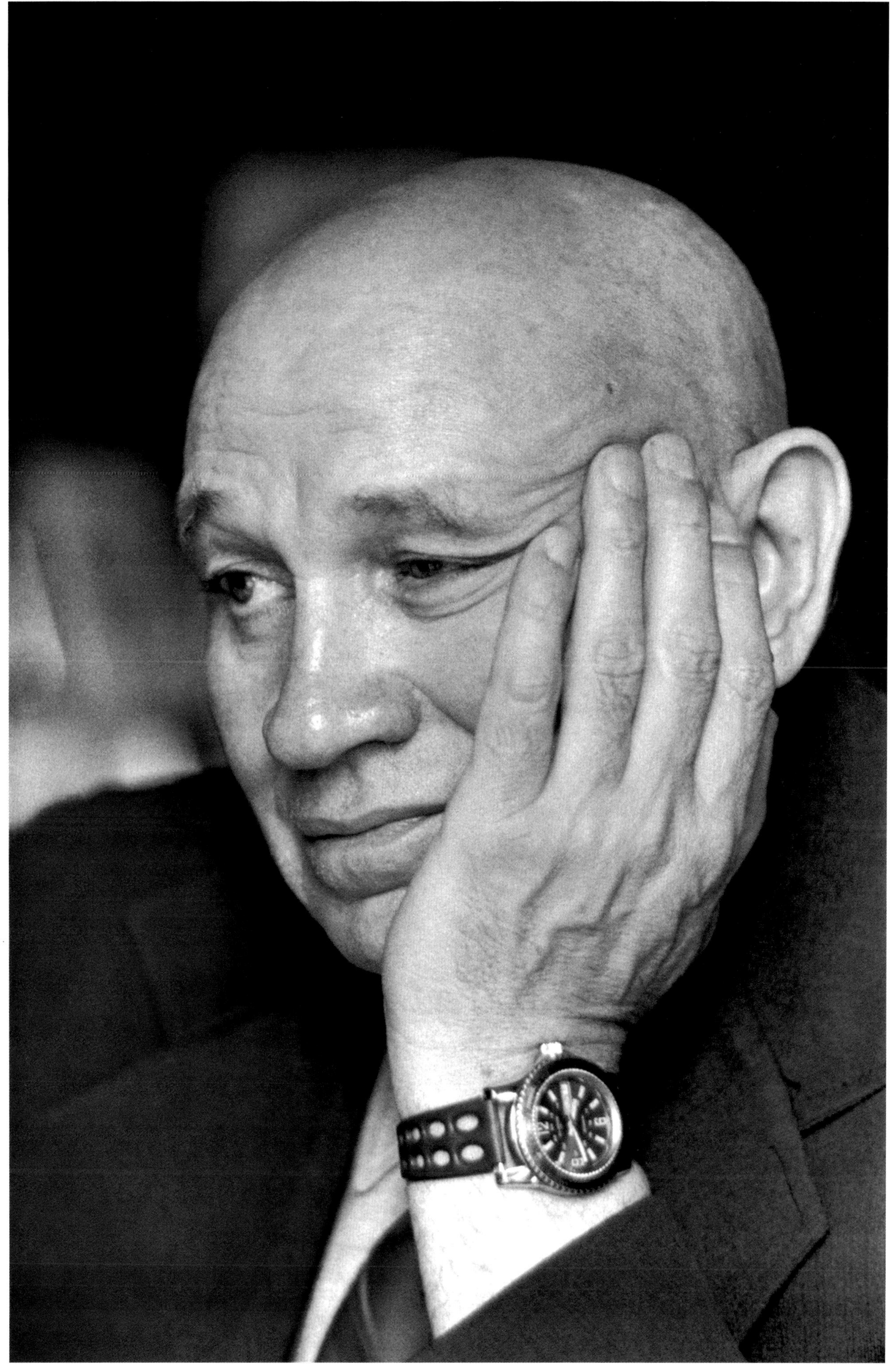

Romare Bearden. 1977

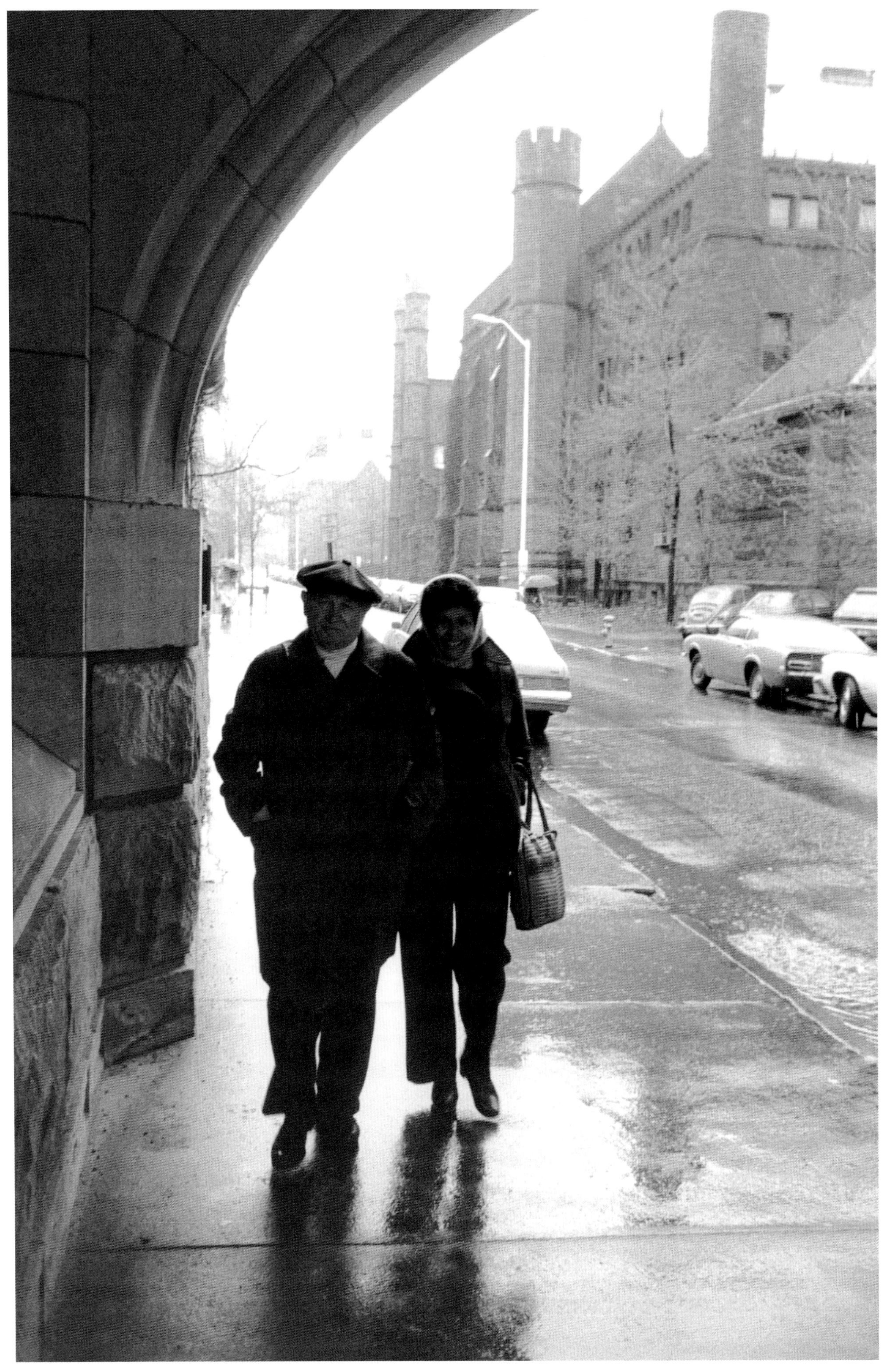

Romie and Nanette are in New Haven on a cold, snowy day, after he taught a class at Yale. They're getting ready to go to the car so I could drive them back to New York. 1980

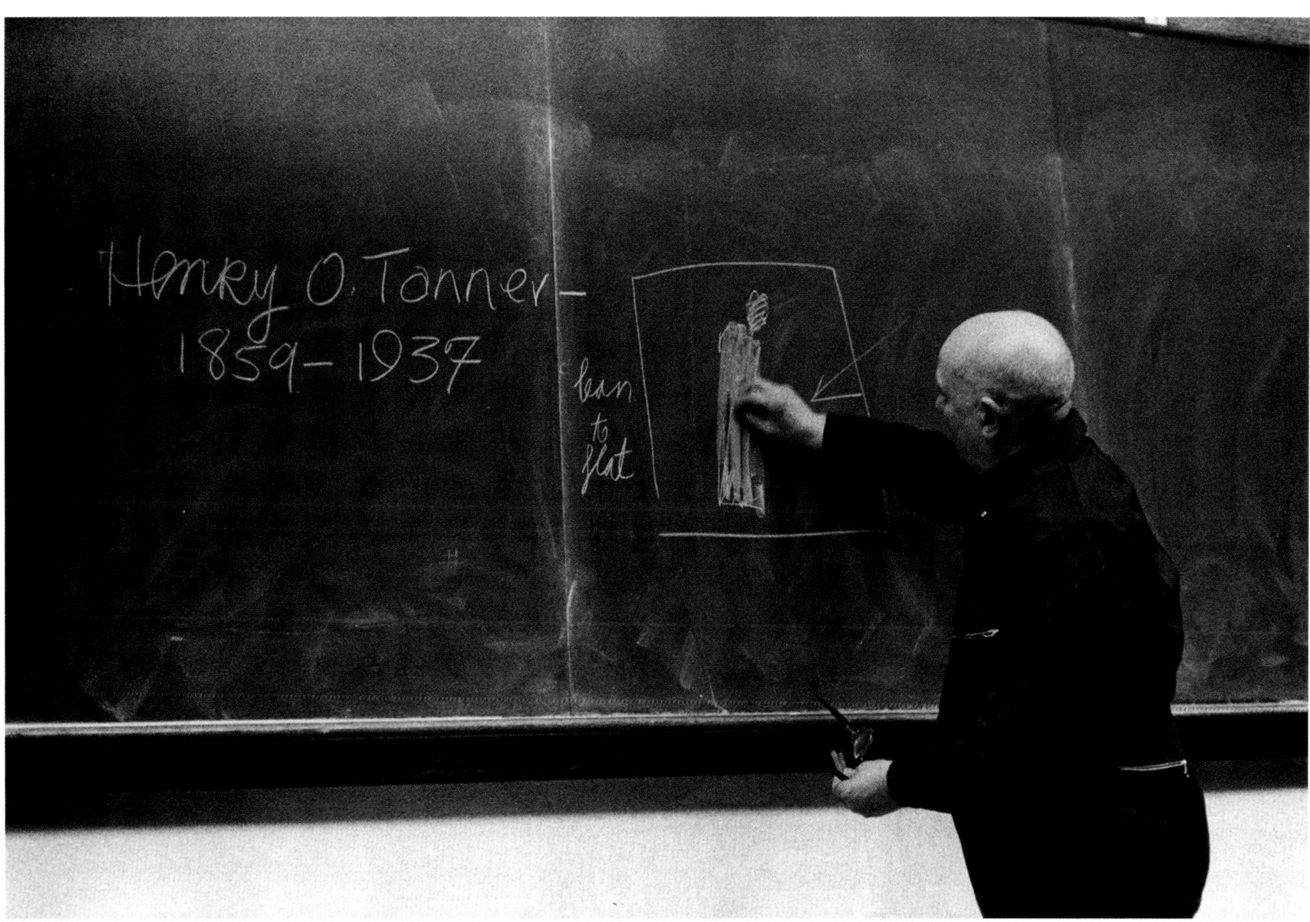

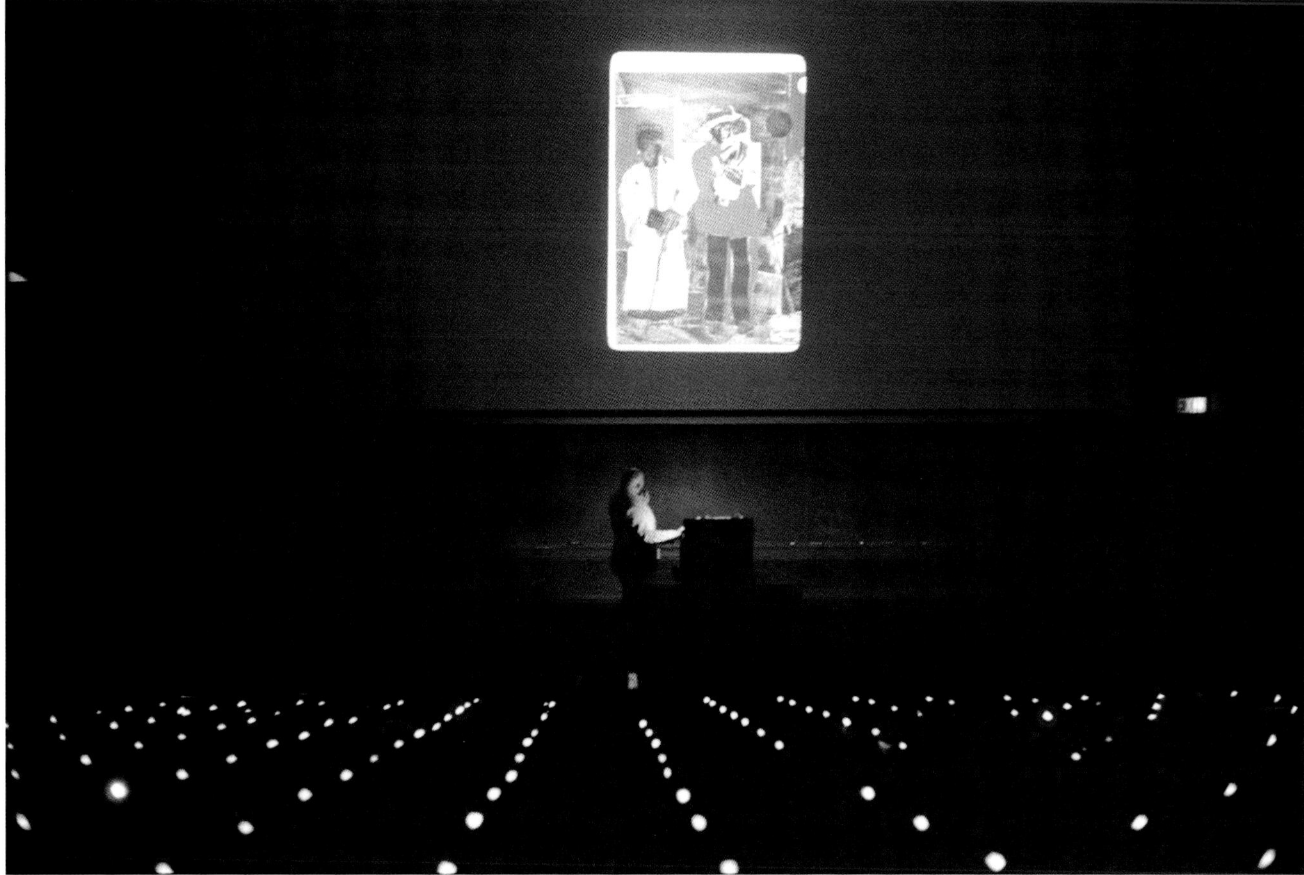

Romie's giving a demonstration of how Tanner would use a brushstroke to glaze, to get this special effect. 1980

Romie's giving a lecture about his work at Vassar College in Poughkeepsie, New York. This is where I would come in, to take pictures of the works, or to copy works by other artists out of books, and then prepare slides for the lectures. *Profile/Part I, The Twenties: Miss Bertha and Mr. Seth*, 1978, is on the screen. The shiny spots are lights by the students' seats so they could see to take notes. 1979

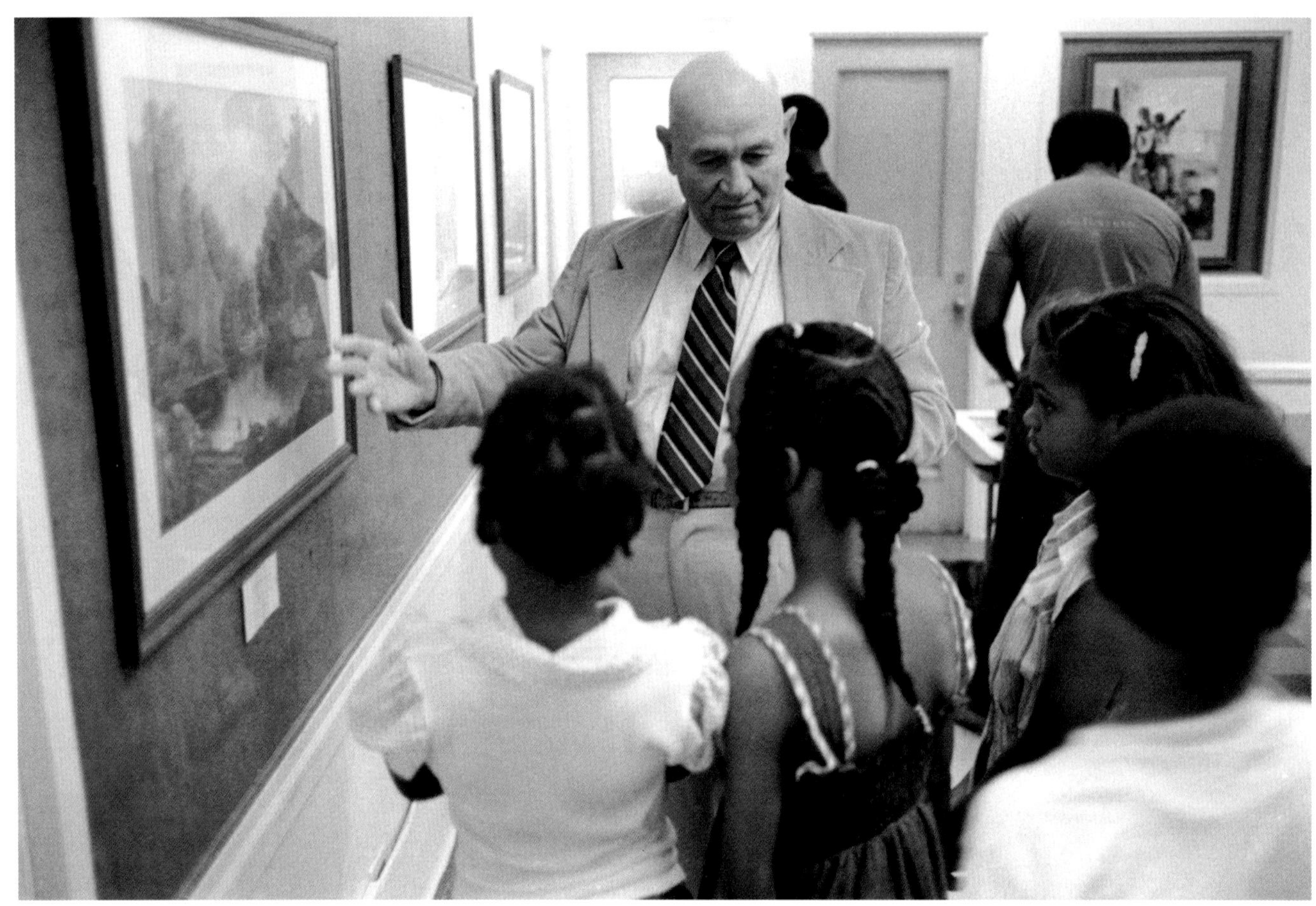

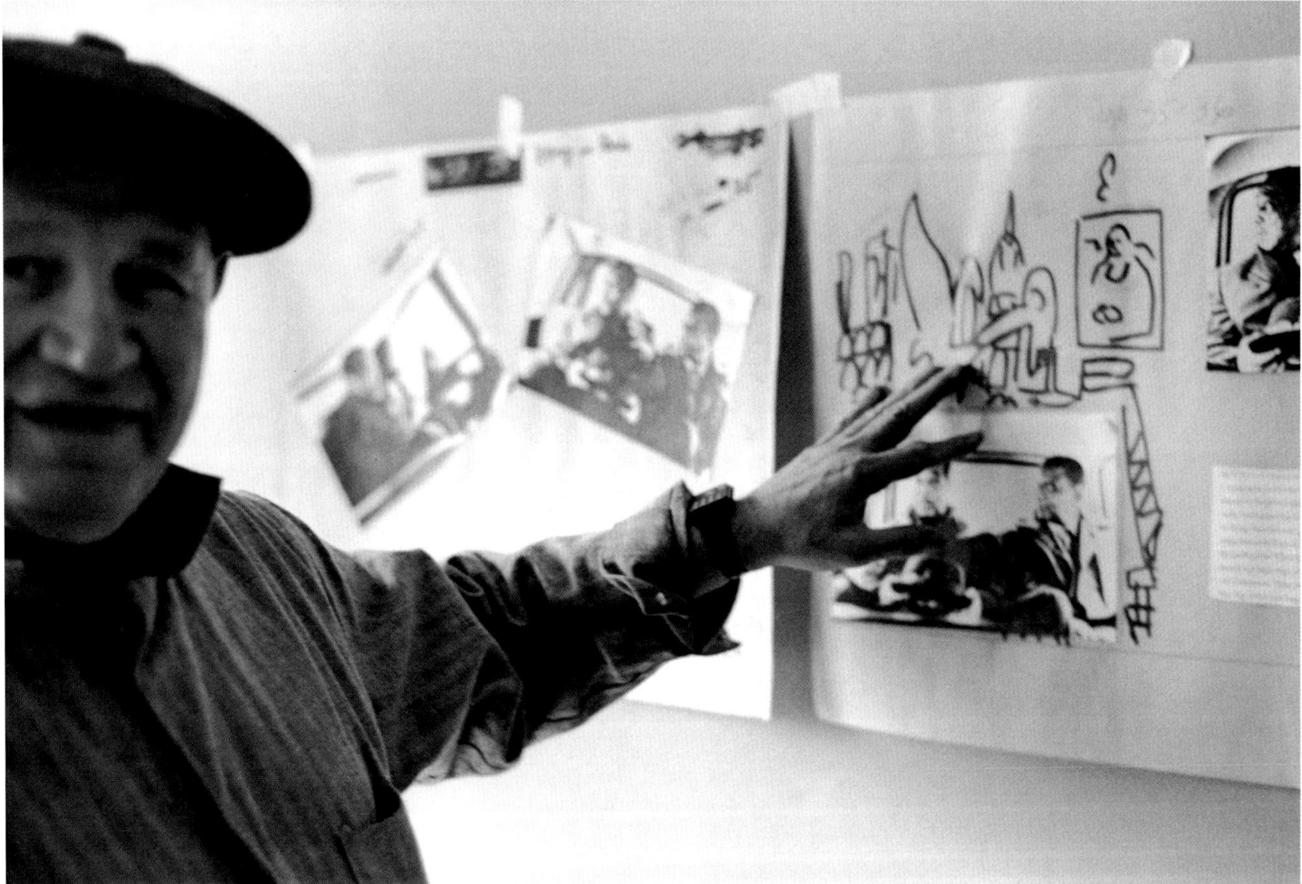

Romie loved children. He took a lot of time introducing them to art when the opportunity was there. At the Mint Museum in Charlotte he's talking about Robert Scott Duncanson. 1980

Romie's talking about book design. He's in his last studio, a second one in the same Long Island City building he'd been in since before I knew him. I think he might have taken this one just to work on this book, *Paris Blues*, which never was published. c. 1987.

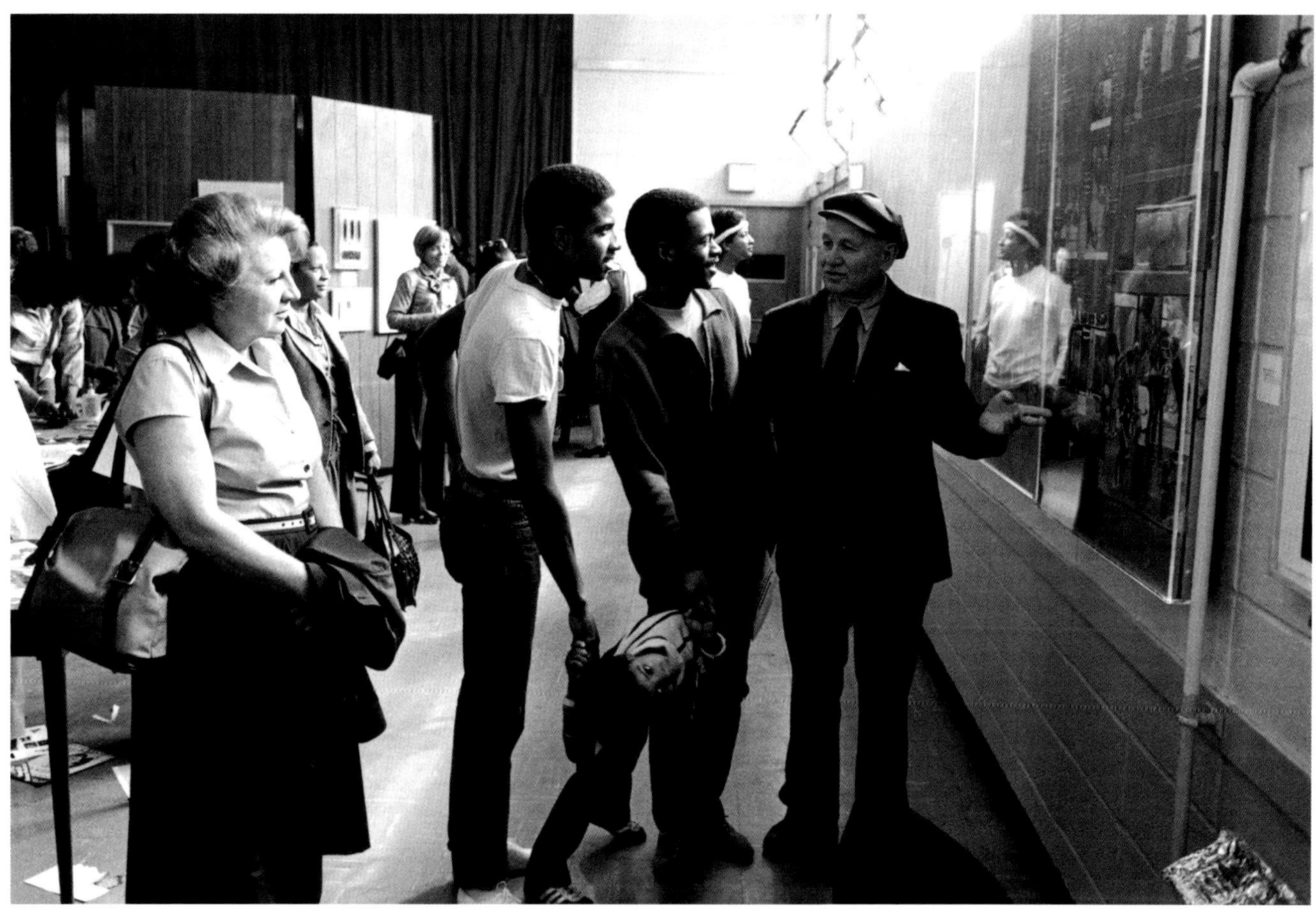

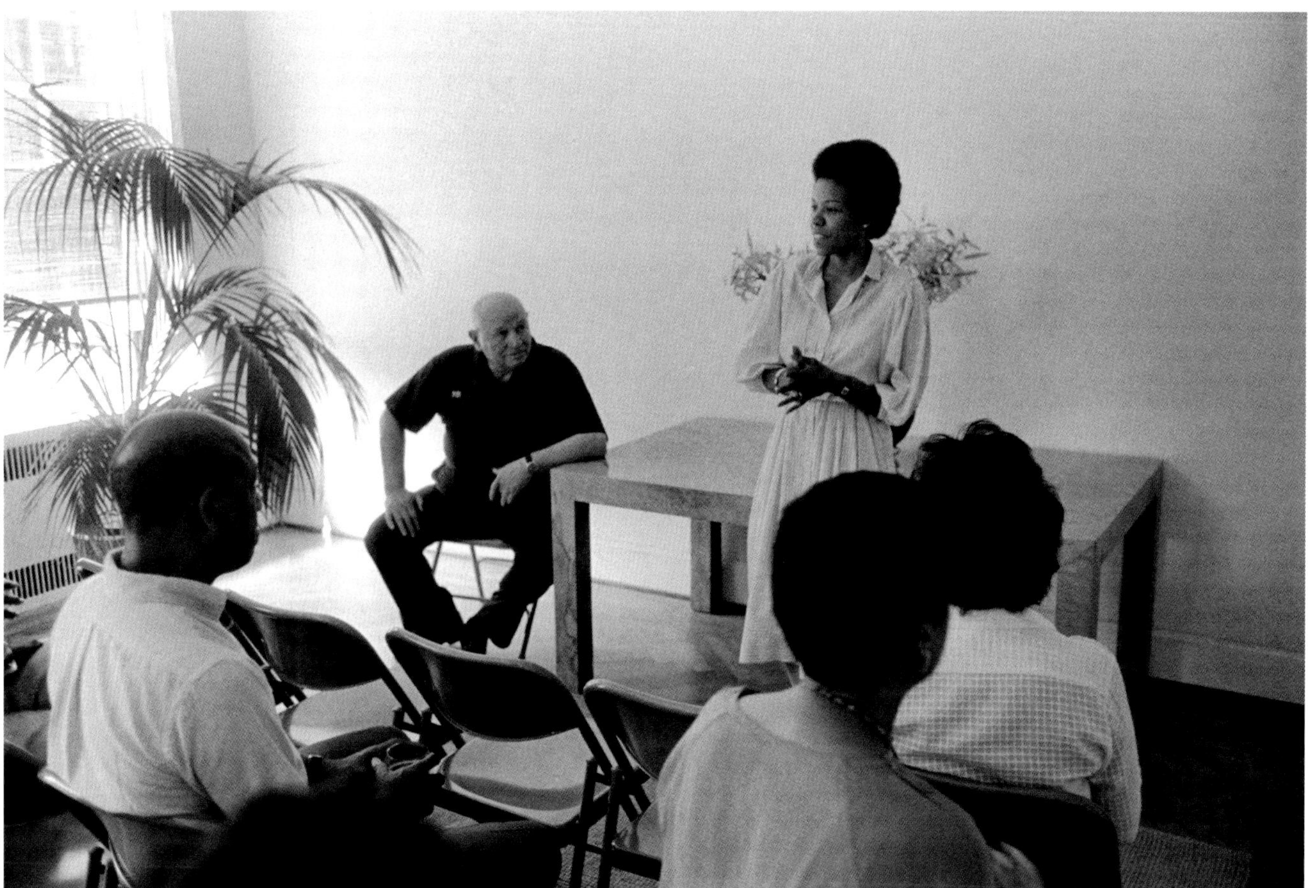

Goddard Riverside Community Center in New York, on the Upper West Side, had borrowed *The Block*. Romie's talking to two young artists. The niece of one of them was getting tired and rambunctious. c. 1977

Mary Schmidt Campbell, director of The Studio Museum in Harlem at the time, is lecturing to young prospective African American collectors. They're in a gallery in Janet Carter's house, for exhibits of emerging artists. Janet was married to the famous bass player with Miles Davis, Ron Carter. I think Romie was there to give a talk on the history of African American art. c. 1982

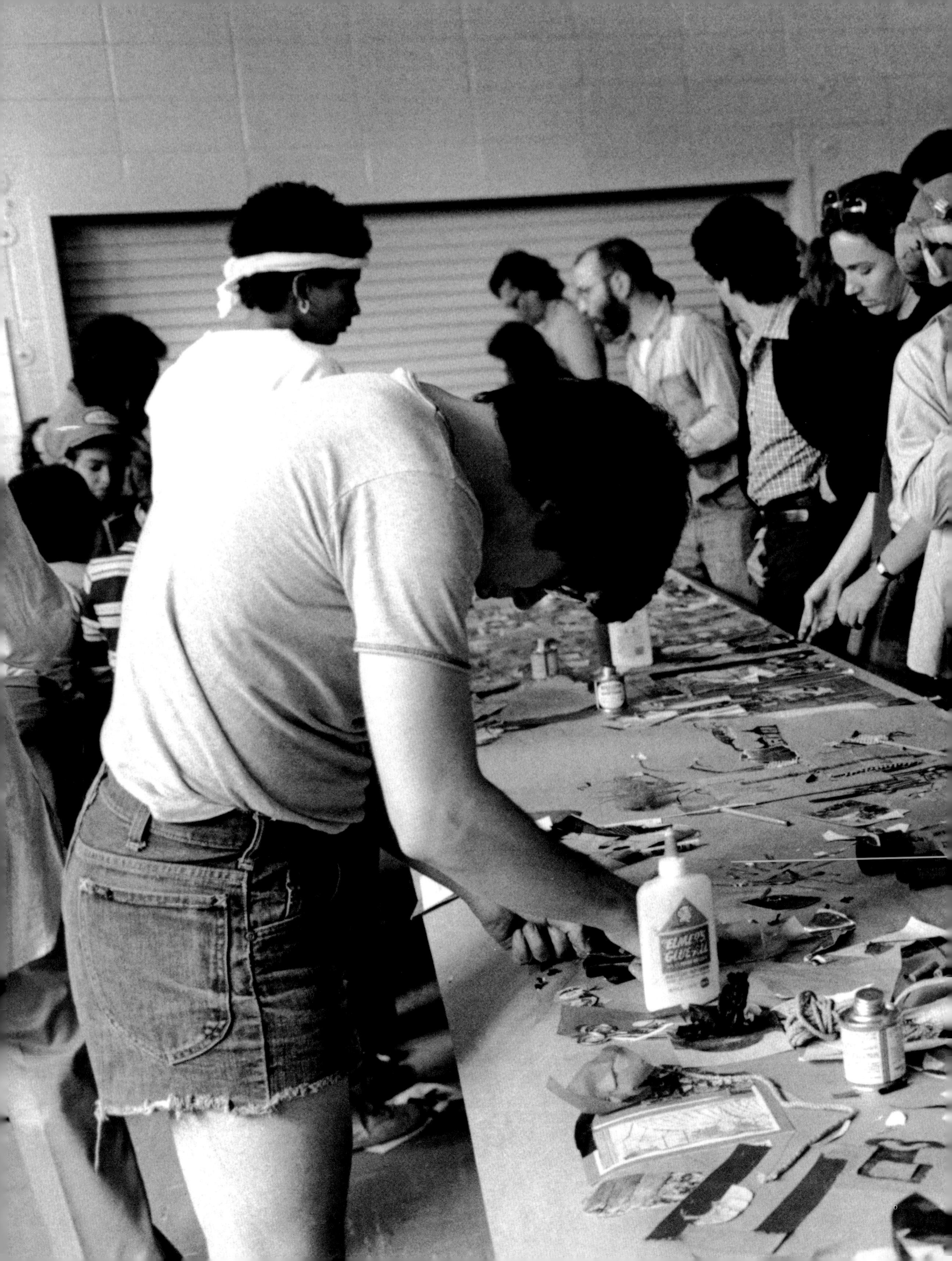

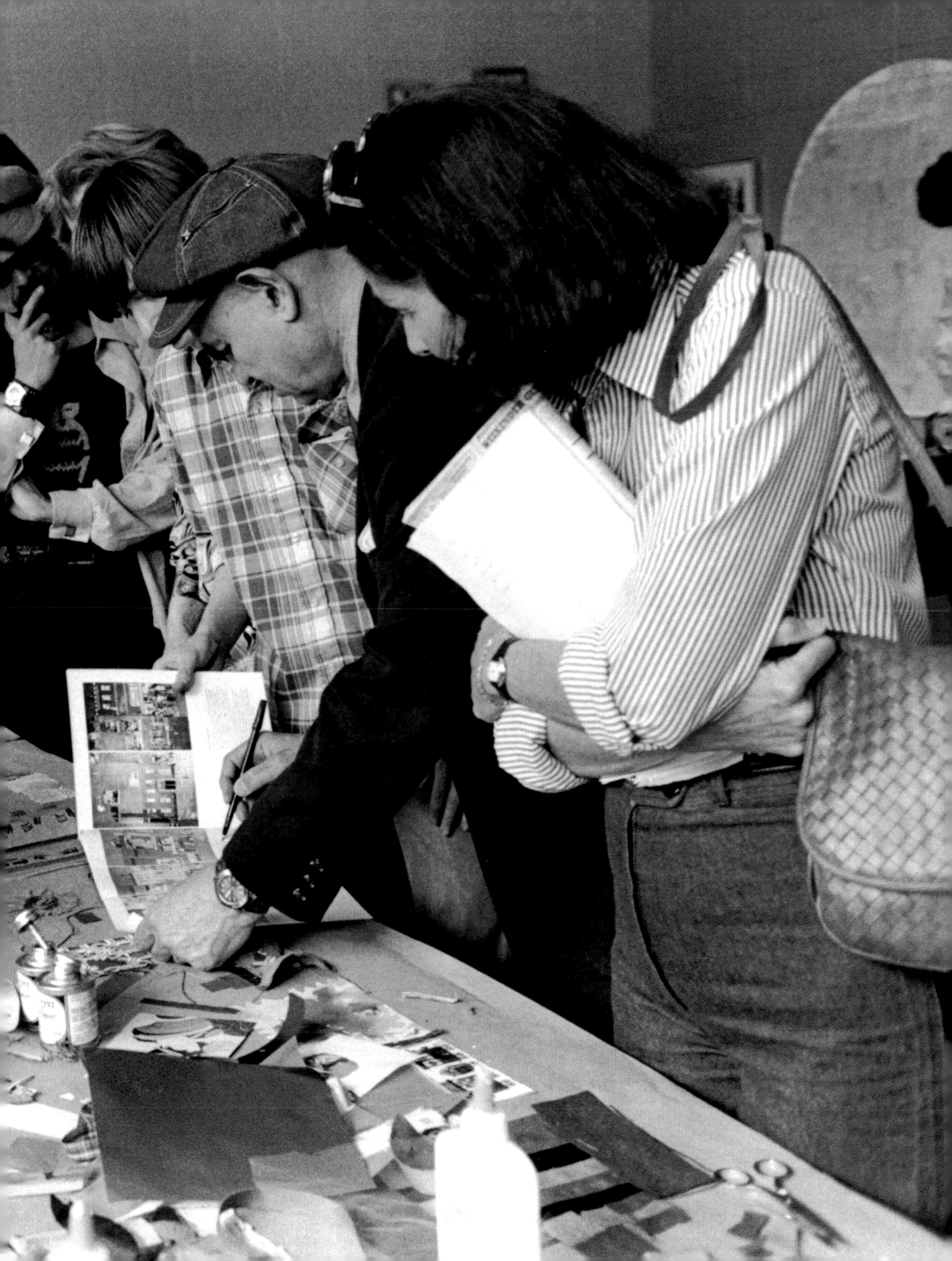

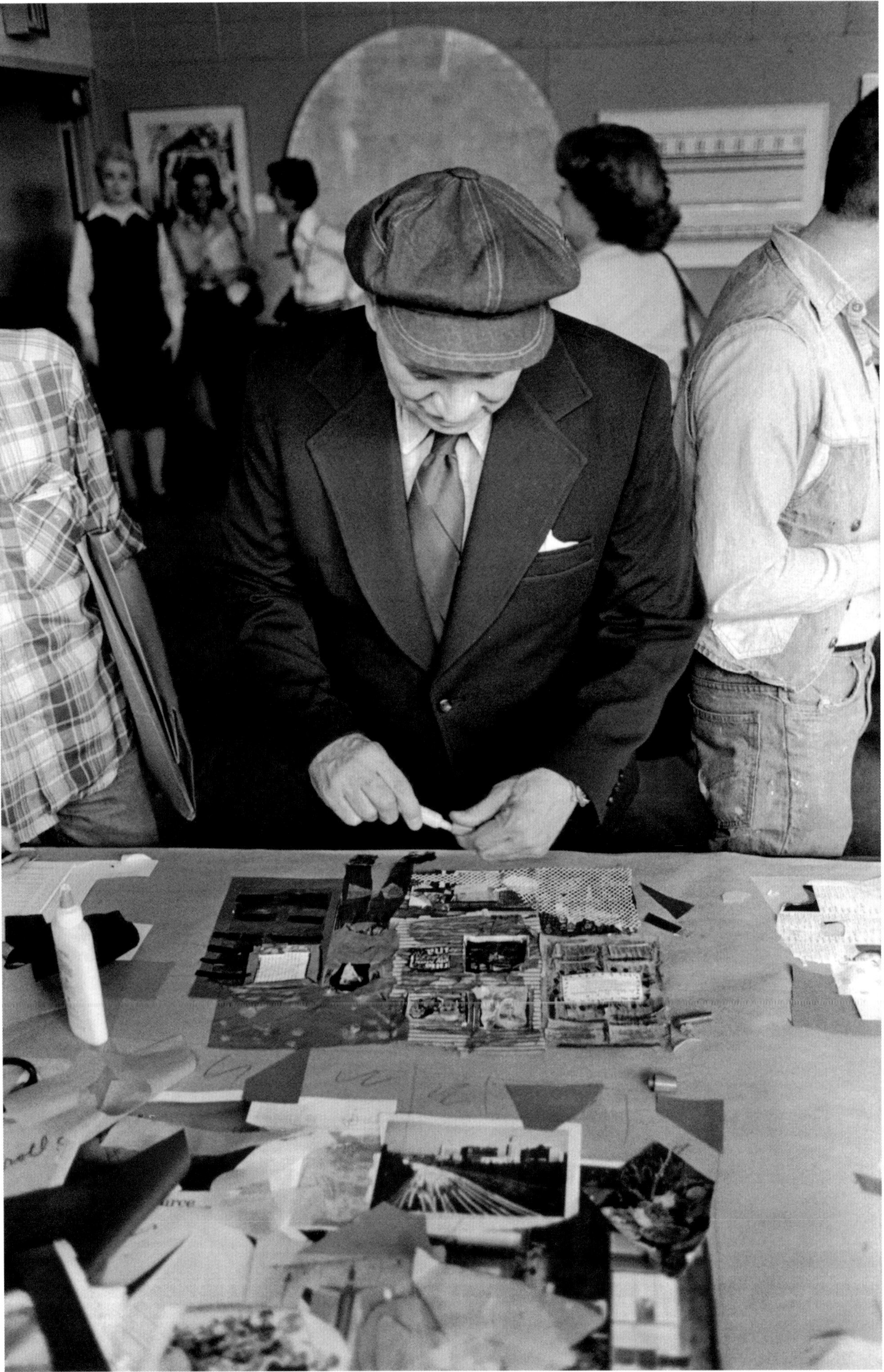

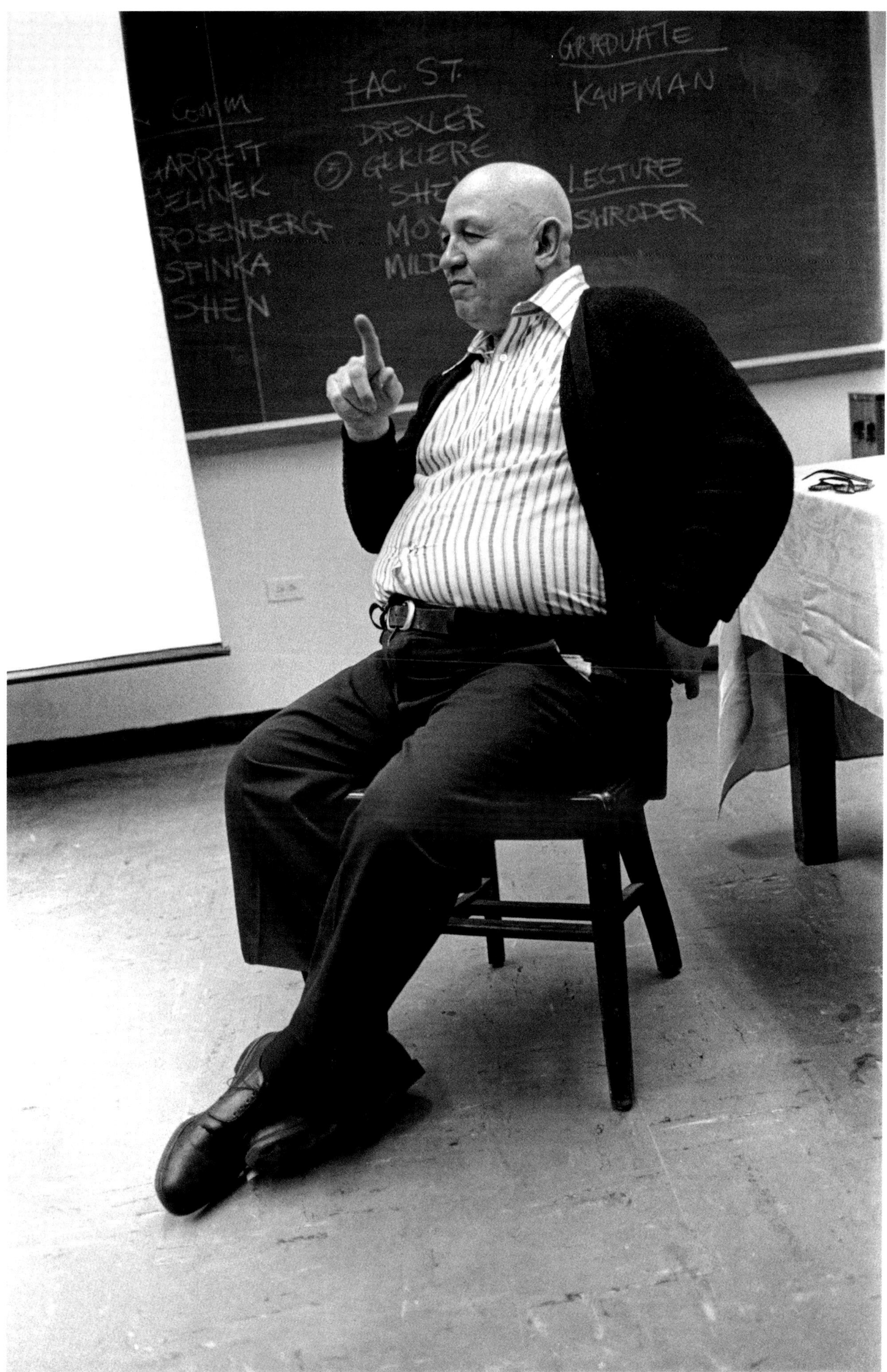
GRADUATE
KAUFMAN
FAC. ST.
DREXLER
LECTURE
SHRODER
ROSENBERG
SPINKA
SHEN

PRECEDING PAGES

Romie's teaching a class on collage making at the Goddard Riverside Community Center while *The Block* was on exhibition there. The class lasted several hours, about half a day. c. 1977

Romie's at Goddard Riverside Community Center. c. 1977

Romie went to colleges to speak a lot, to go and visit art classes. Here he's at City College of New York in Harlem. He would give instructions, and he would pay particular attention to any of the students who were black. 1975

FRIENDS

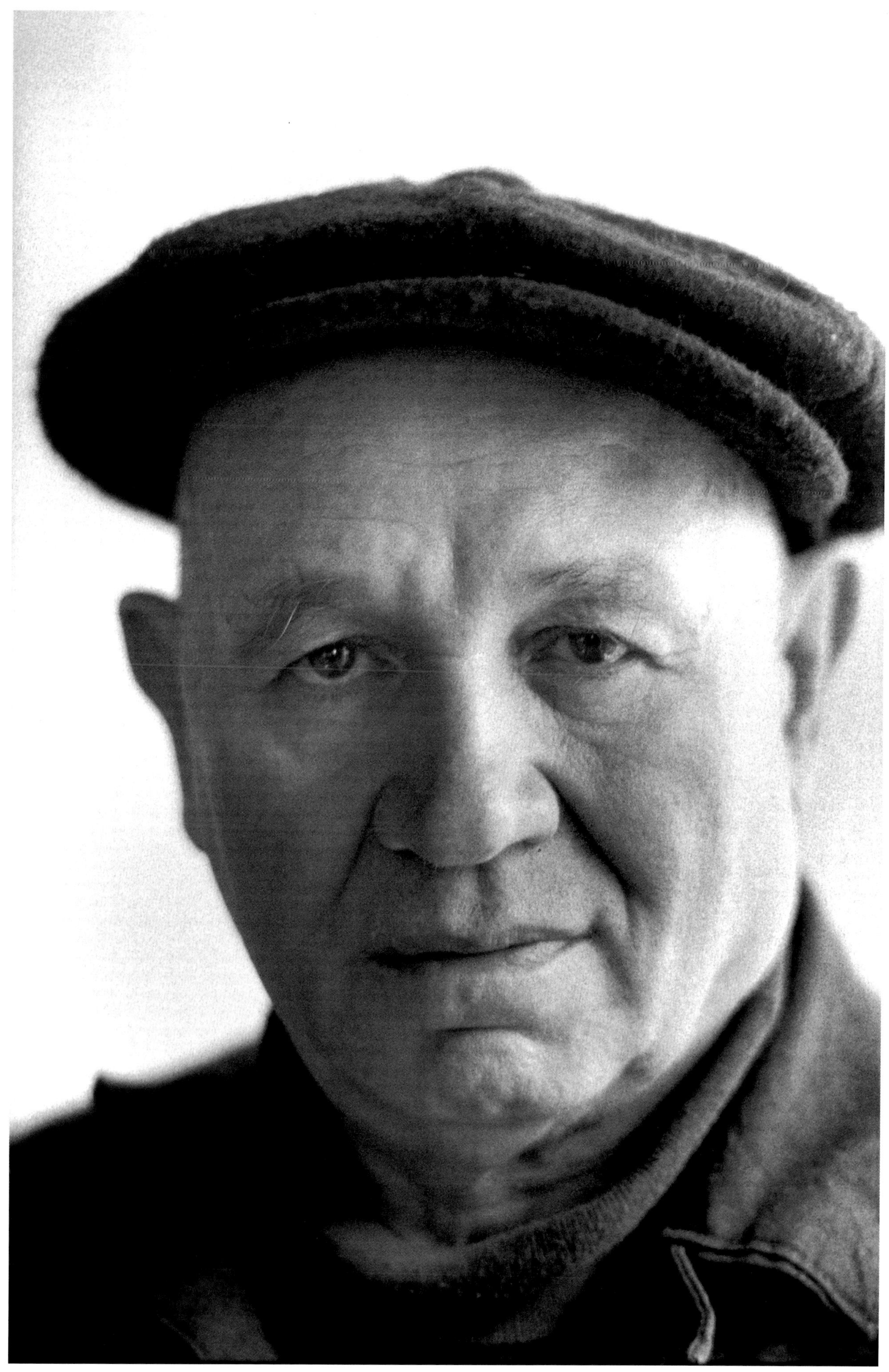

Romare Bearden. 1979

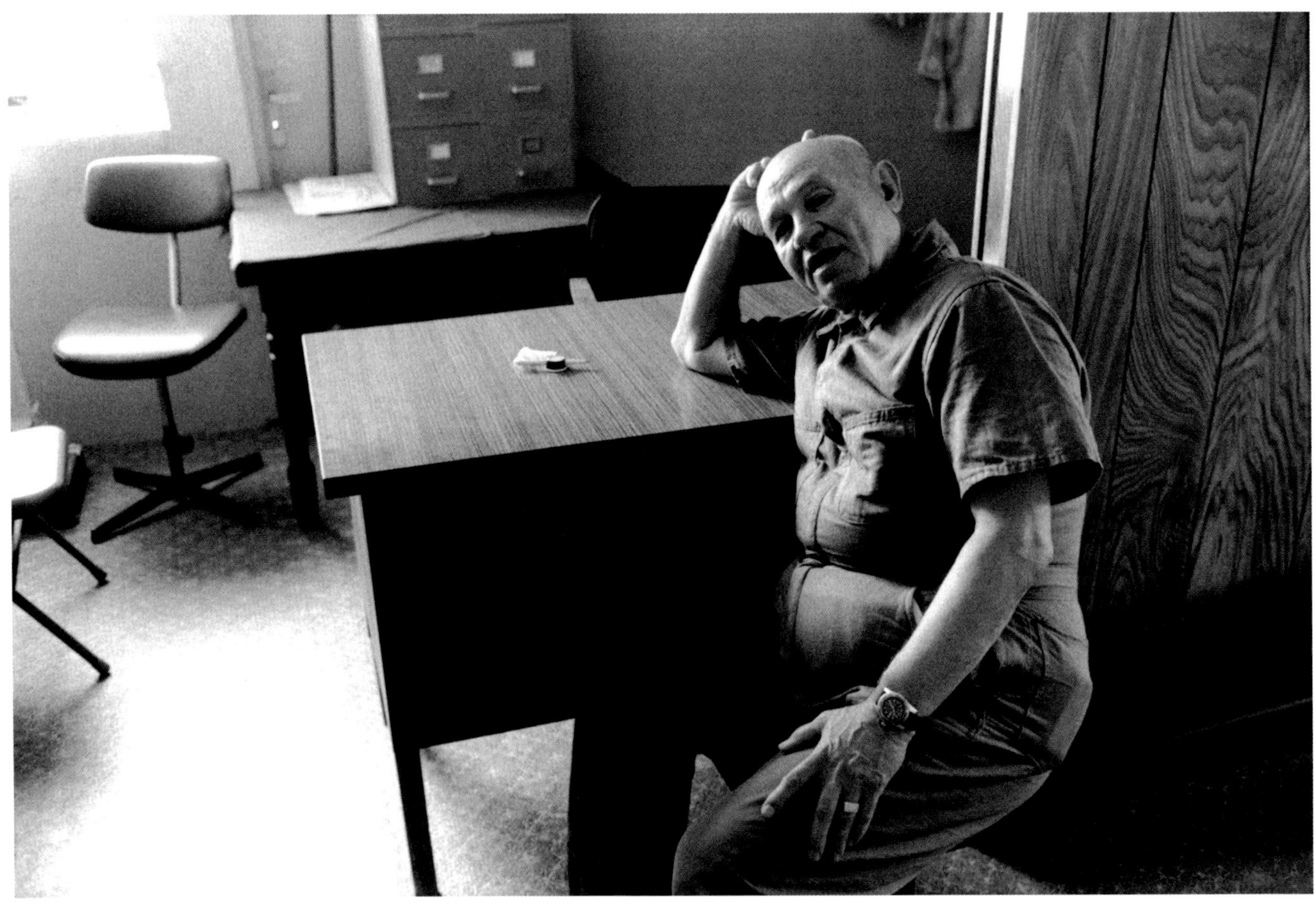

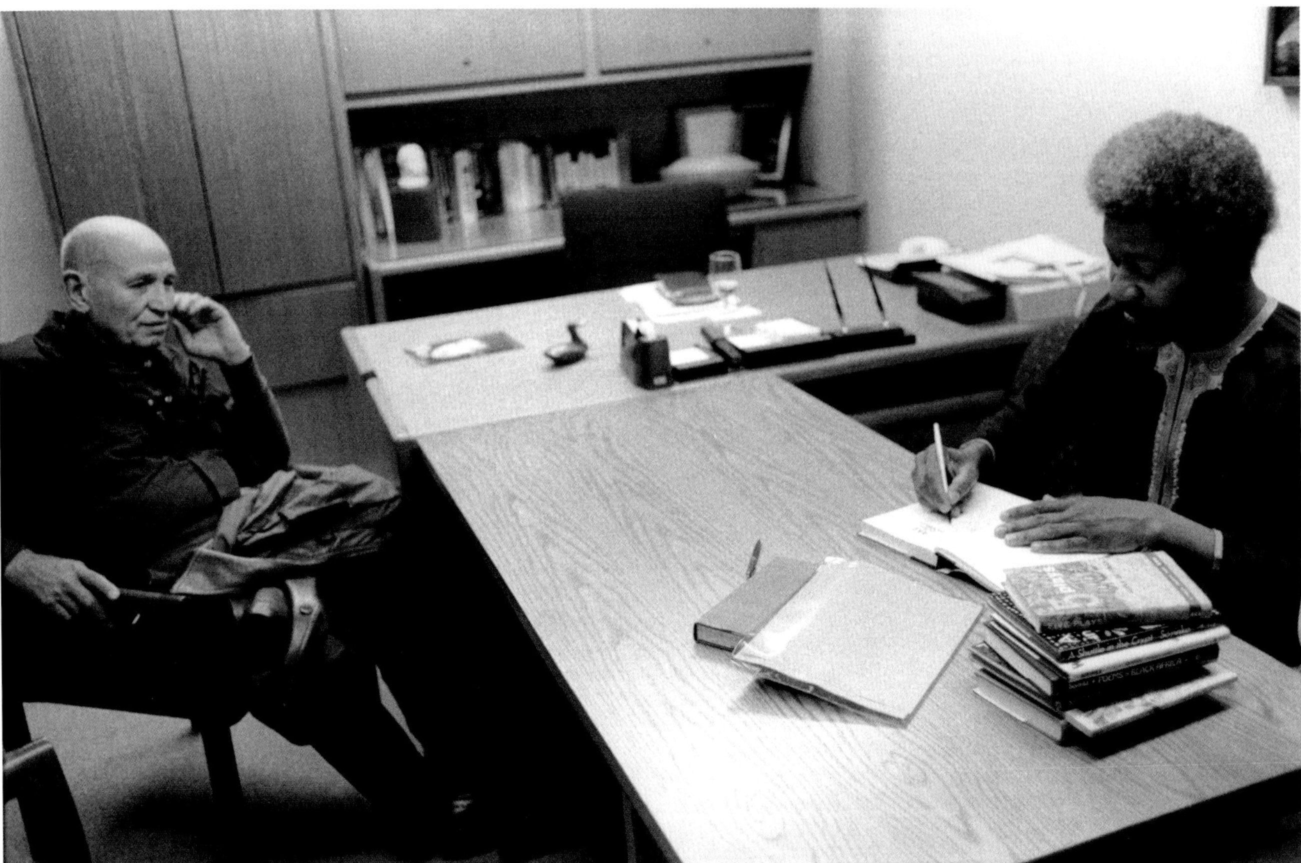

Romie's at an office in Long Island City. He and I were both from the South, and being from the South, you learn how to —what they say—take a bone and carry a bone. He'd have these stories that he would embellish, that he would hear from somebody, and he'd make them like they were his own. They were always interesting. He would like put yeast in them, yeast them up. c. 1986

Romie's meeting the writer Wole Soyinka for the first time, at the Schomburg Center for Research in Black Culture, New York Public Library. Mid-1980s

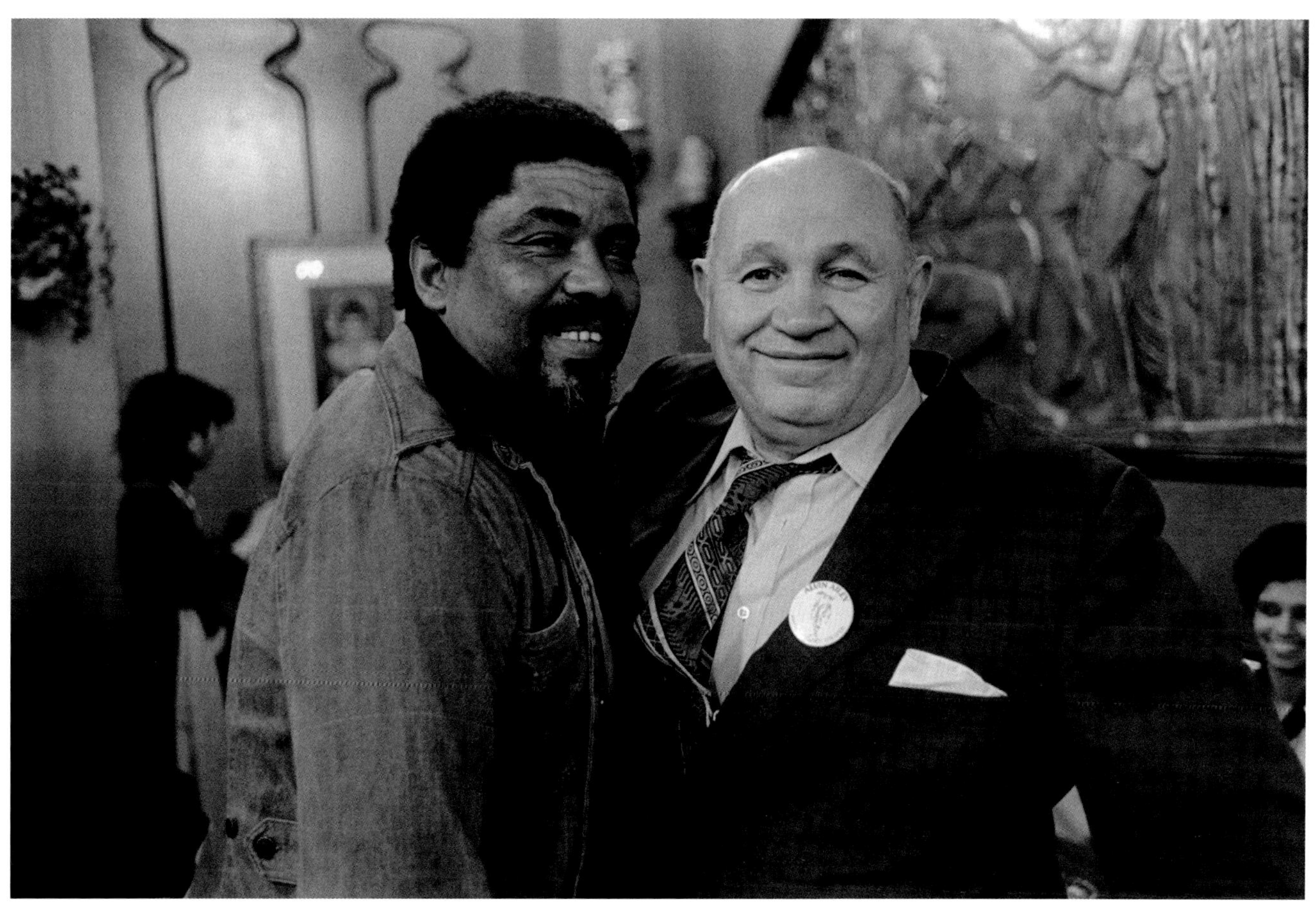

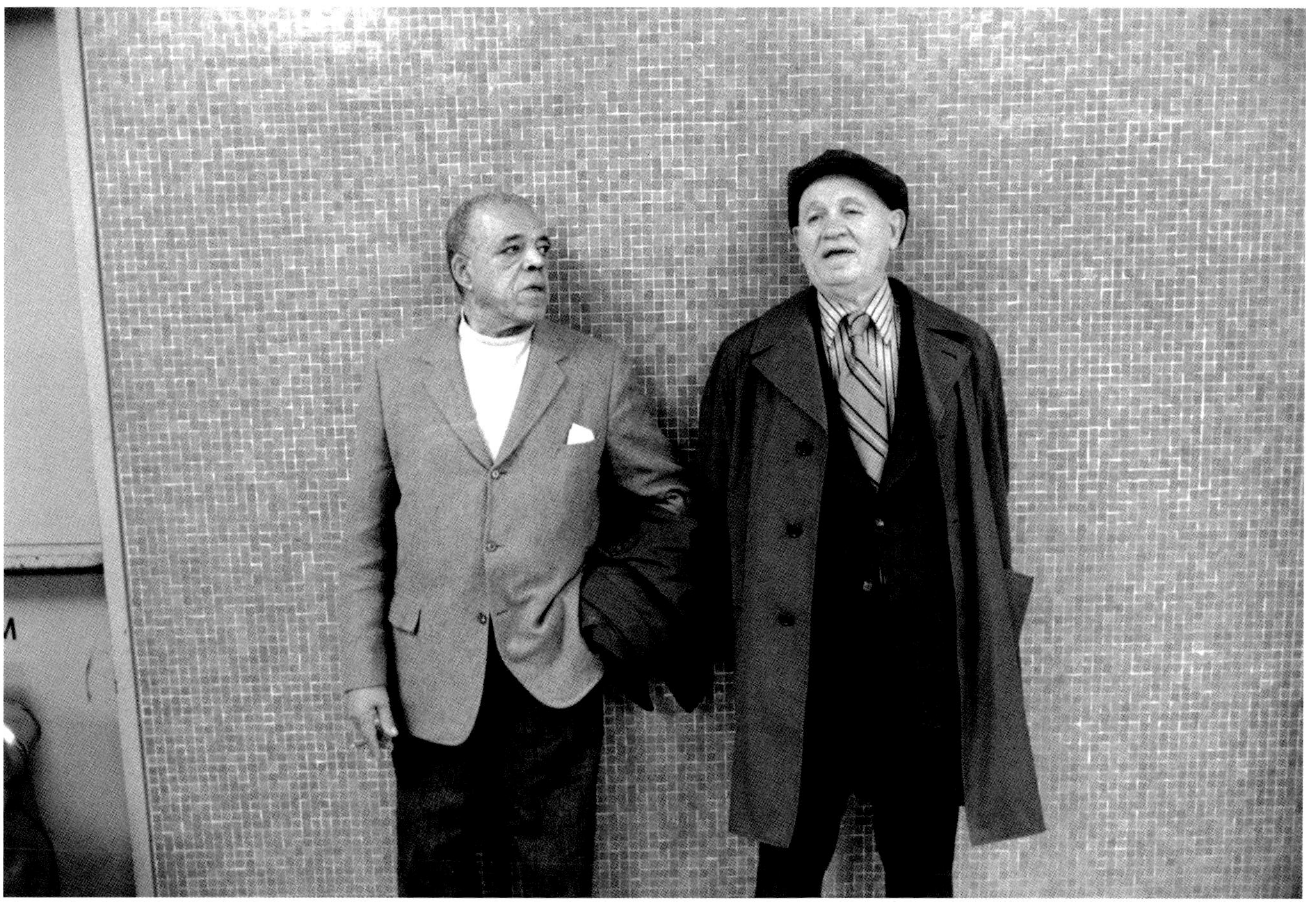

Alvin Ailey and Romie were good friends. Romie was interested in backing Nanette's dance company, and other dance companies, too. He would give them a print to sell. c. 1982

Addison Bates, who was responsible for Romie's first solo show in 1940, and Romie in New York City. 1978

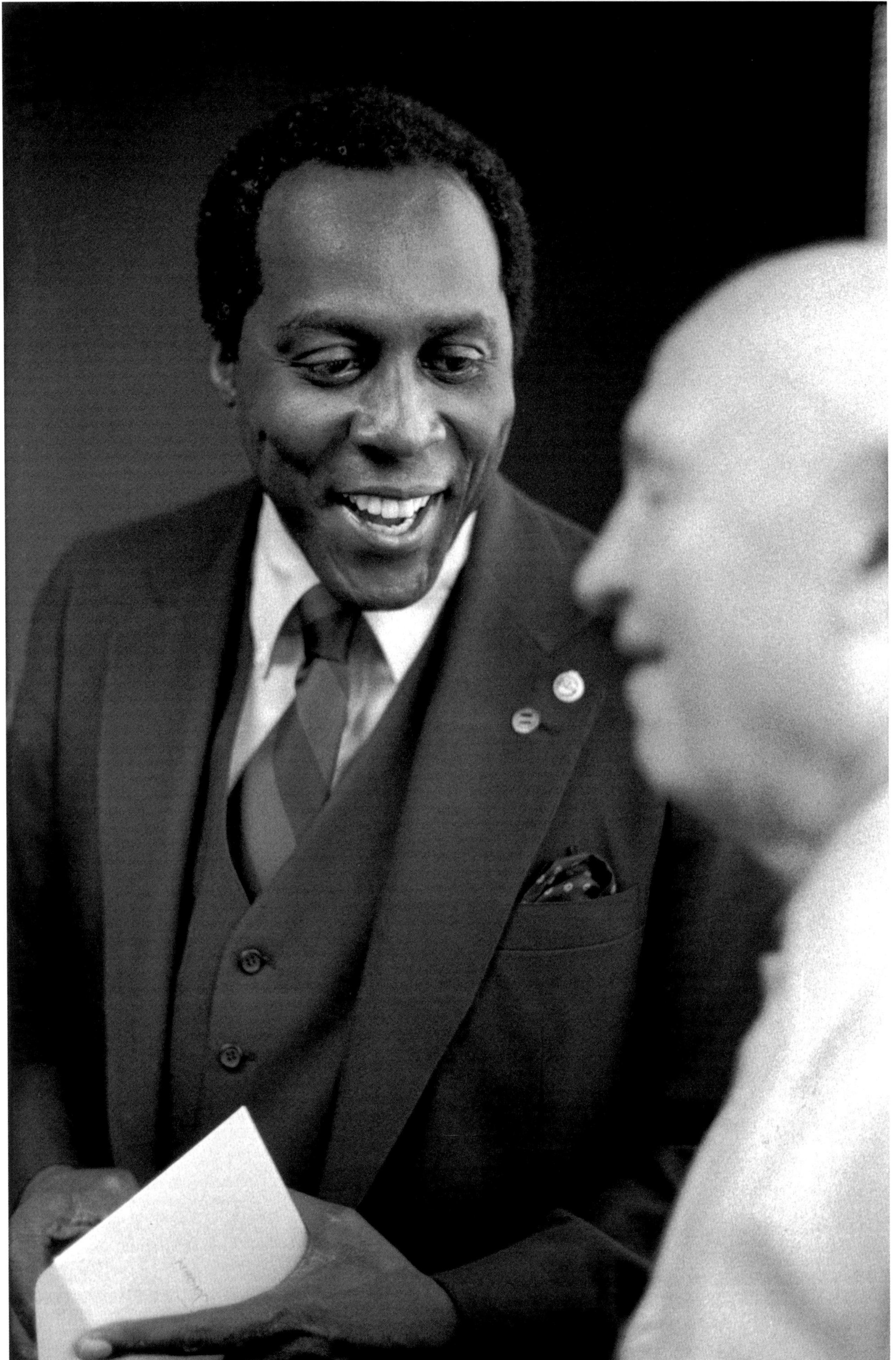

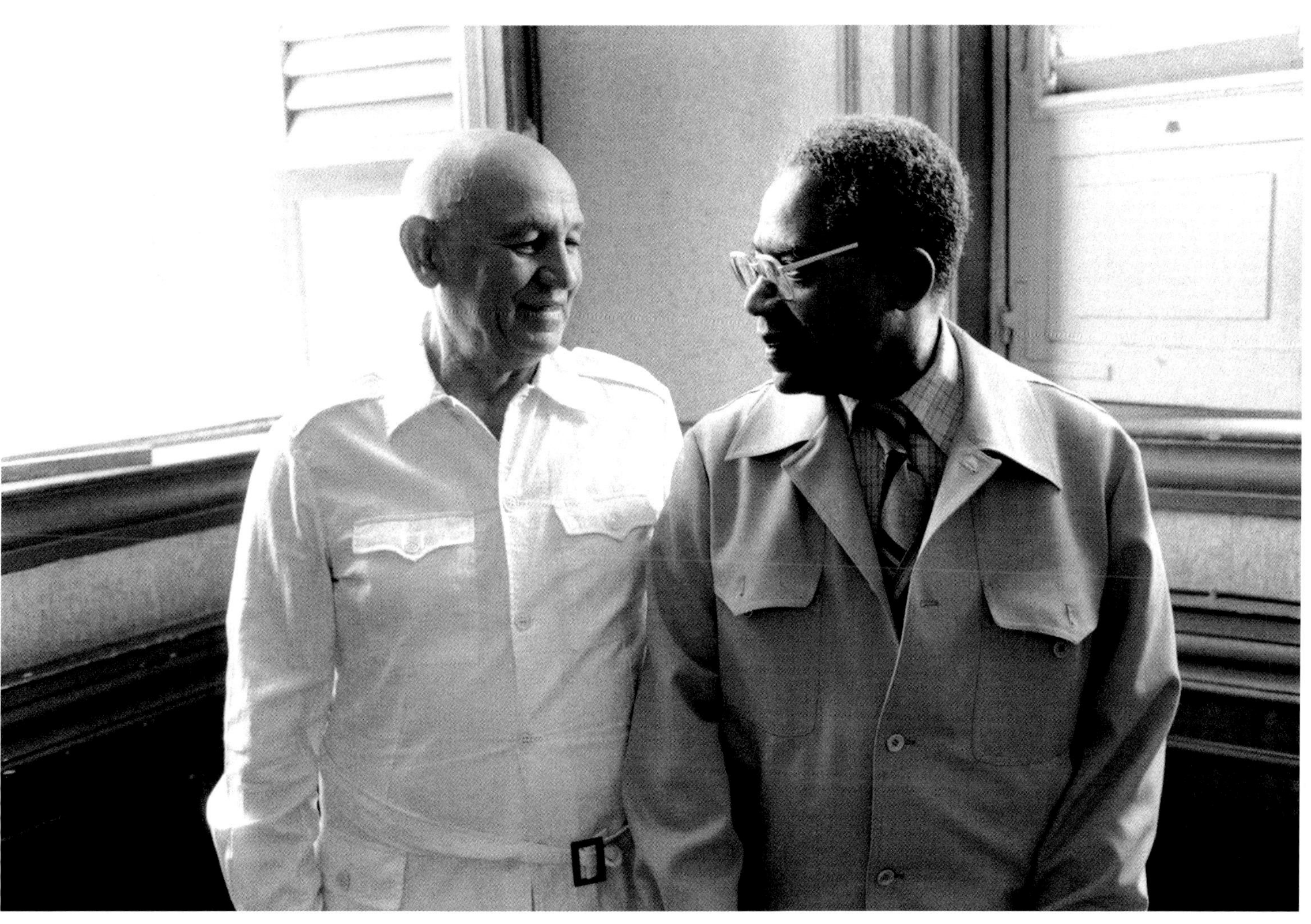

Romie's meeting Aimé Césaire for the first time, in his office in Fort-de-France, Martinique. 1979

FACING PAGE
Romie was on his way to an exhibit at Gallery 62 in the lobby of the Urban League building when he bumped into Vernon Jordan. Jordan was director of the Urban League at the time. c. 1978

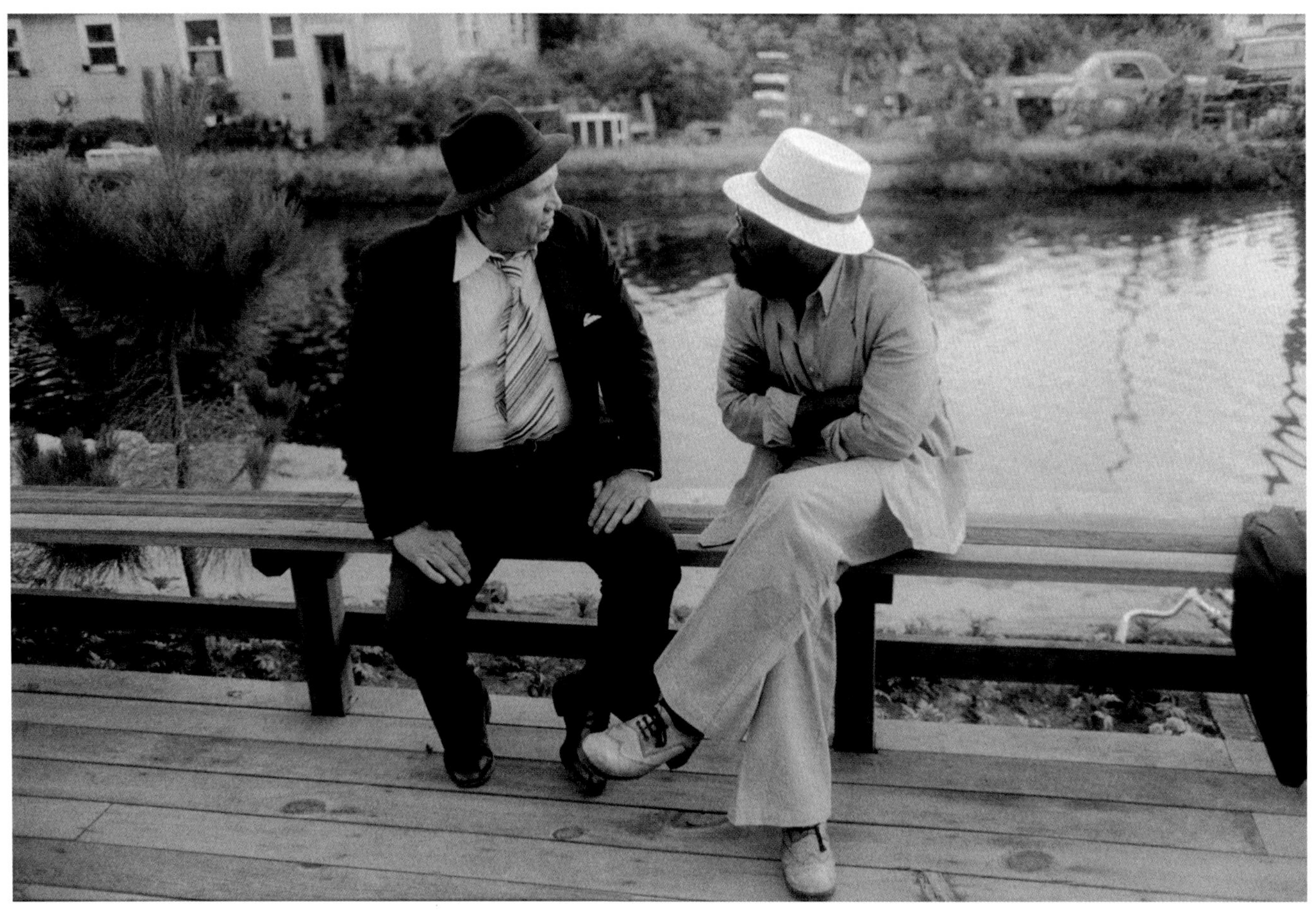

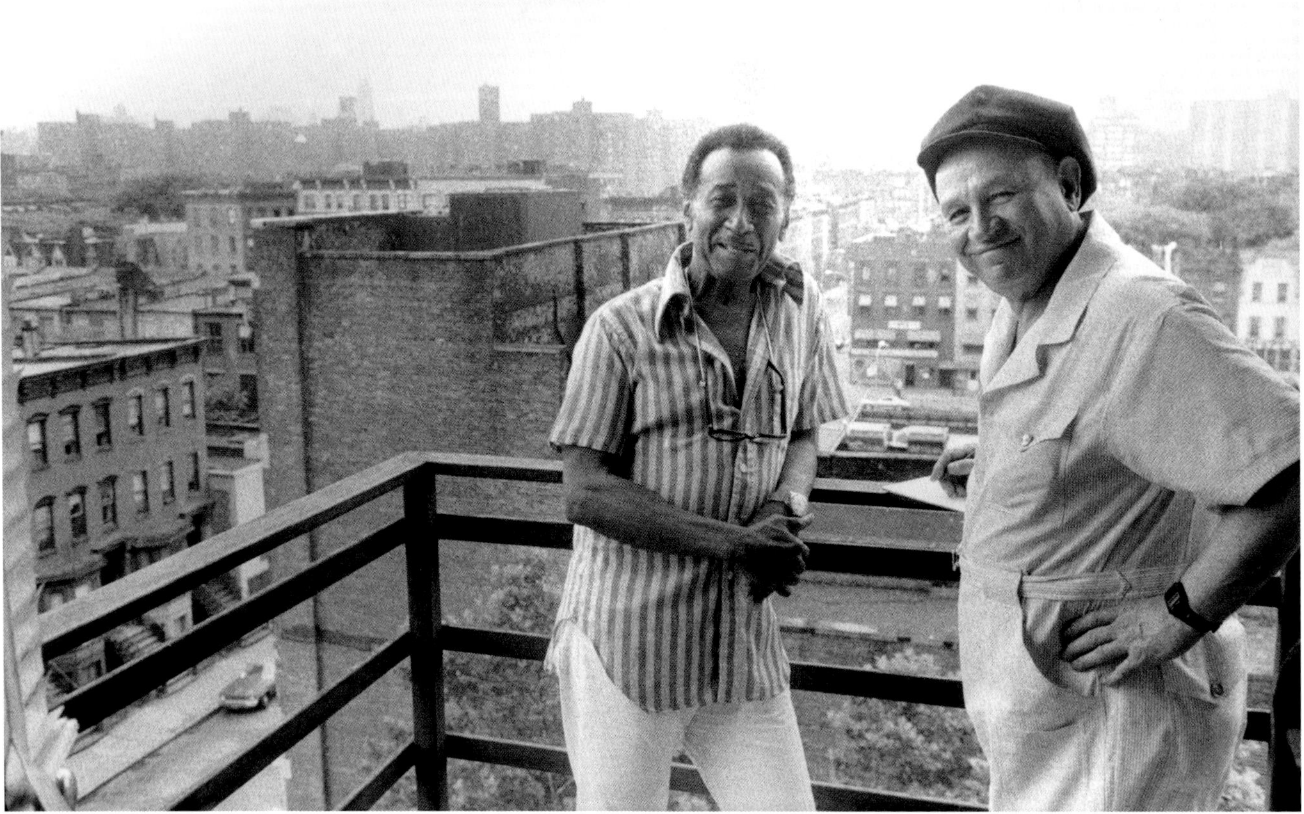

Romie's with painter Raymond Saunders by a canal in Venice, California. Ray came down from Oakland to the opening of Romie's show at the Art Garden. 1980

Albert Murray and Romie are on Al's balcony looking out over Lenox Avenue, where *The Block* was actually conceived, but this was ten years later. Al's giving his running commentary of what it's like living on "the block," and Romie's reenacting how he constructed the collage. 1980

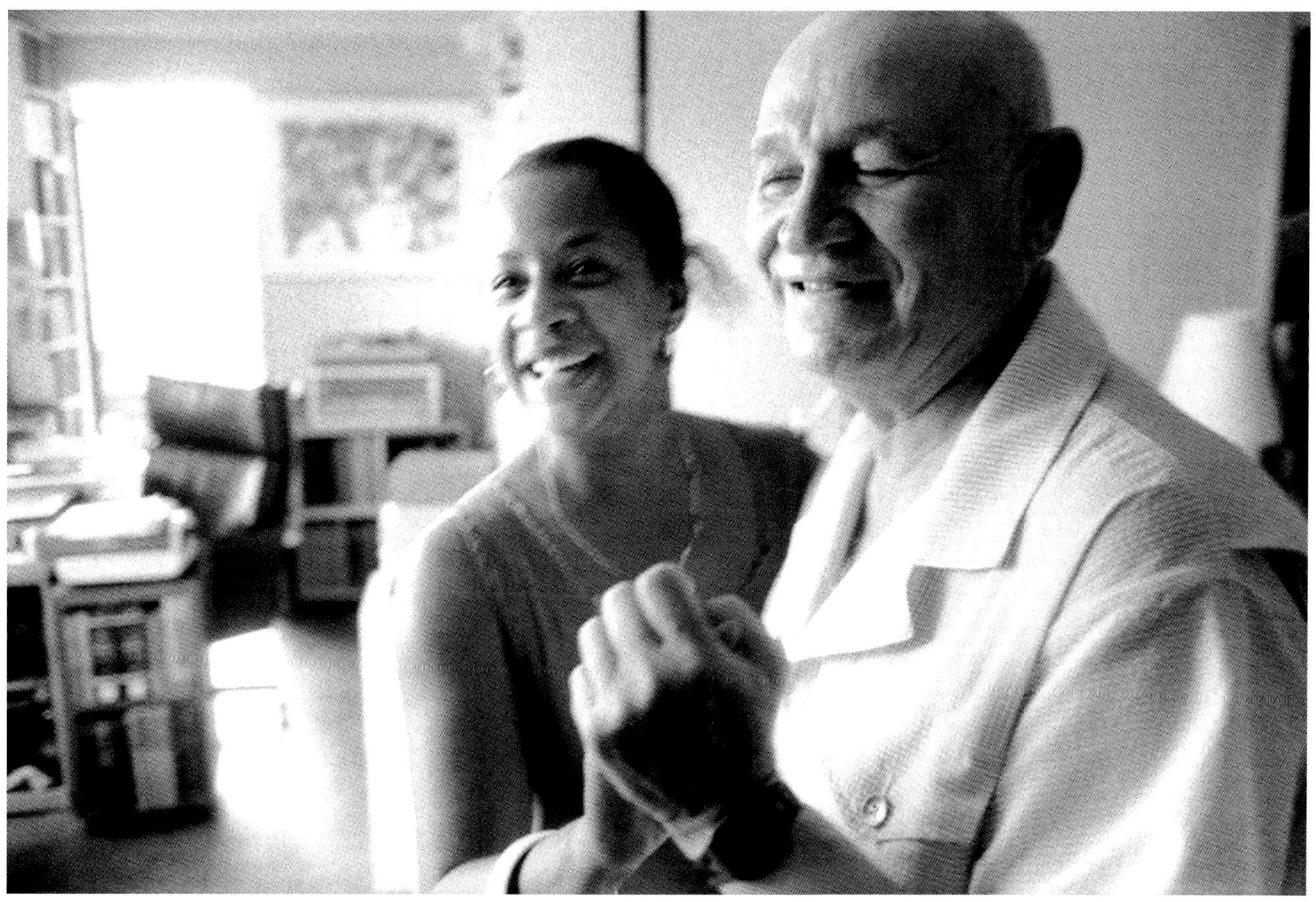

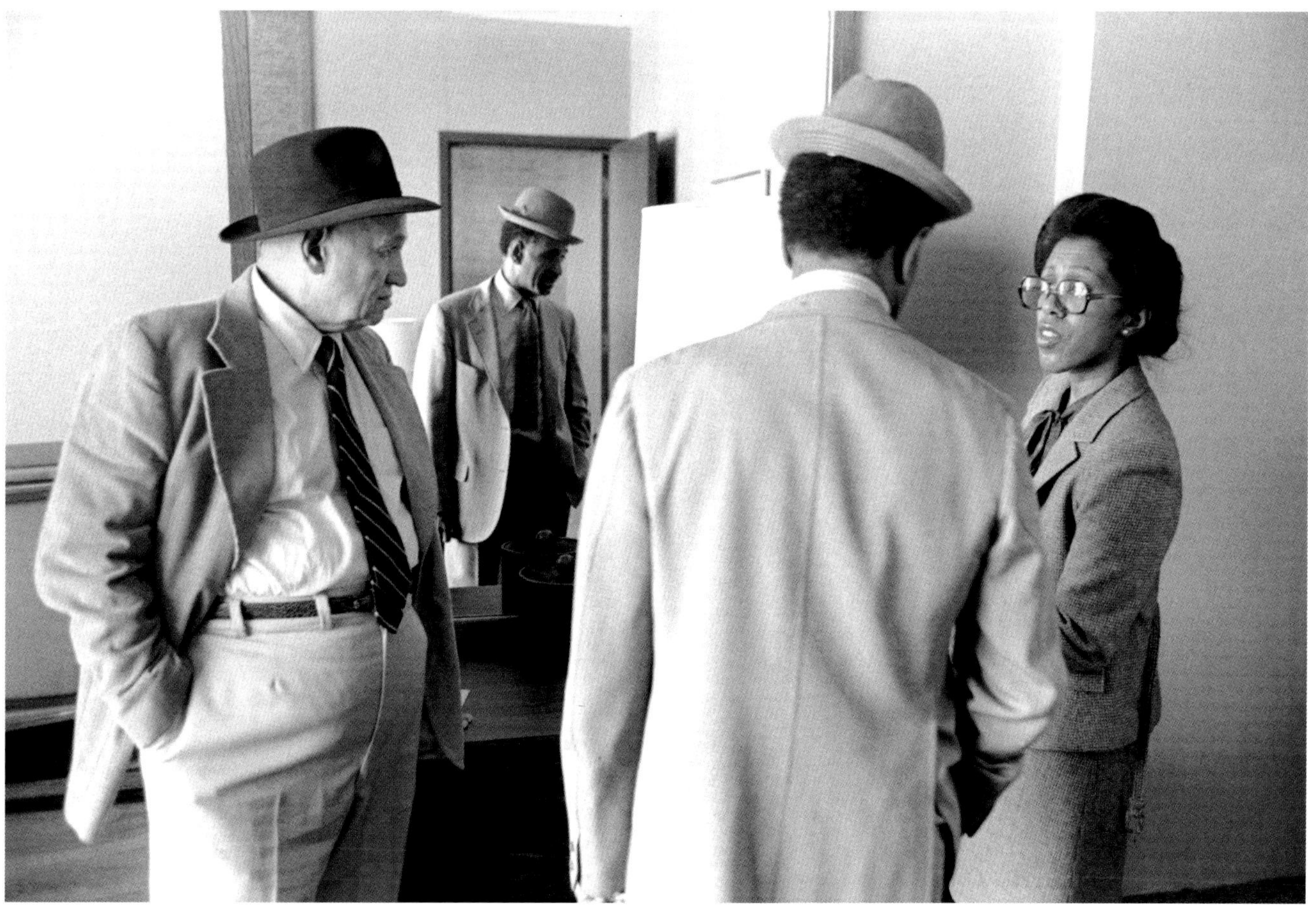

Romie liked to dance. Here he's with Billie Allen at the time we were filming *Bearden Plays Bearden.* They're at Albert Murray's, dancing to Ellington. 1980

Romie, Albert Murray, and June Kelly in a hotel room in Charlotte, at the time of the Mint Museum opening. Romie had to sign prints, and Al had to give a lecture. They're going over the schedule and the places where they had to be. 1980

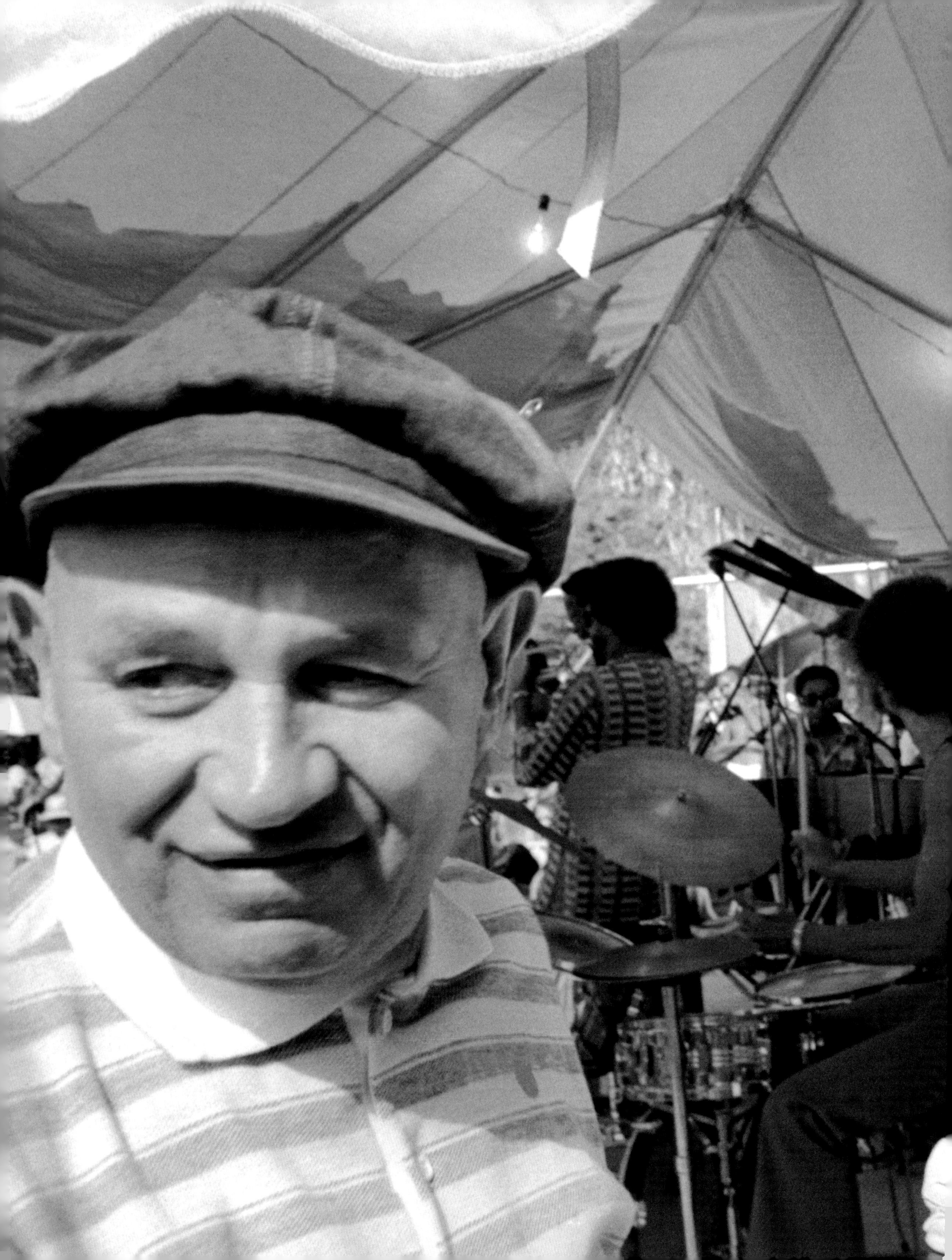

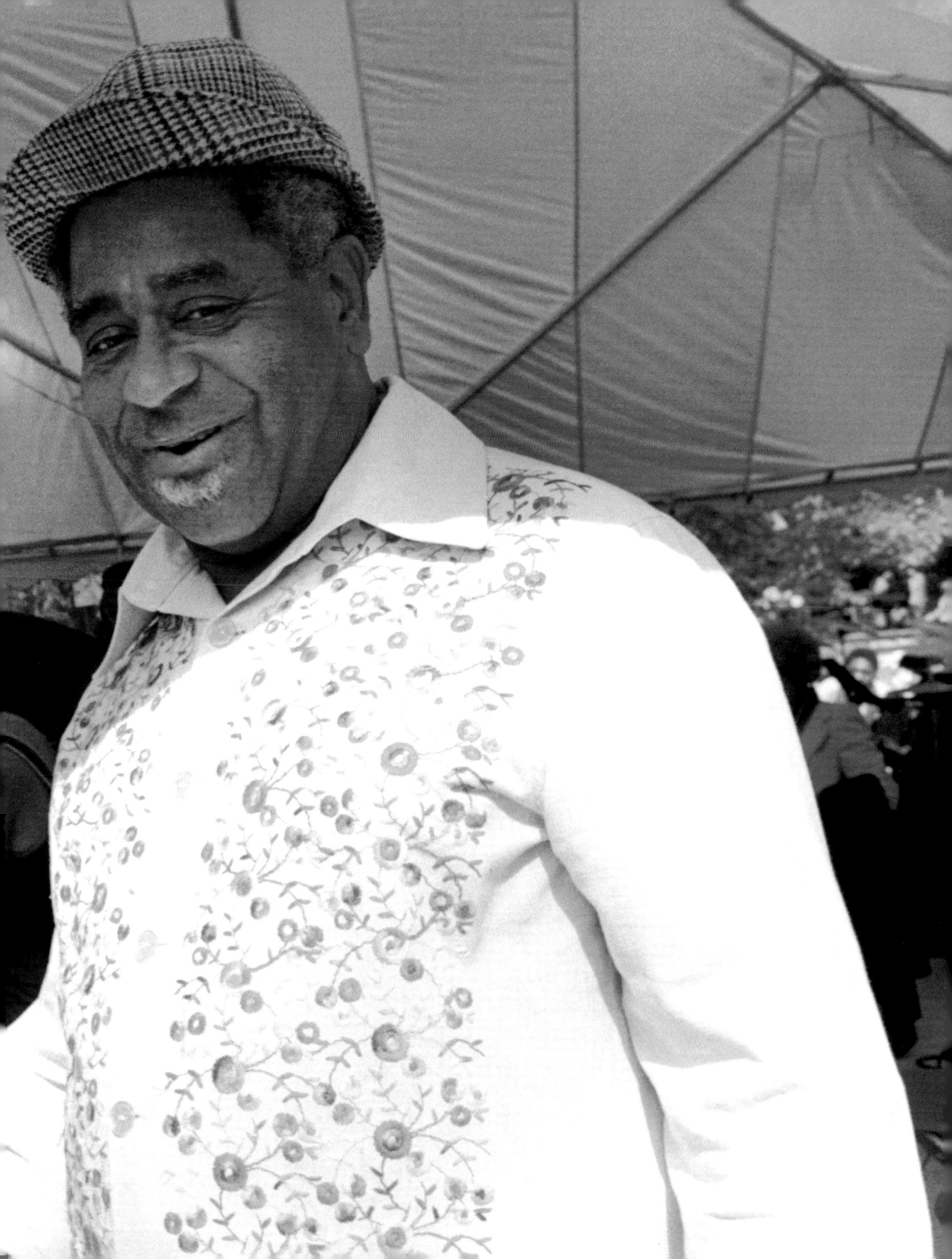

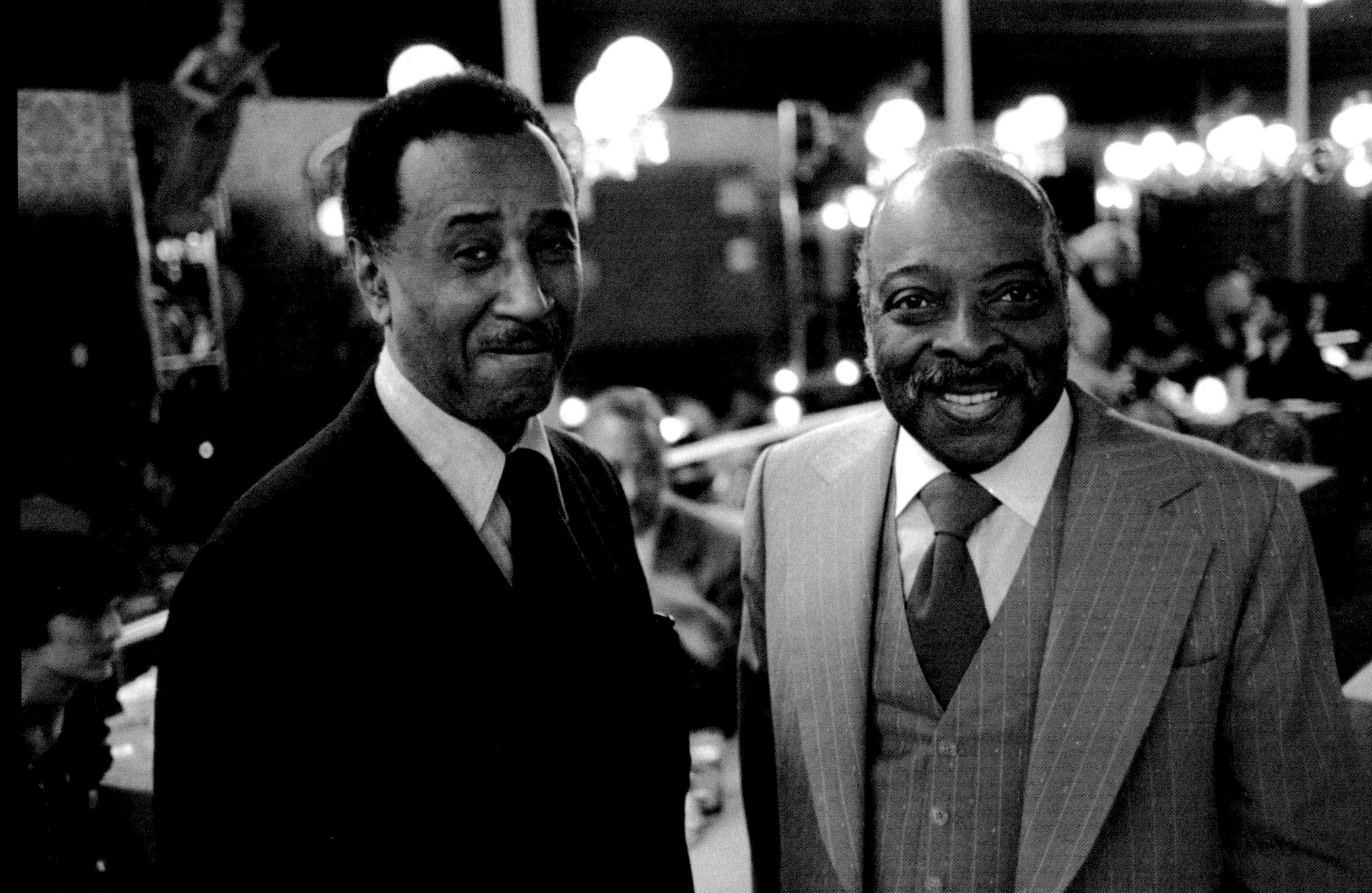

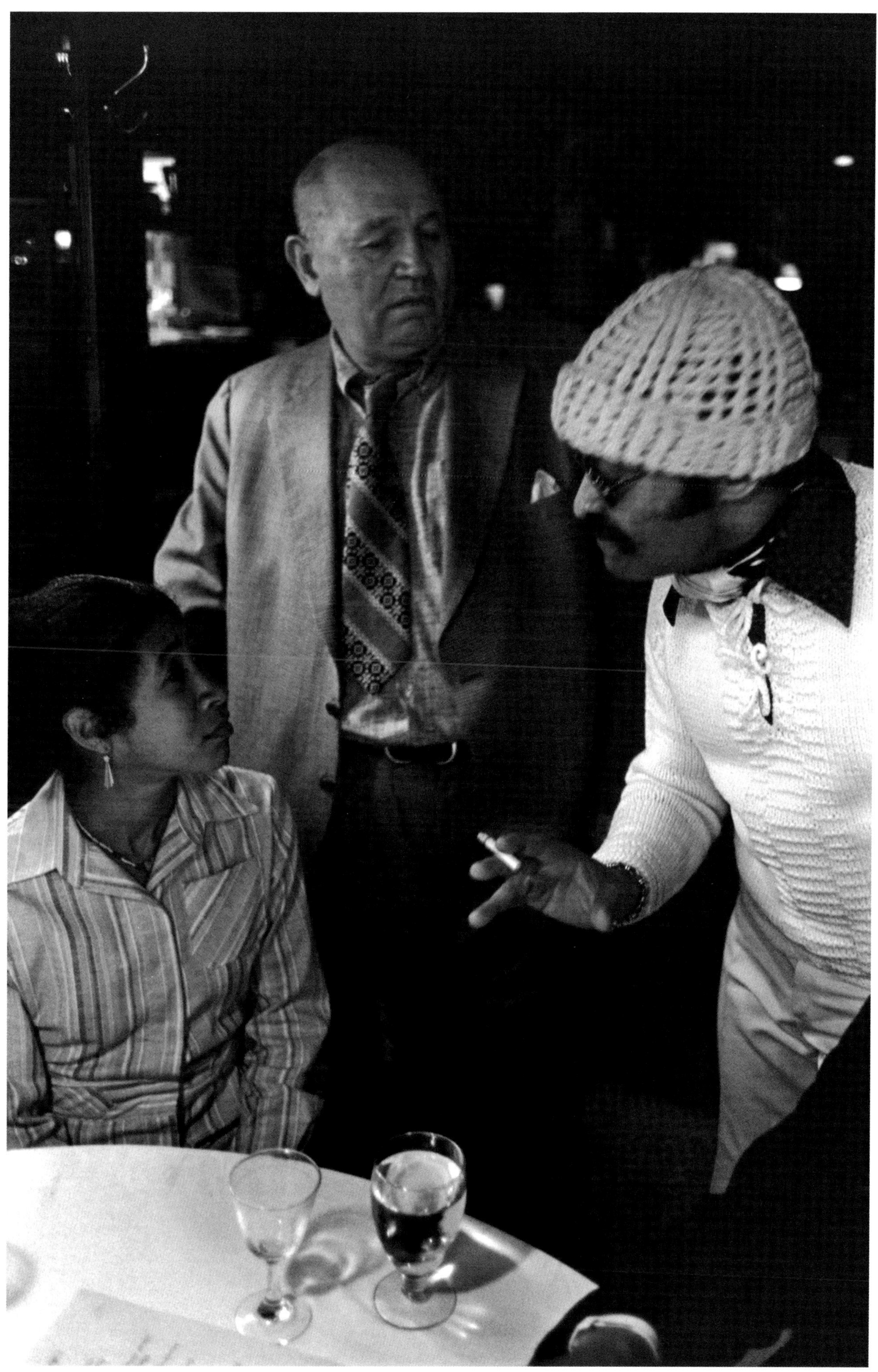

Diane McIntyre's with Romie and Cecil Taylor in New York City. 1982

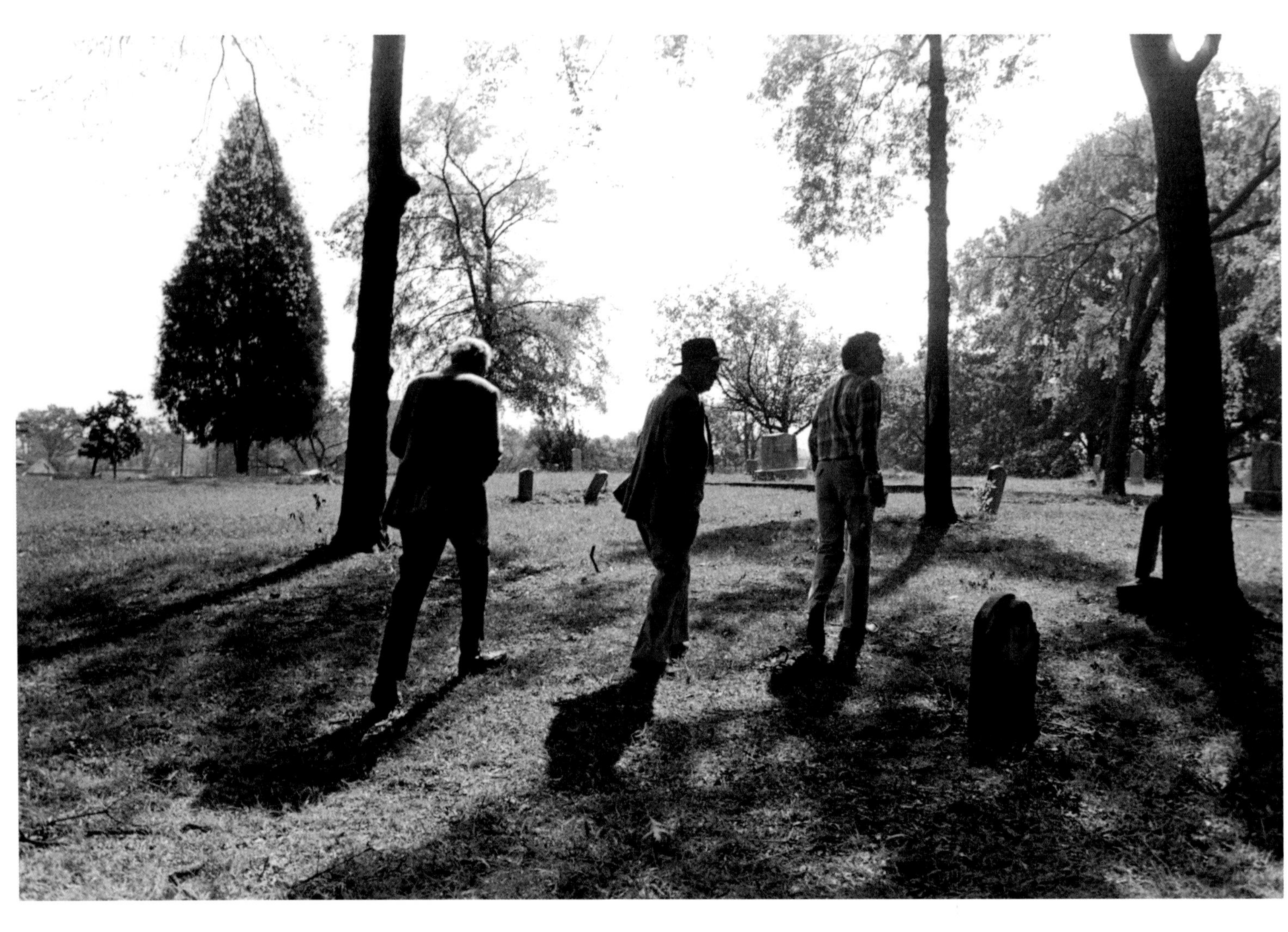

Harry Henderson and Romie are with a Pinewood Cemetery caretaker, in Charlotte, looking for the Alston-Bearden family gravestone. 1980

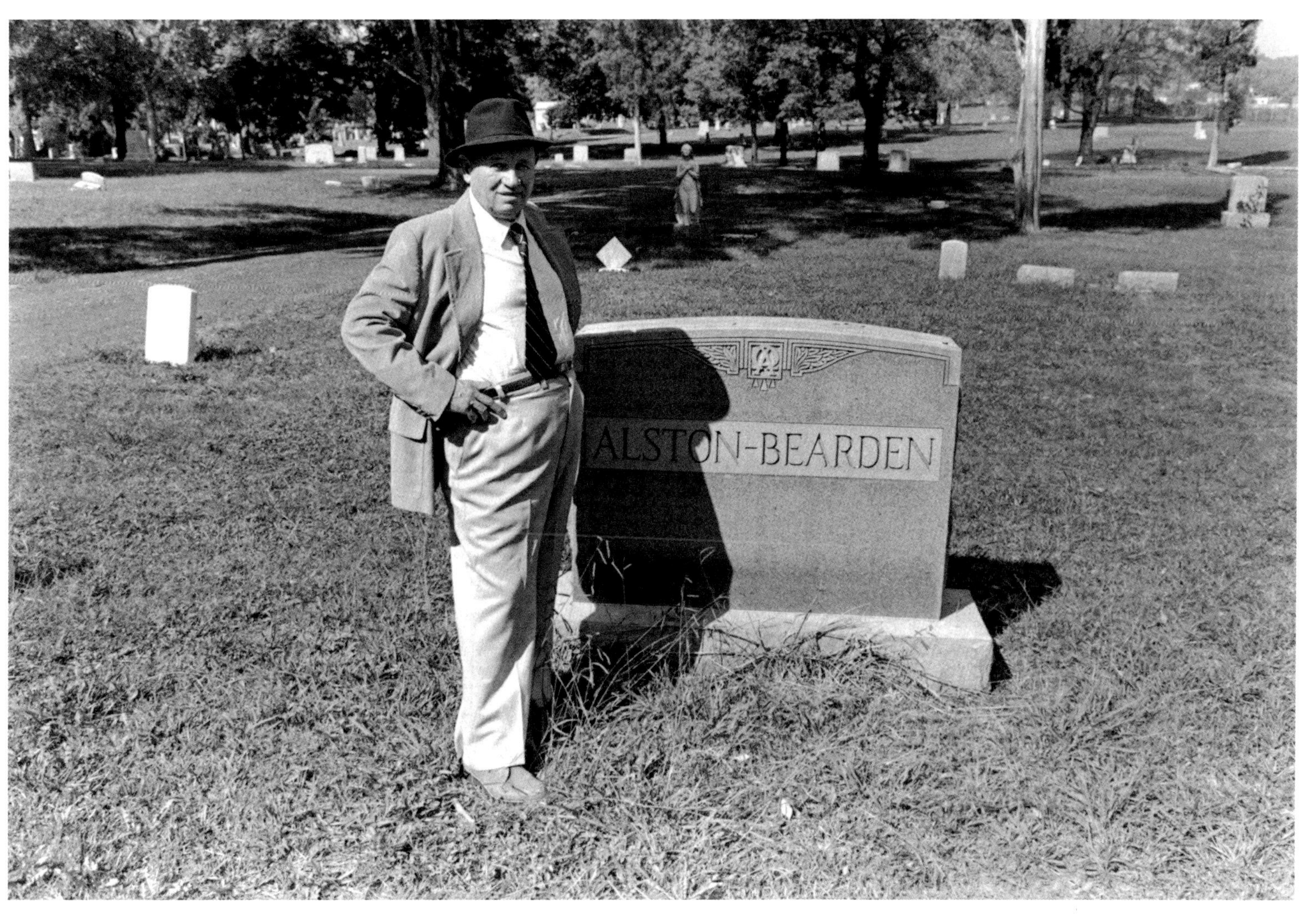

Romie with the Alston-Bearden family gravestone. Painter Charles Alston was Romie's cousin. 1980

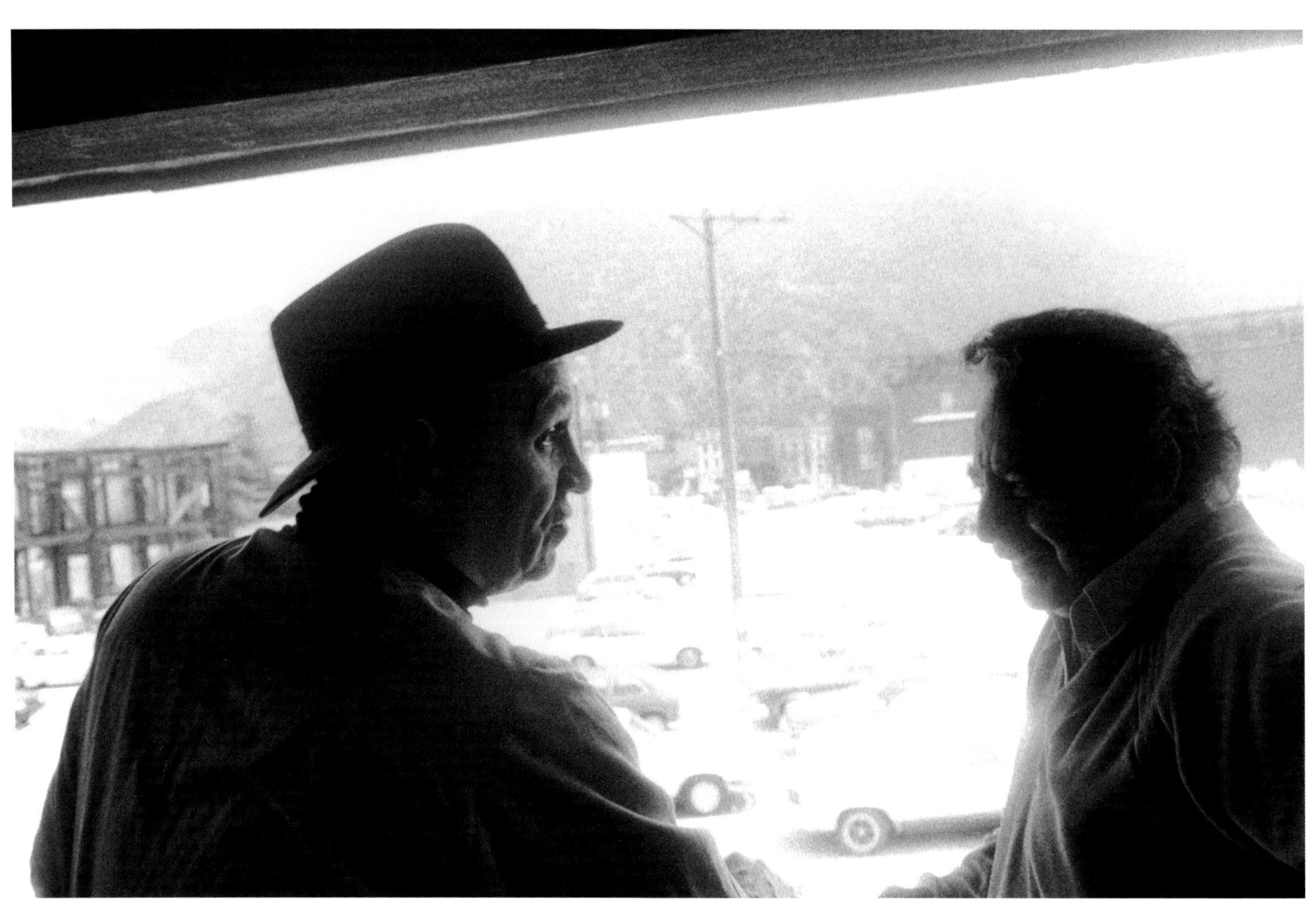

Romie's talking with Sam Shaw. I don't know how they met, but they went back a long way. Sam shot those early photographs of Romie on 125th Street, and in the studio with the model. 1980.

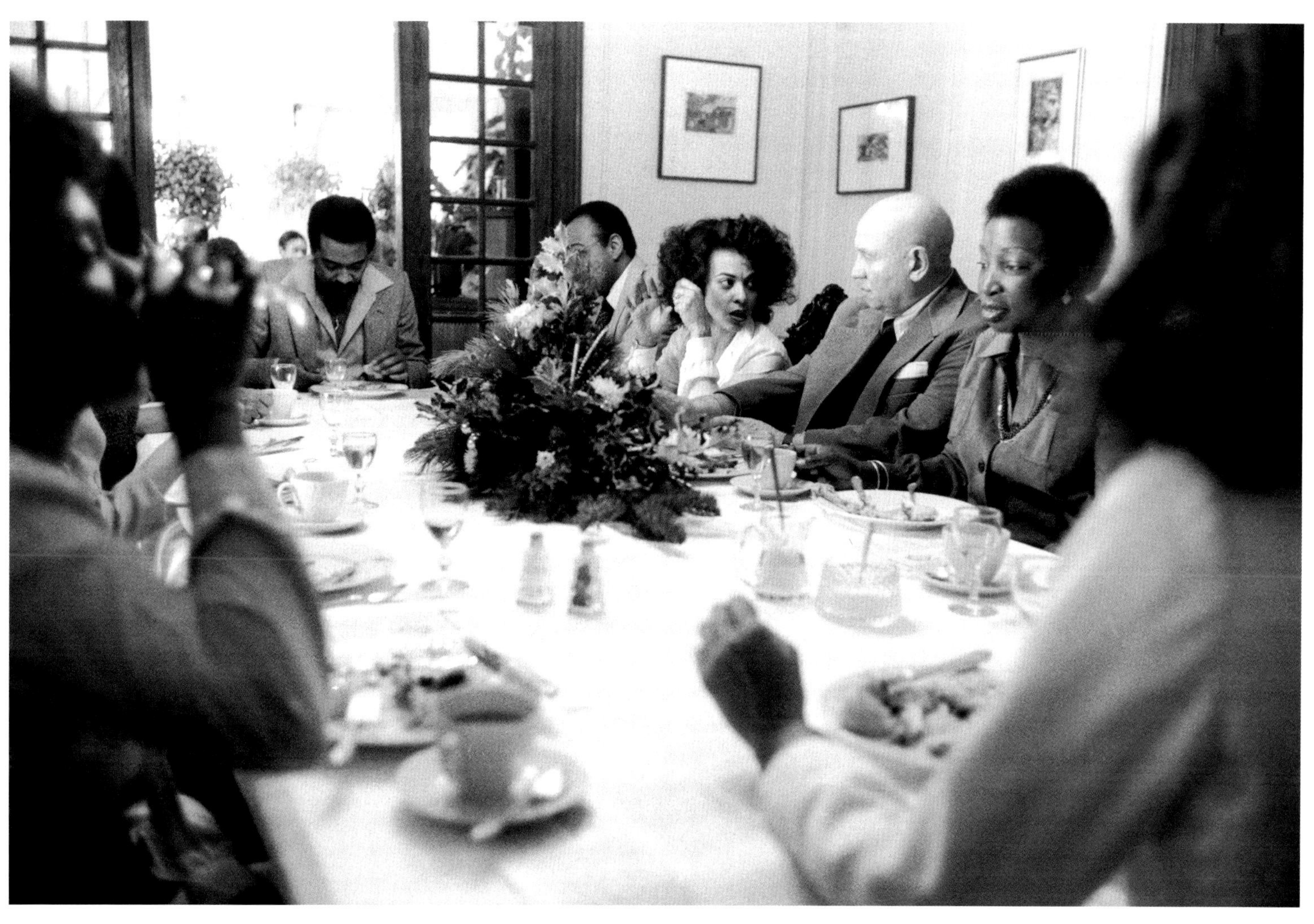

Romie's at dinner in Walter O. Evans' house in Detroit. 1977

OVERLEAF
Romie's being presented with a portrait of himself in Philadelphia. I don't recall the name of the artist who painted the portrait. 1986/87

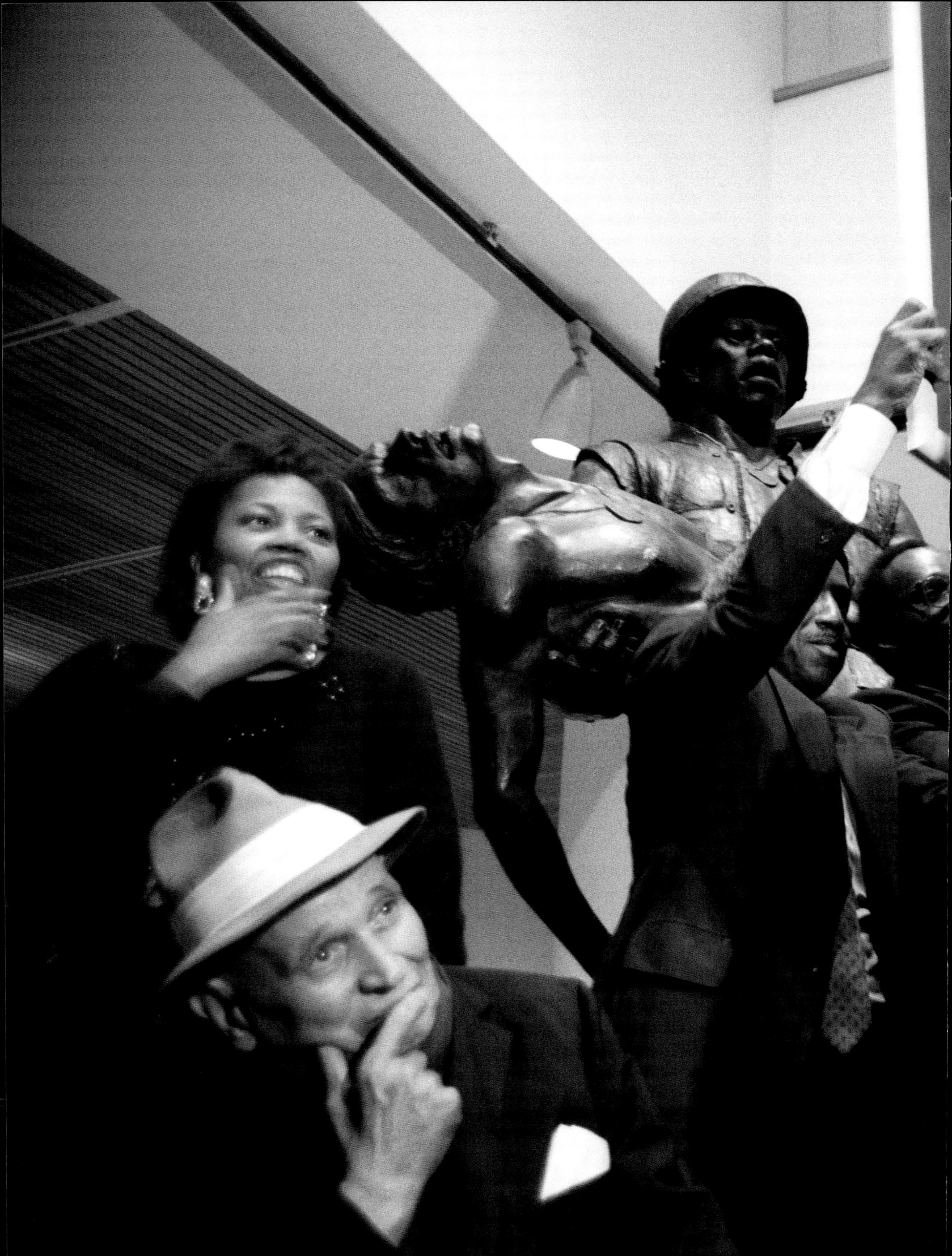

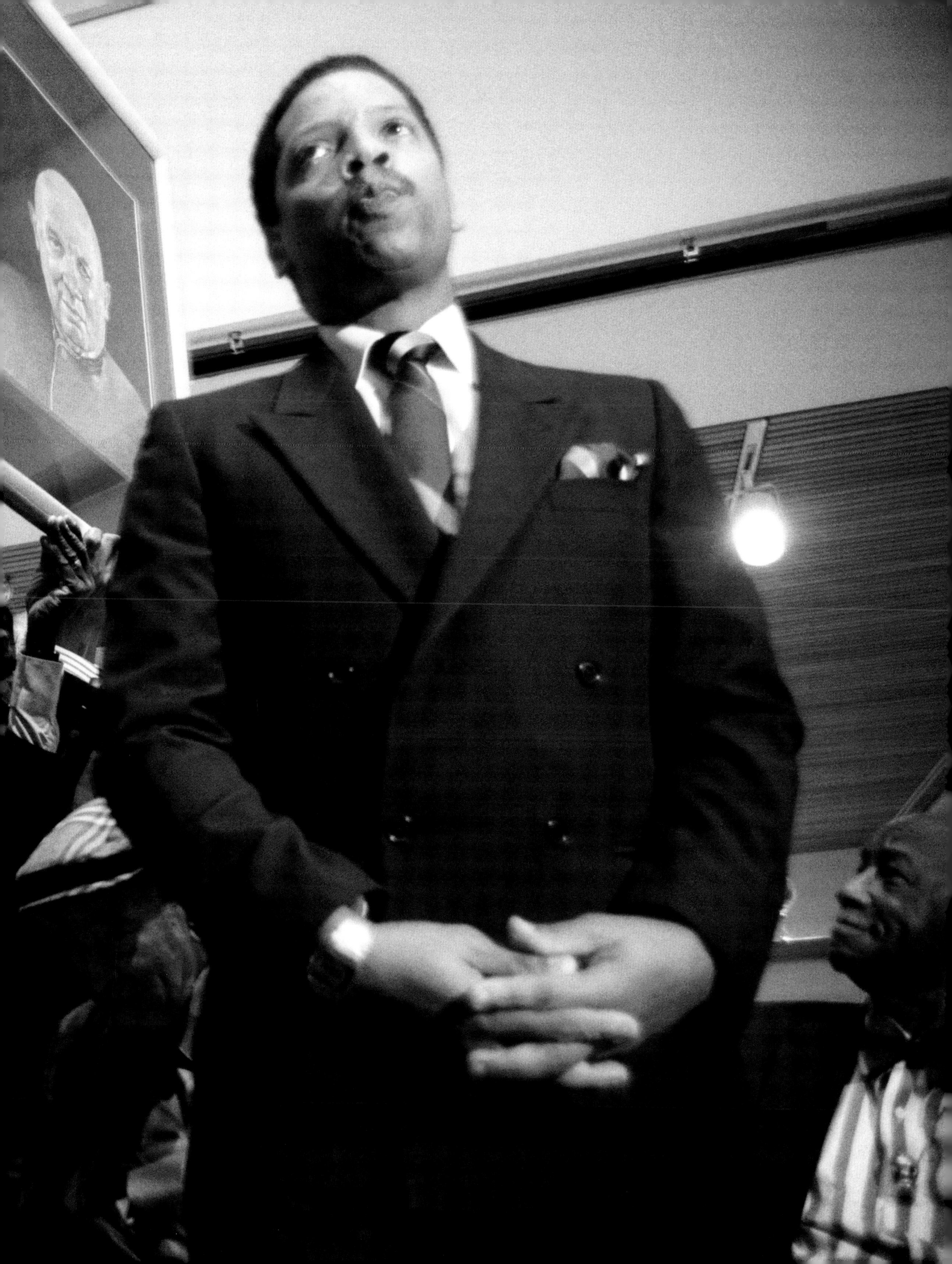

STATEN ISLAND

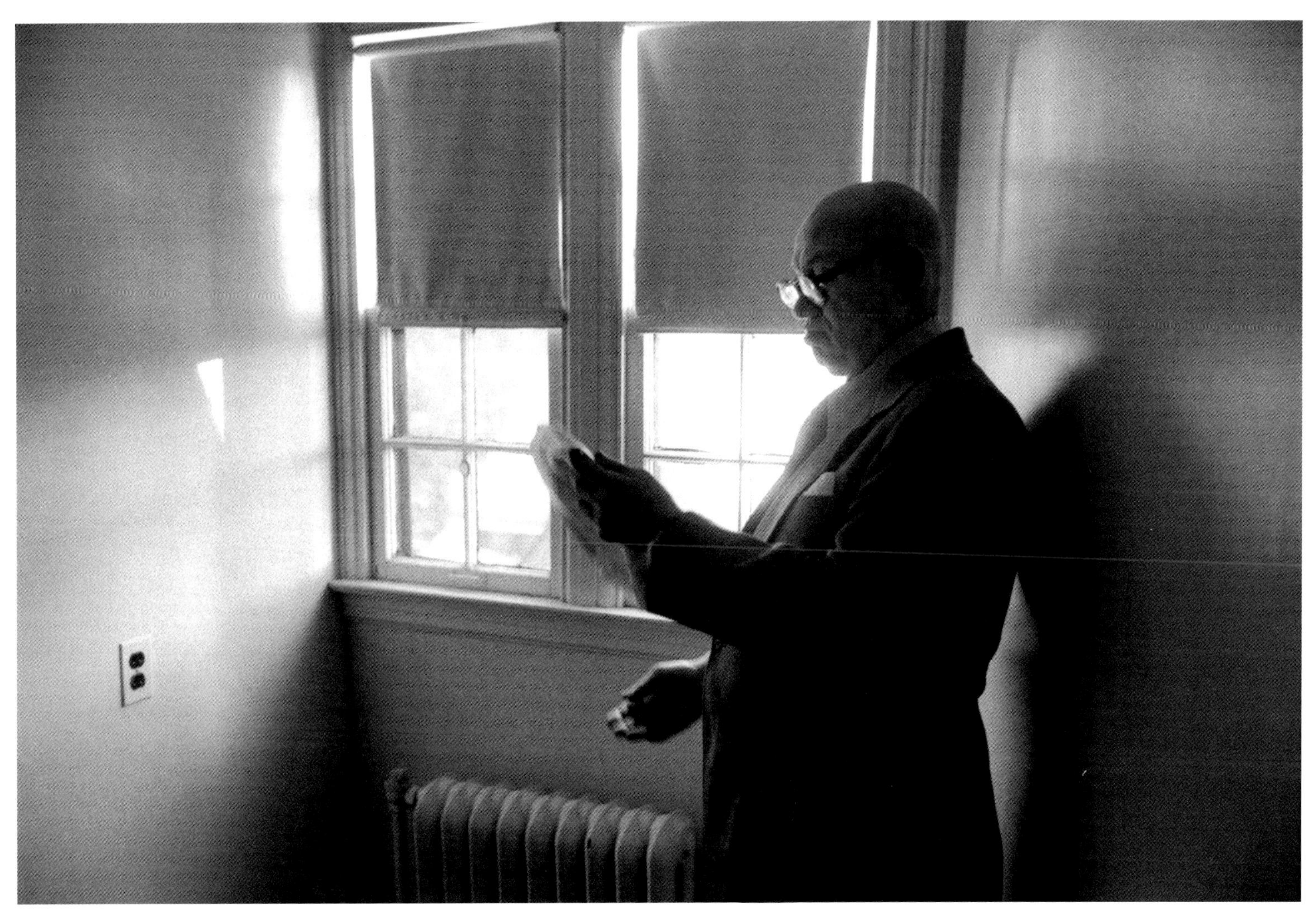

Romie's reading a letter. 1978

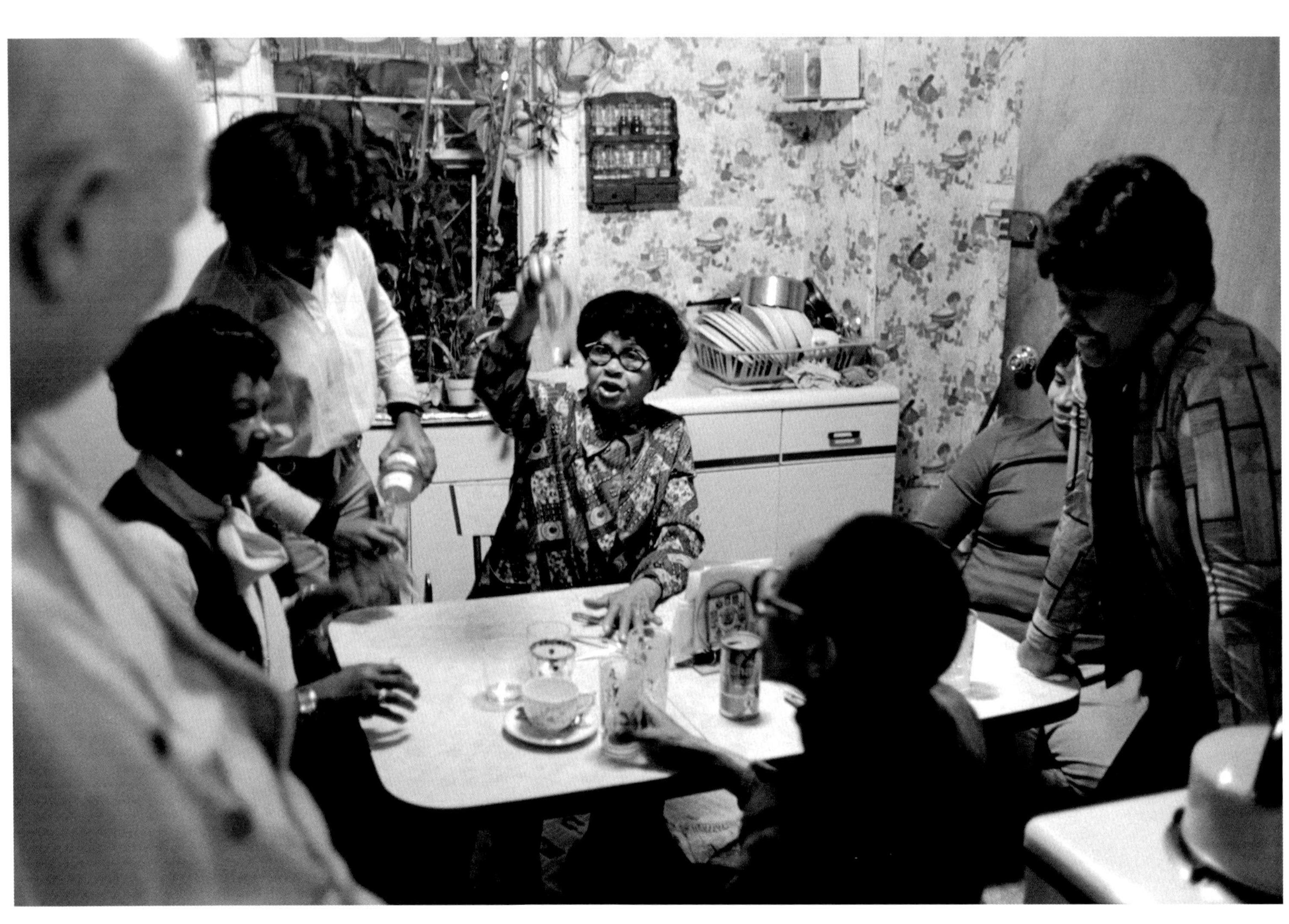

Romie and Nanette with her mother, Eleeza, and her sisters and niece,
Dorothy, Donna, Sheila, and Marie. 1976

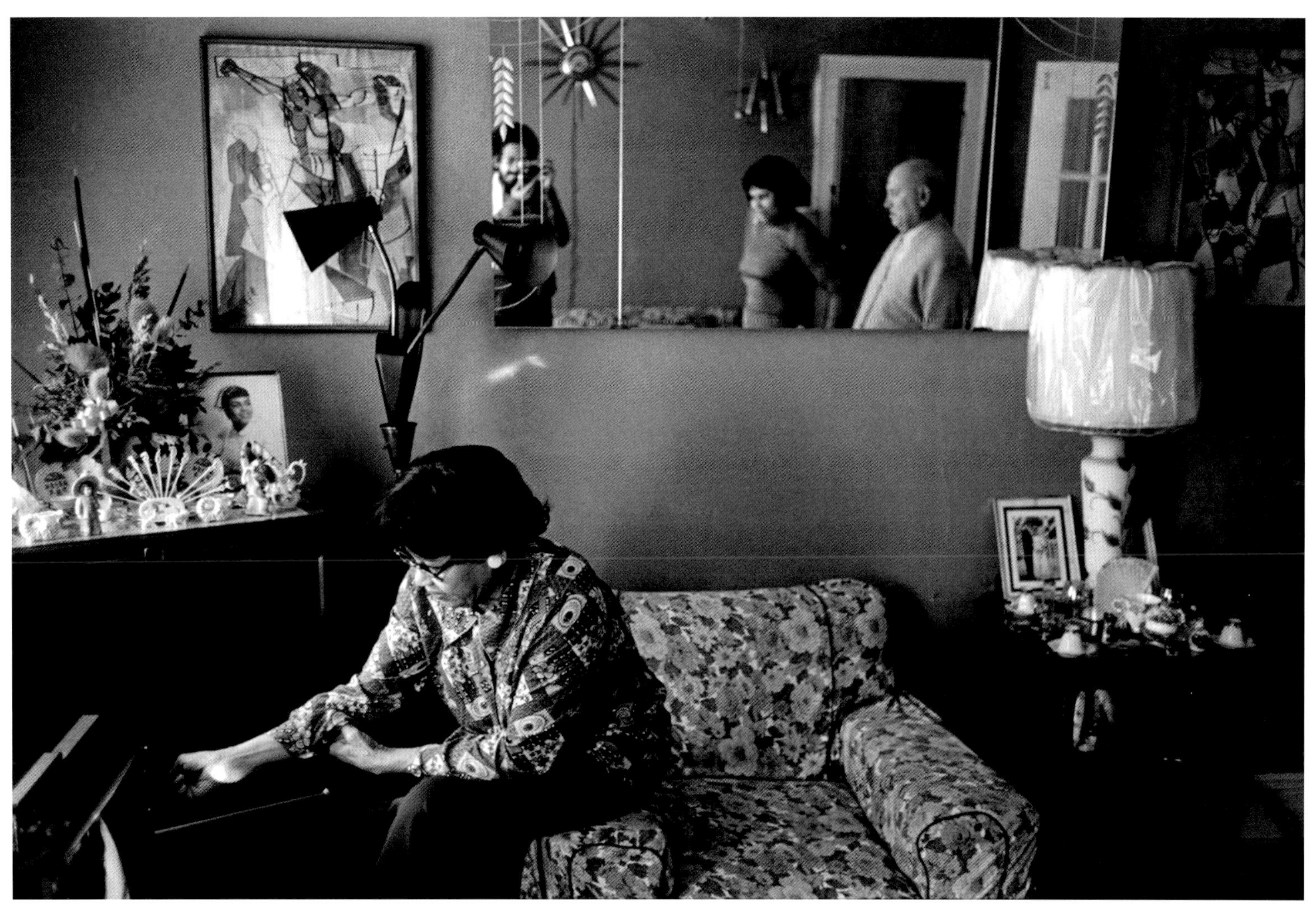

Eleeza Rohan and (in mirror) Frank Stewart, Nanette, and Romie. 1982

OVERLEAF
Romie and Nanette had a joint passport. It's the first time and the last time I've ever seen that, where two people shared one passport. So they never went too far from each other, especially when they traveled. 1977

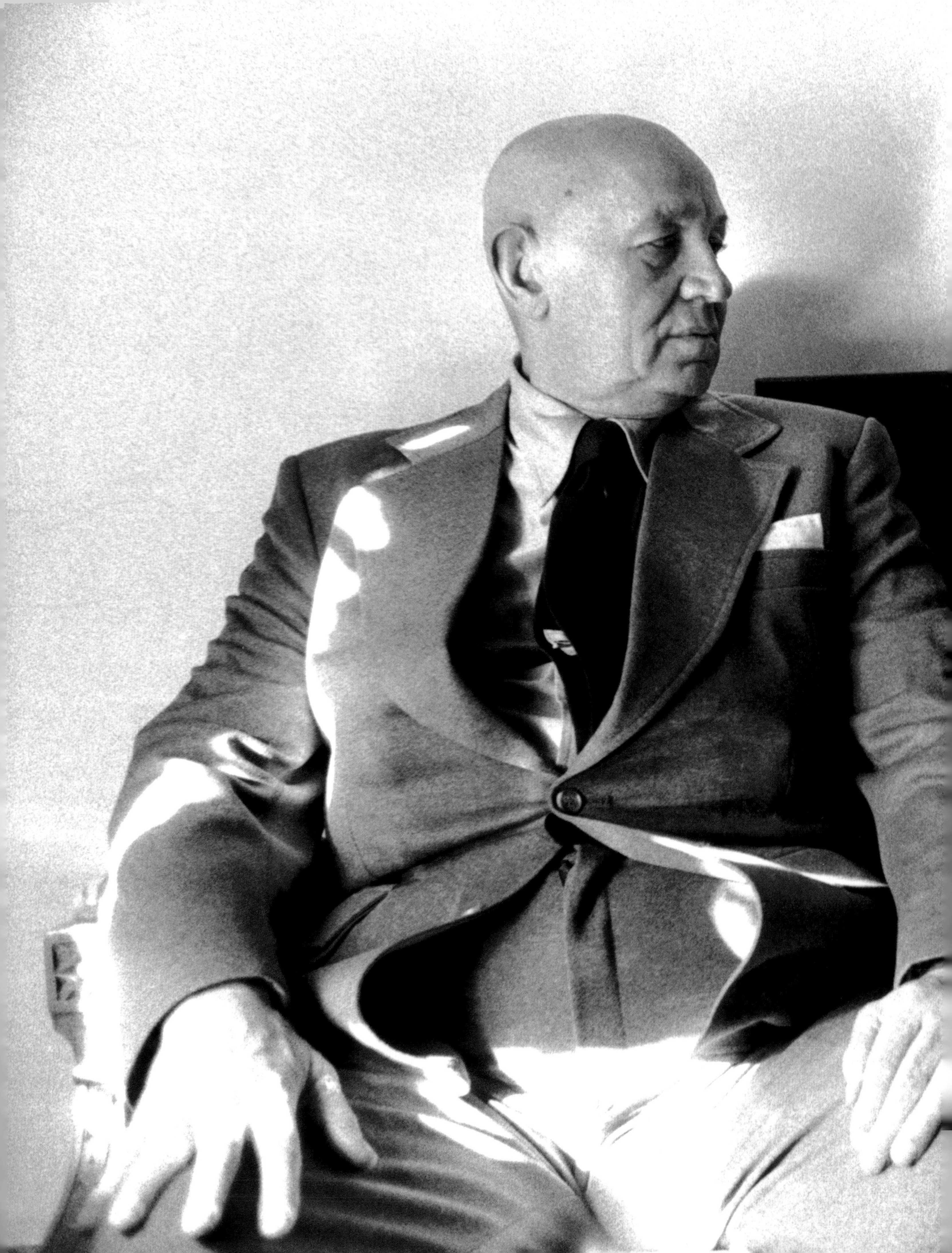

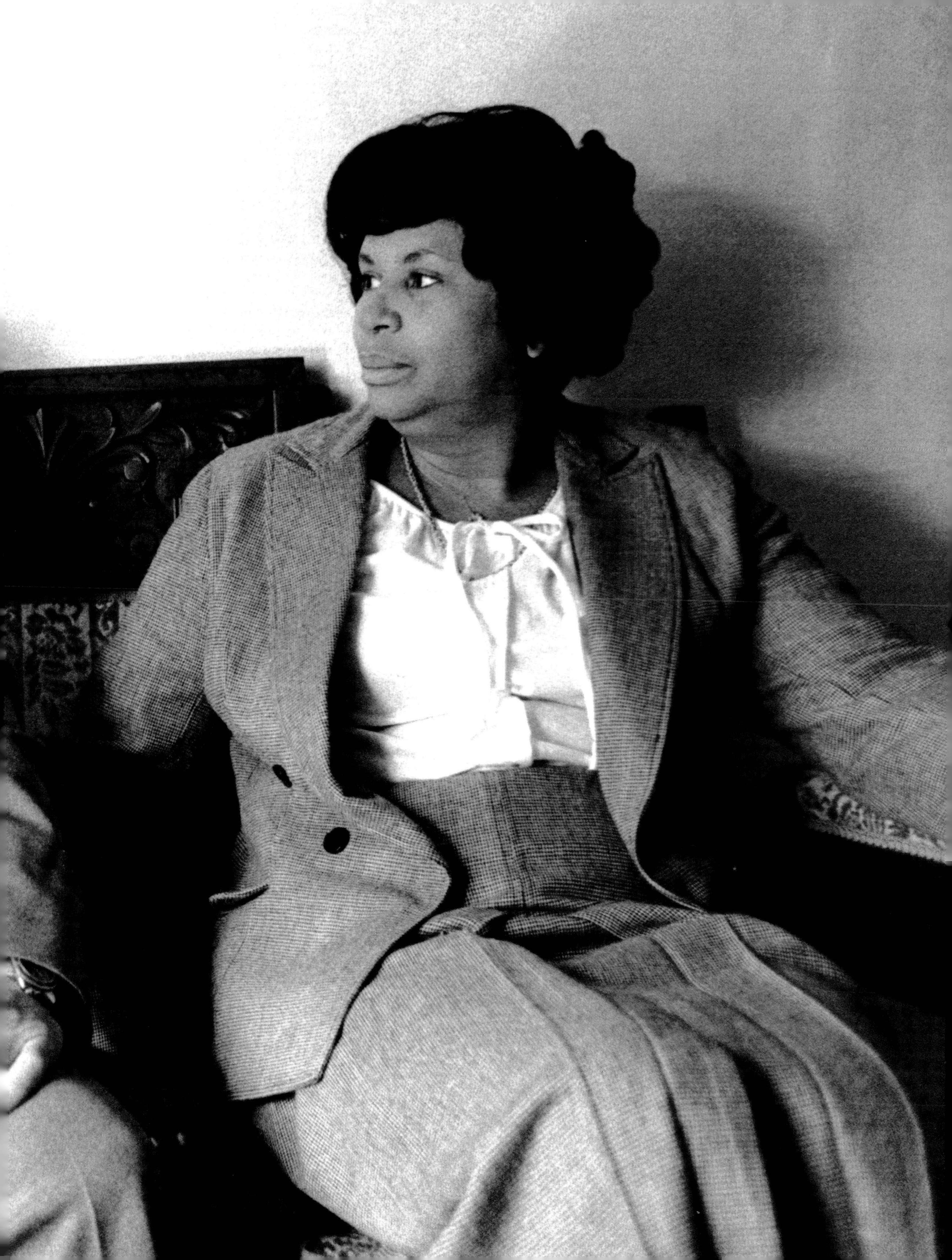

ST. MARTIN

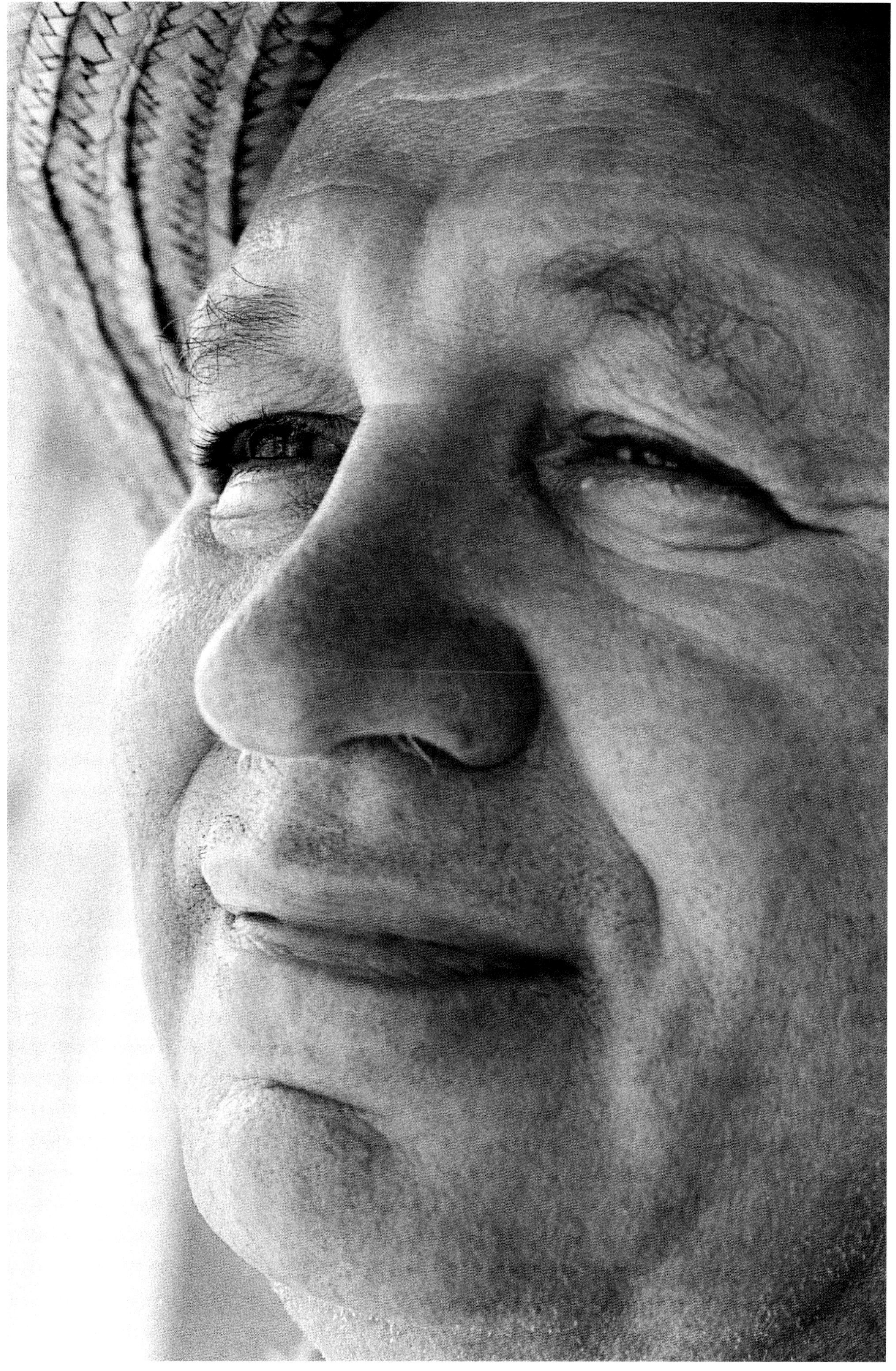

Romare Bearden. 1977

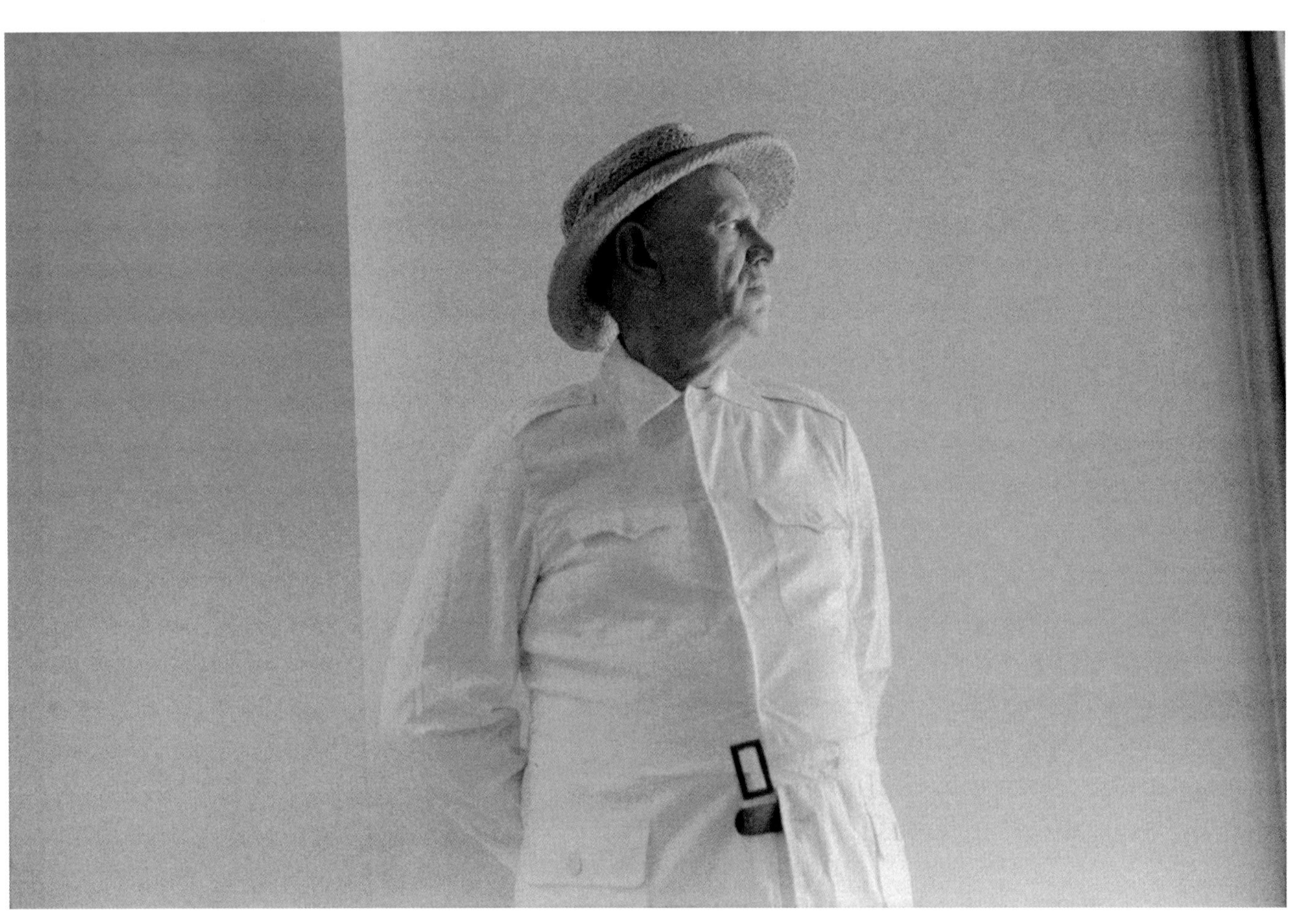

Here's Romie as a "plantation owner." He'd get down to the islands and go native. 1980

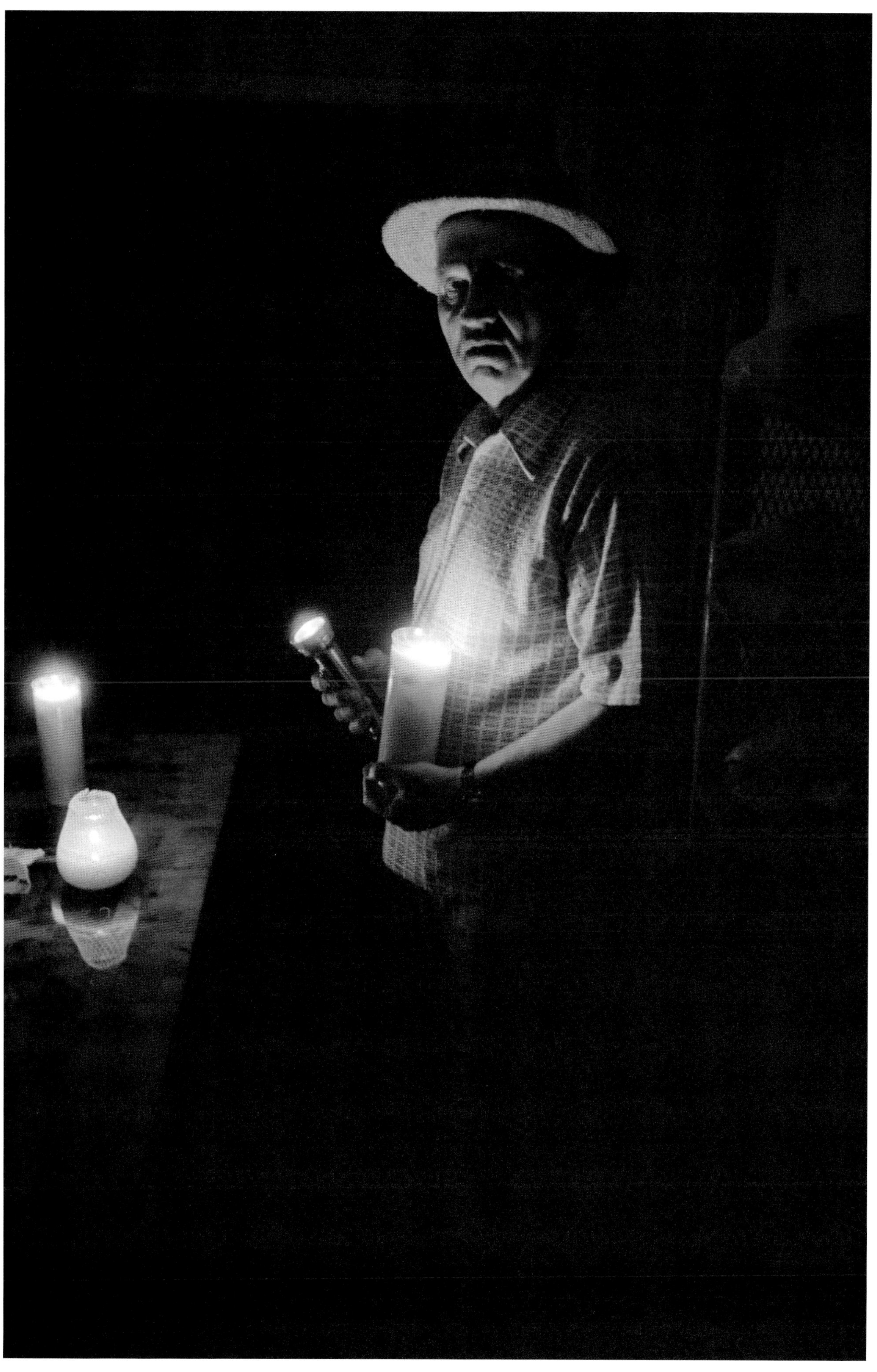

Romie in candlelight during a blackout. c. 1975

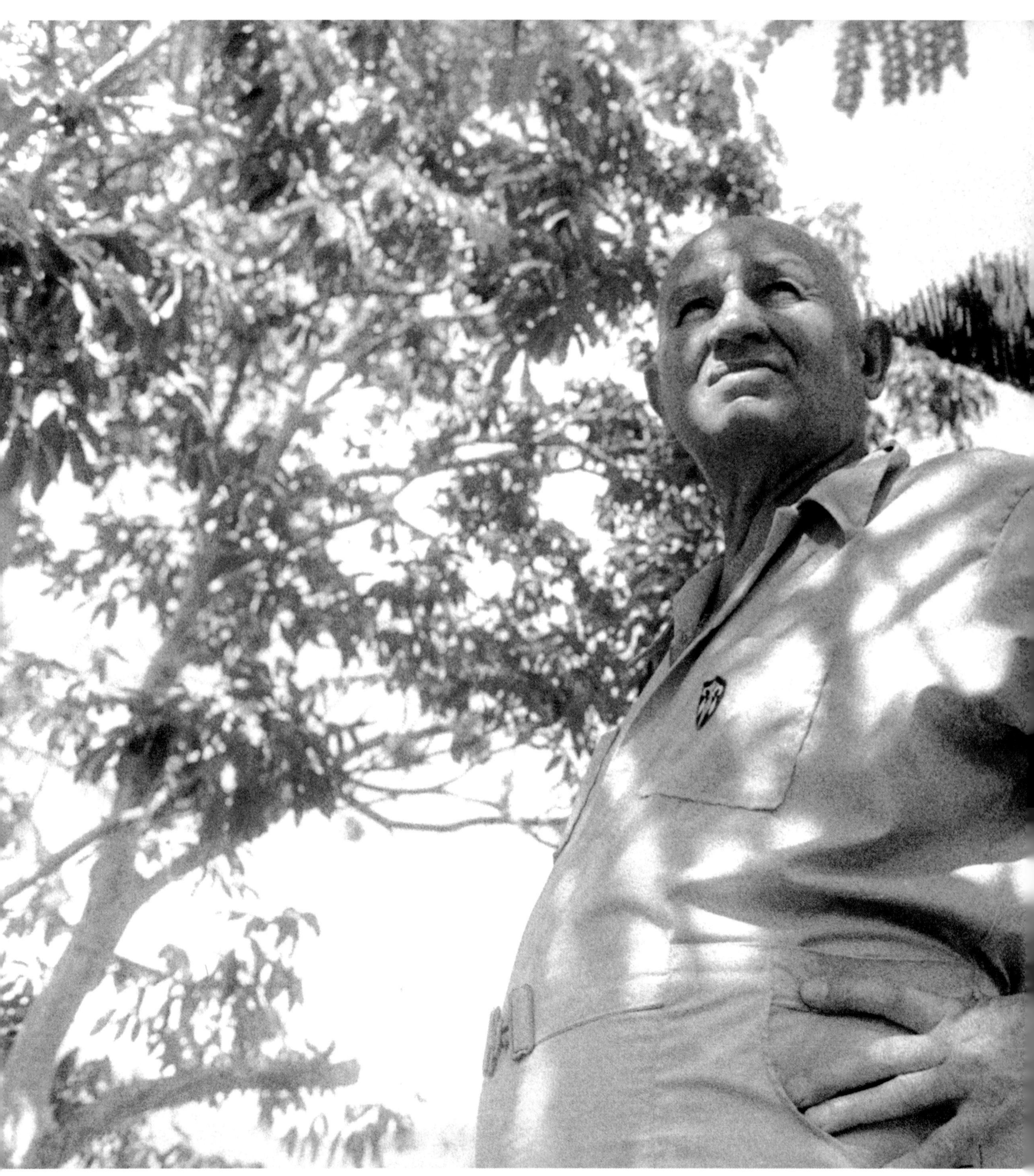

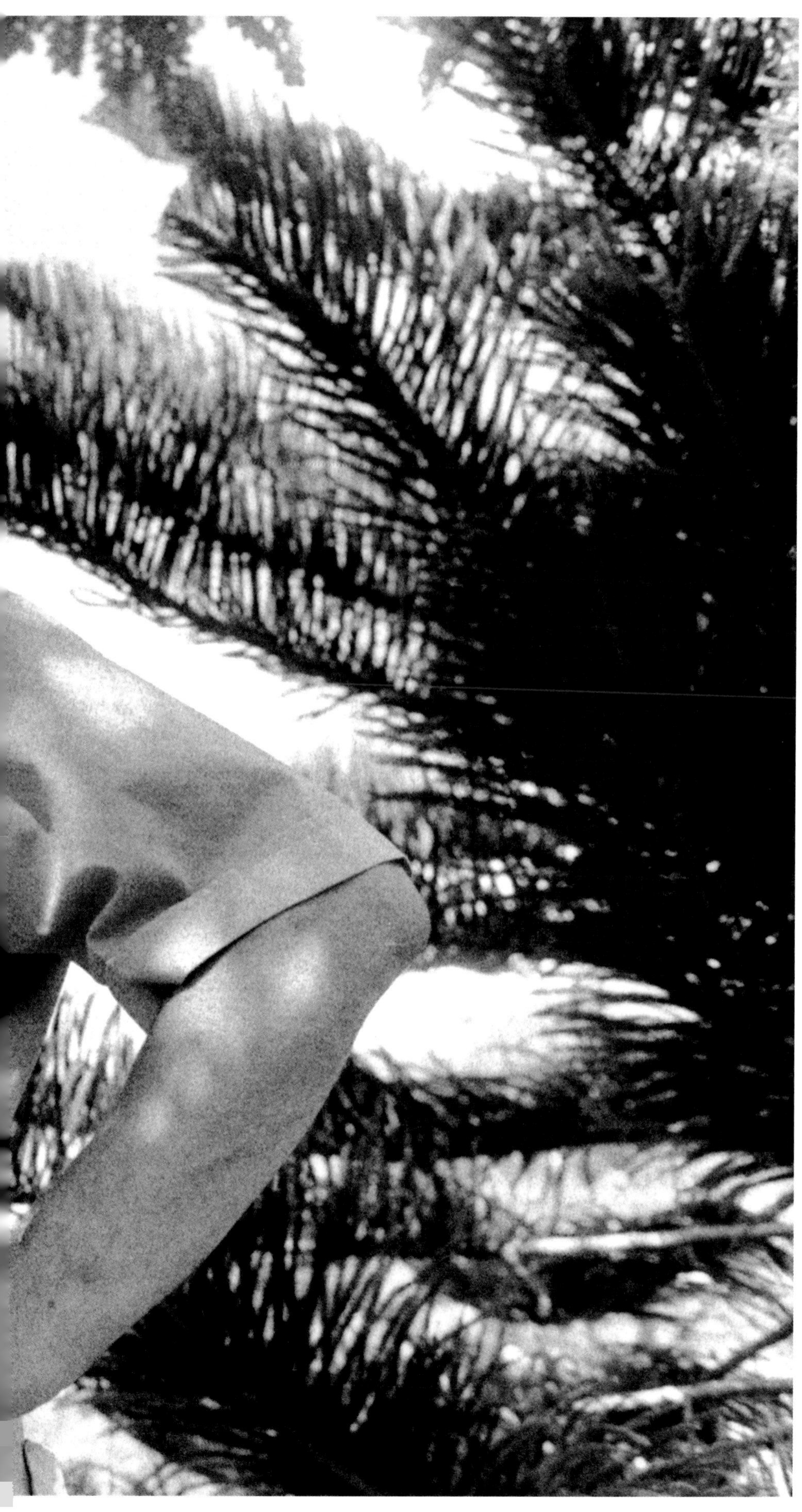

Romie's on property owned by painter Roland Richardson's uncle, Vare Richardson. 1975

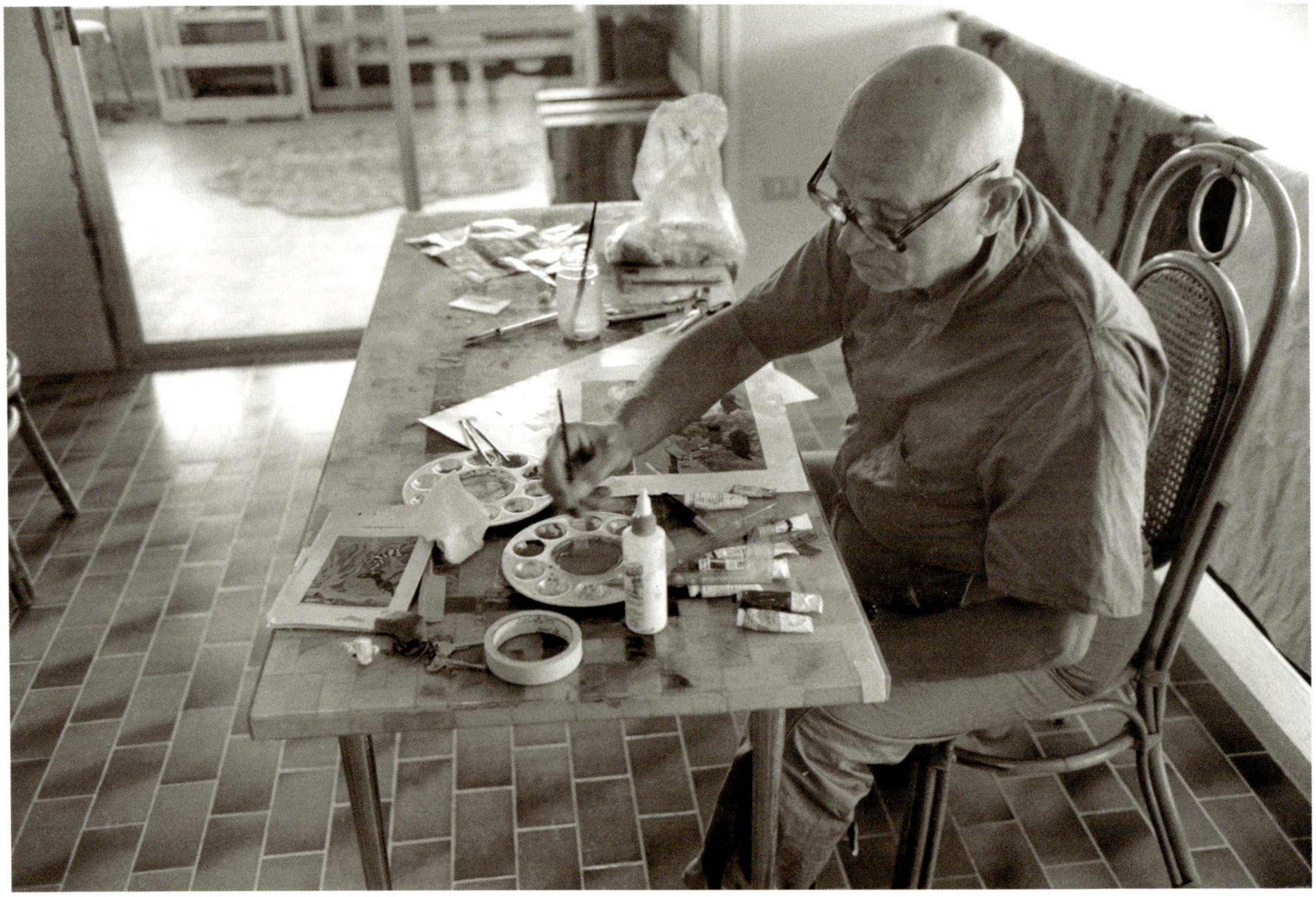

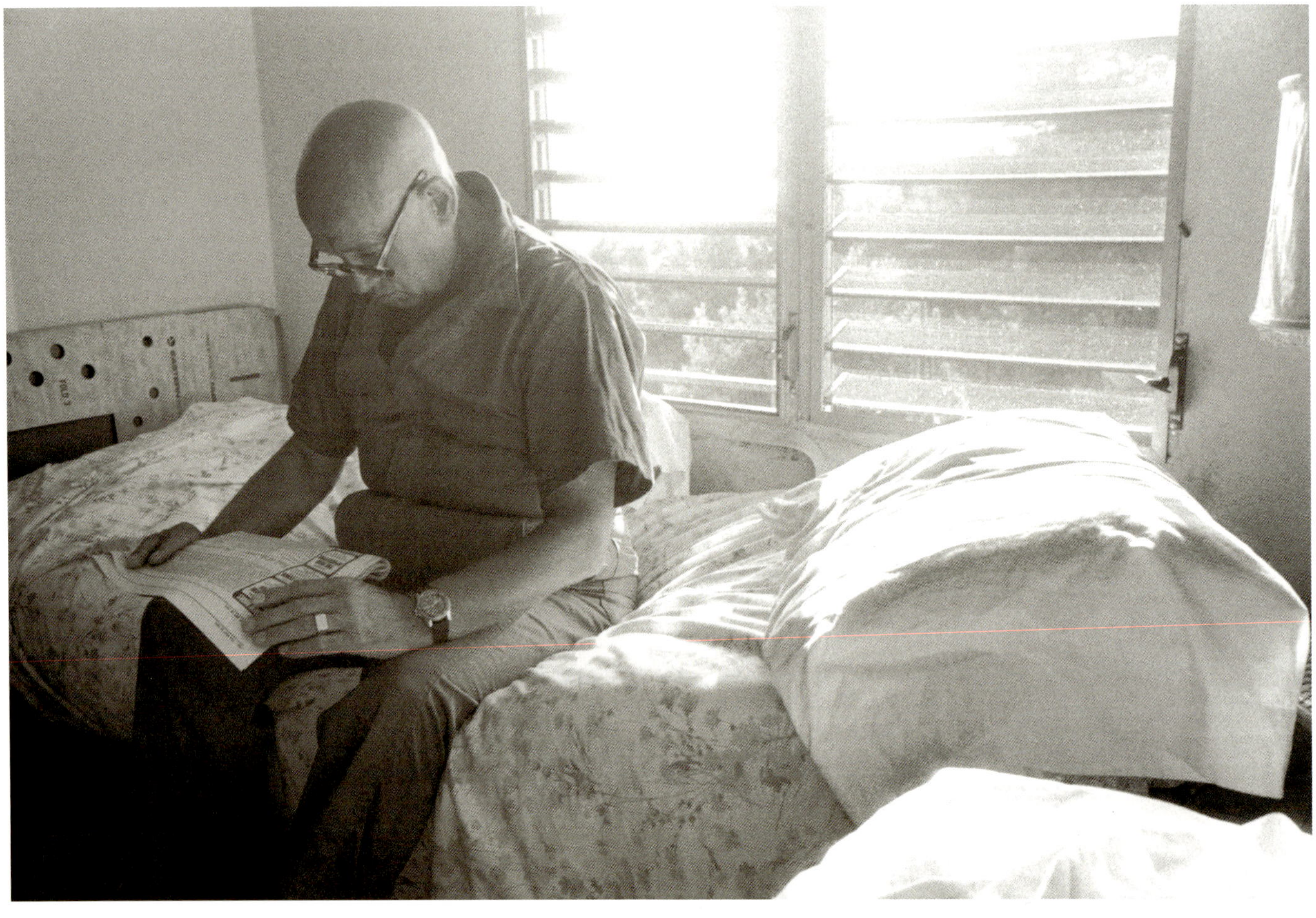

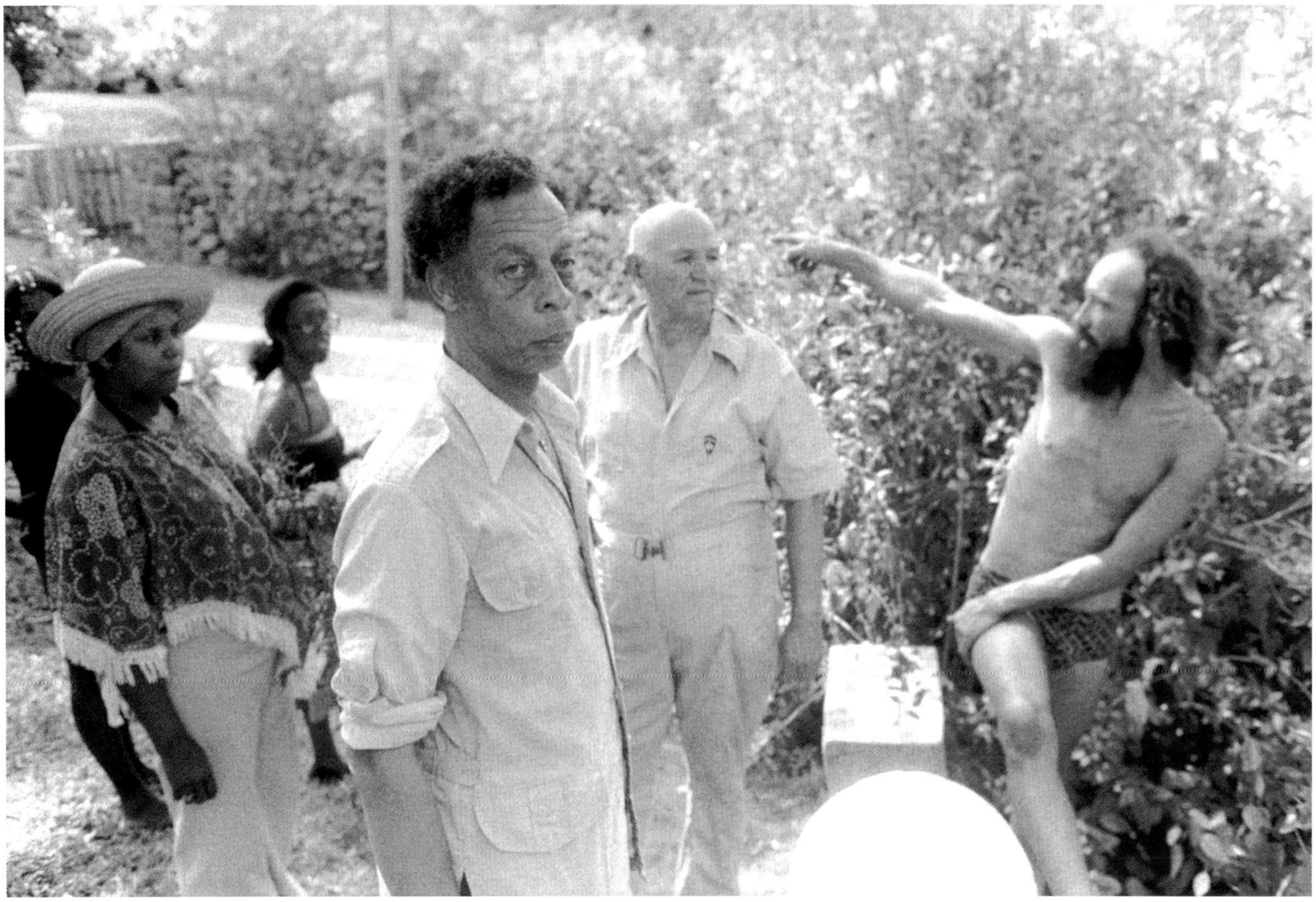

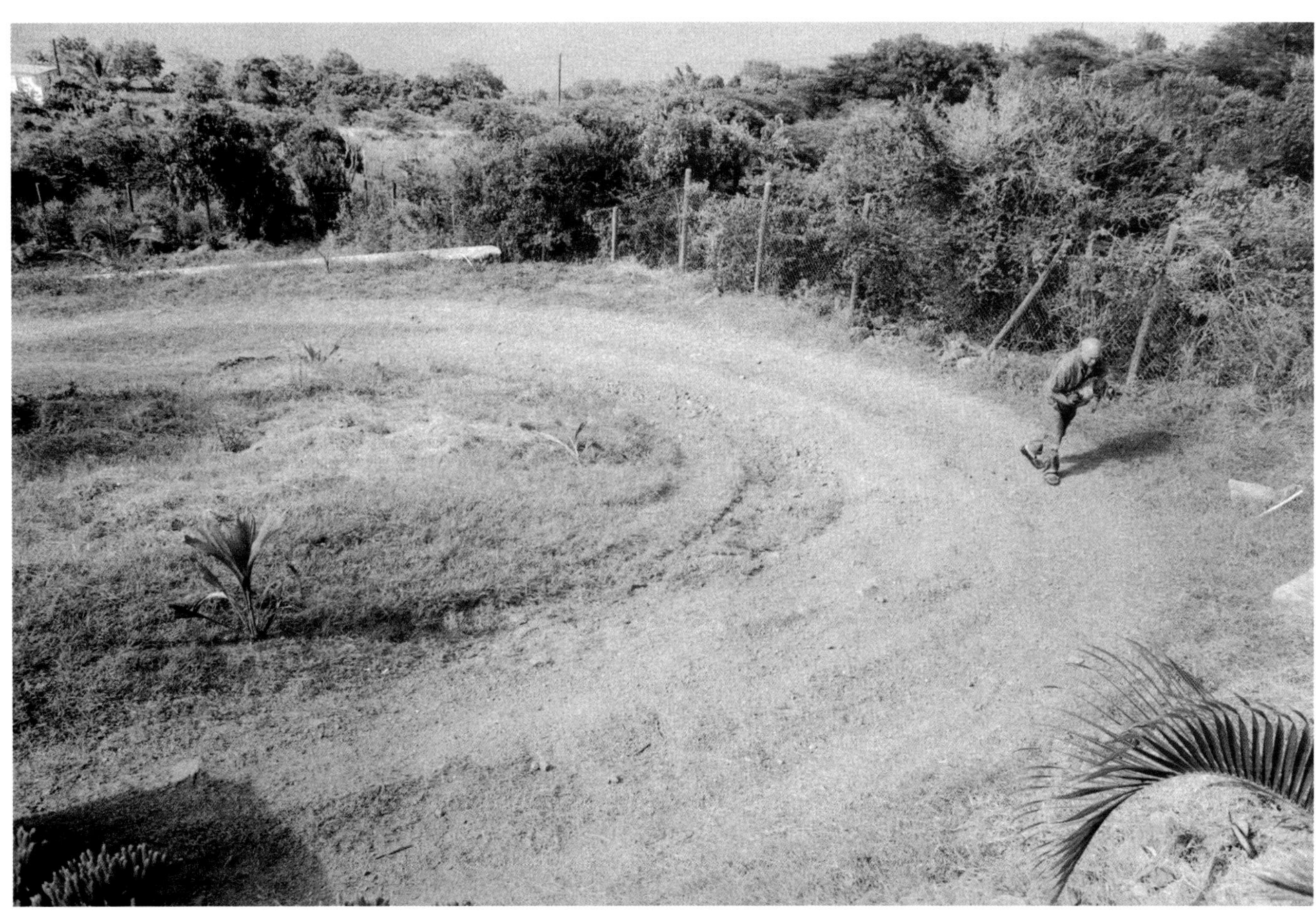

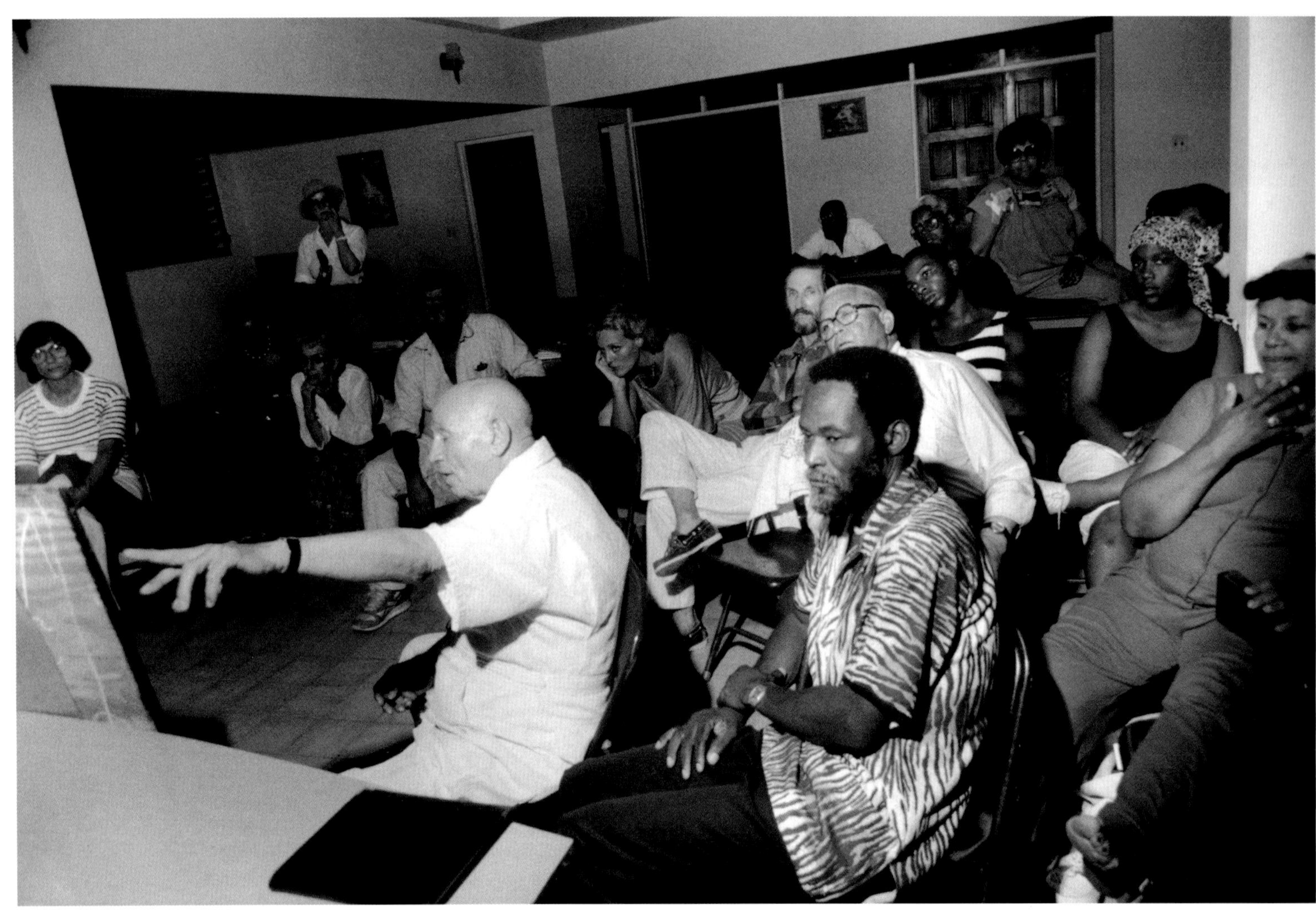

This discussion was taking place while a play of Derek Walcott's was being produced. Romie's probably talking about something the actors are doing. 1987

PRECEDING PAGE, TOP
The pieces Romie painted in St. Martin were watercolors. Here he's working on the *Odysseus* series, remaking them in miniature, copying them line for line sometimes. c. 1978

PRECEDING PAGE
Romie's reading a newspaper. 1979

PRECEDING PAGE, TOP
Nanette, June Kelly, Richard Long, Romie, and Roland Richardson at Roland's family's place. 1987

PRECEDING PAGE
Romie's house in St. Martin was a split-level on a hill. Here's Romie on the road leading up at the back, where you'd come in on the second, top level. In the front of the house you'd come in on the first floor. c. 1982

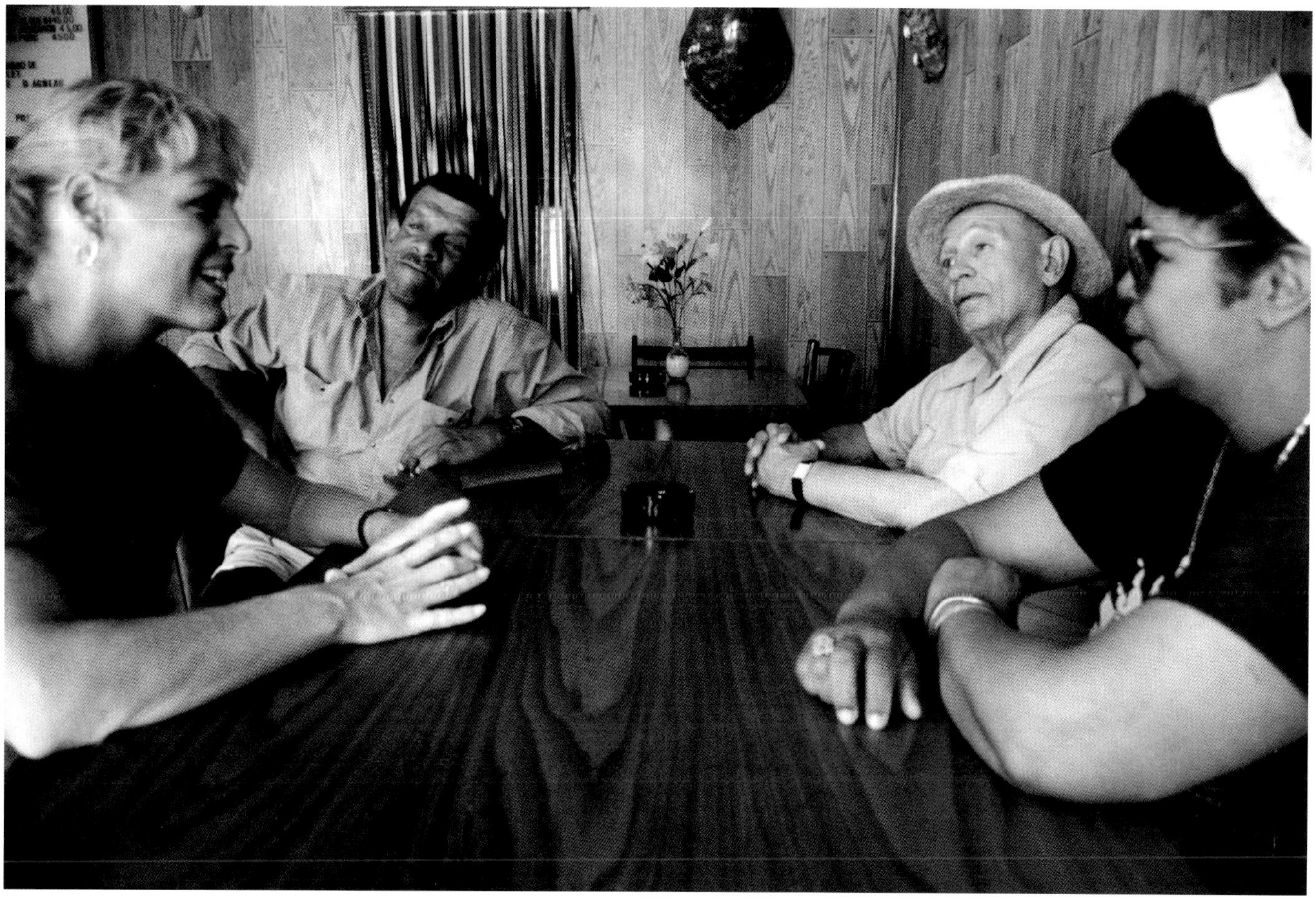

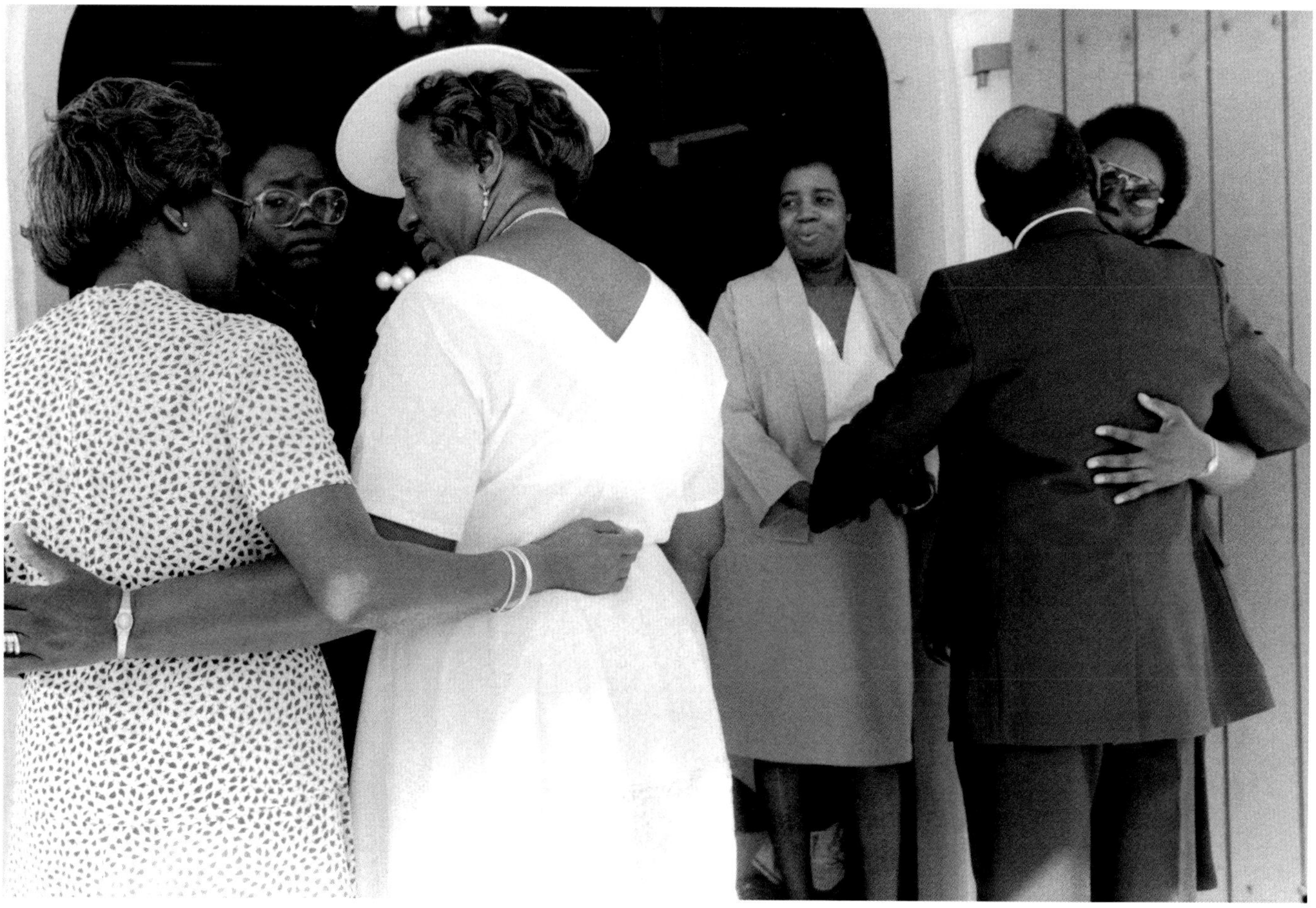

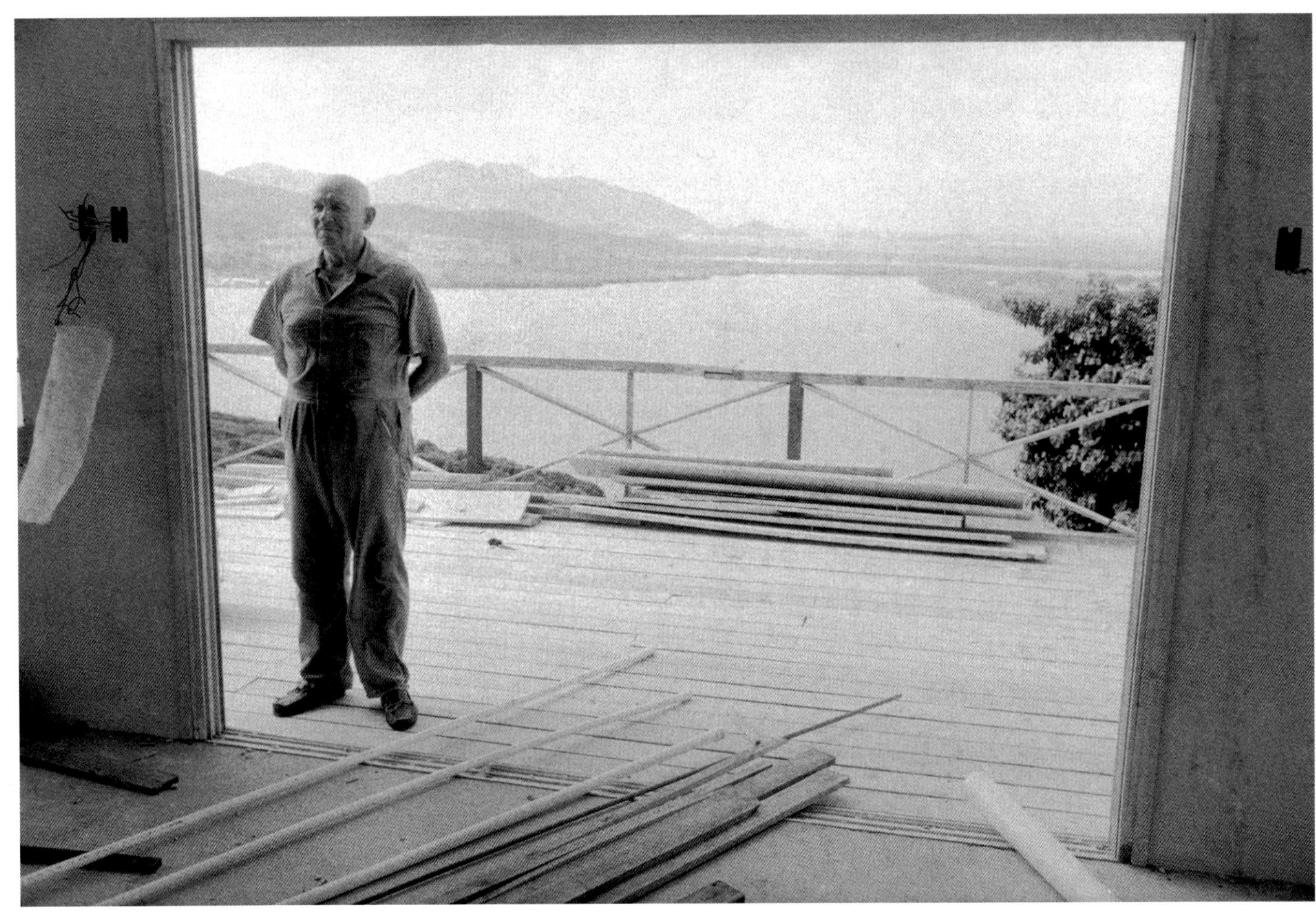

Romie's looking into the studio that was being built by this contractor who'd work while Romie was there but the rest of the time didn't work. It wasn't until the middle 1980s that Romie actually had this place to work in. c. 1985

PRECEDING PAGE, TOP
Sigrid Nama, Derek Walcott, Romie, and Nanette at the time of an interisland festival. We went from St. Martin to Martinique and to Haiti. Nanette had her dancers, Romie had art shows, Richard Long gave lectures, and I think there was a play by Derek. 1987

PRECEDING PAGE
At church after the wedding of Nanette's cousin. 1984

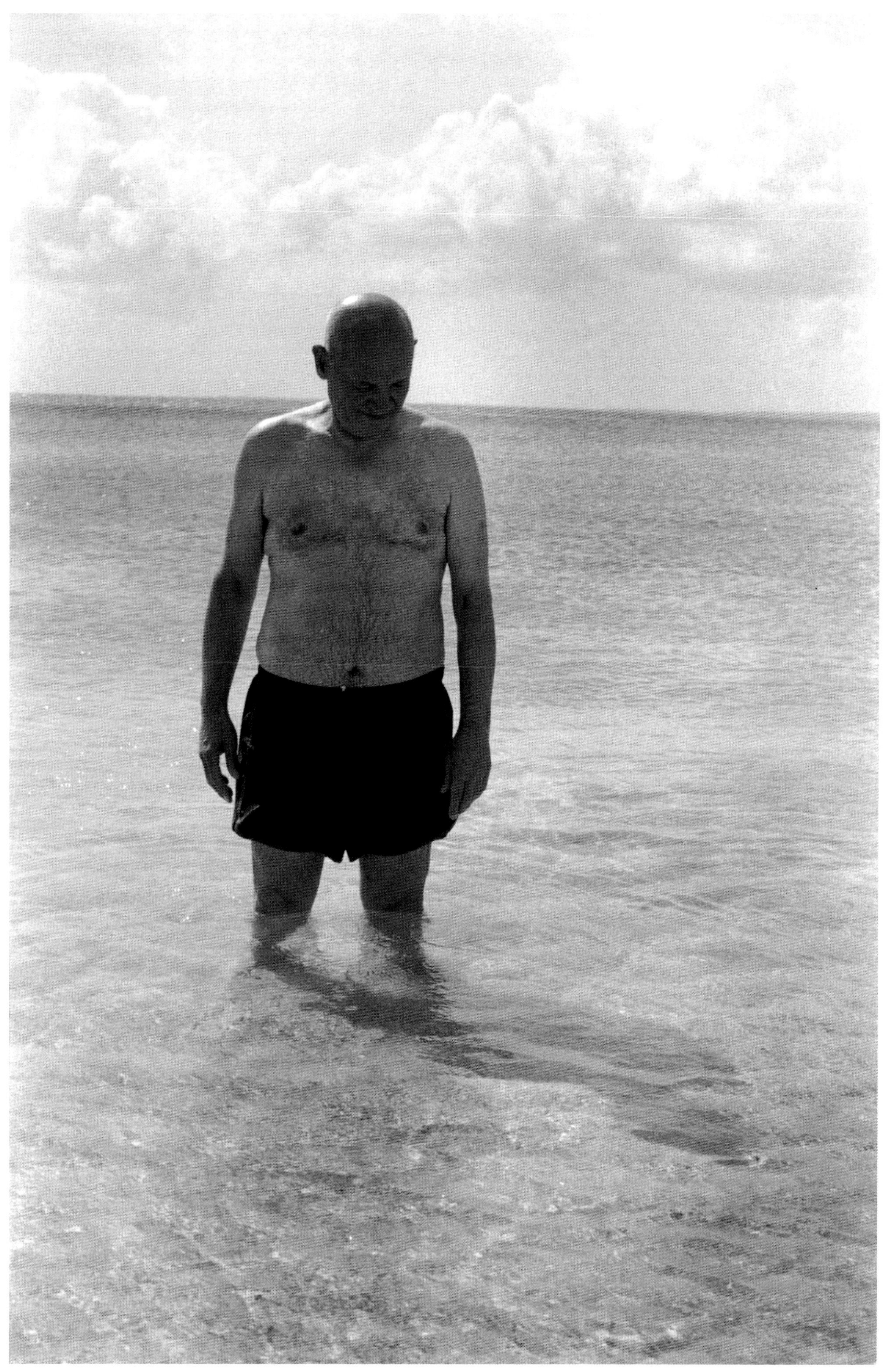

St. Martin was a magical place for Romie. He said that he went down there and got rejuvenated. c. 1977

CANAL STREET
LAST DAYS

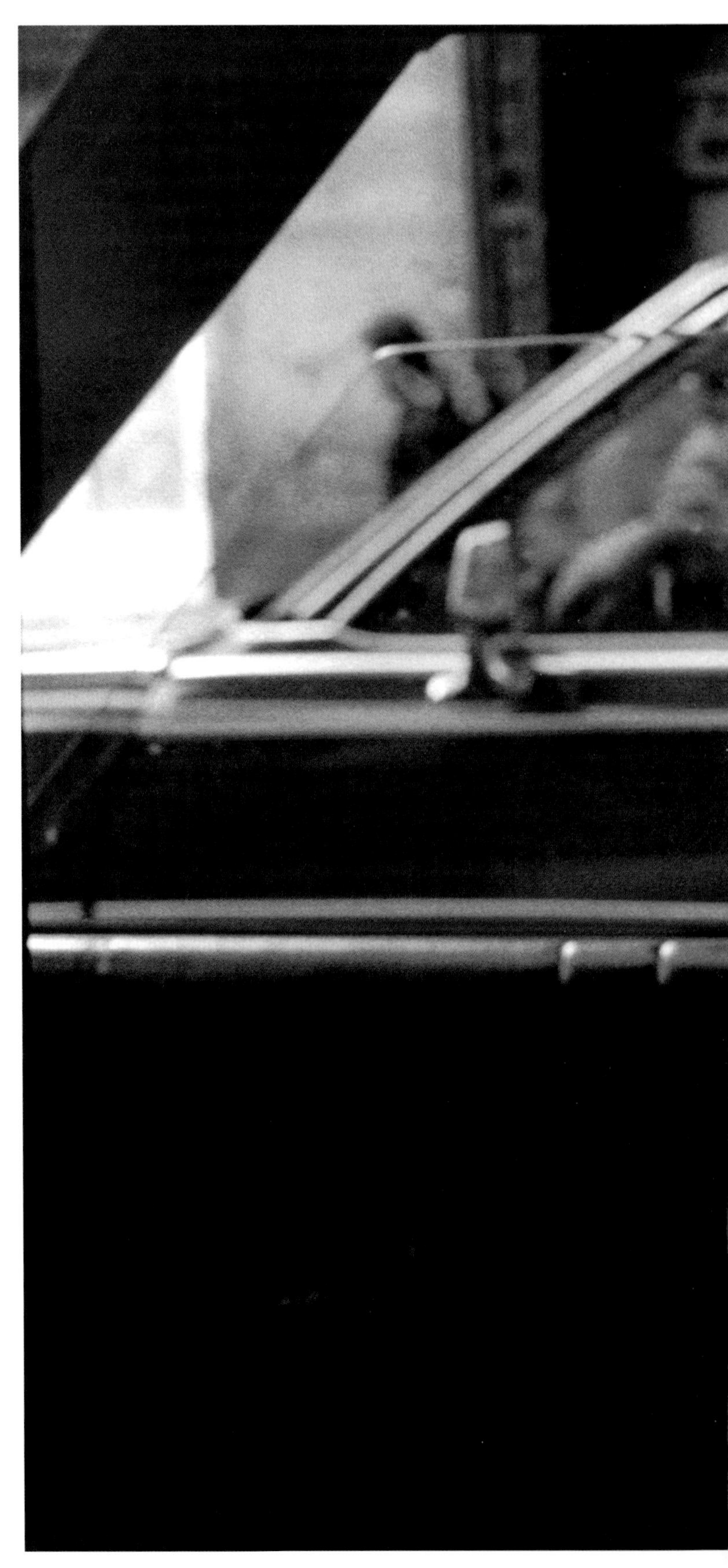

Here's Romie in my car. 1987

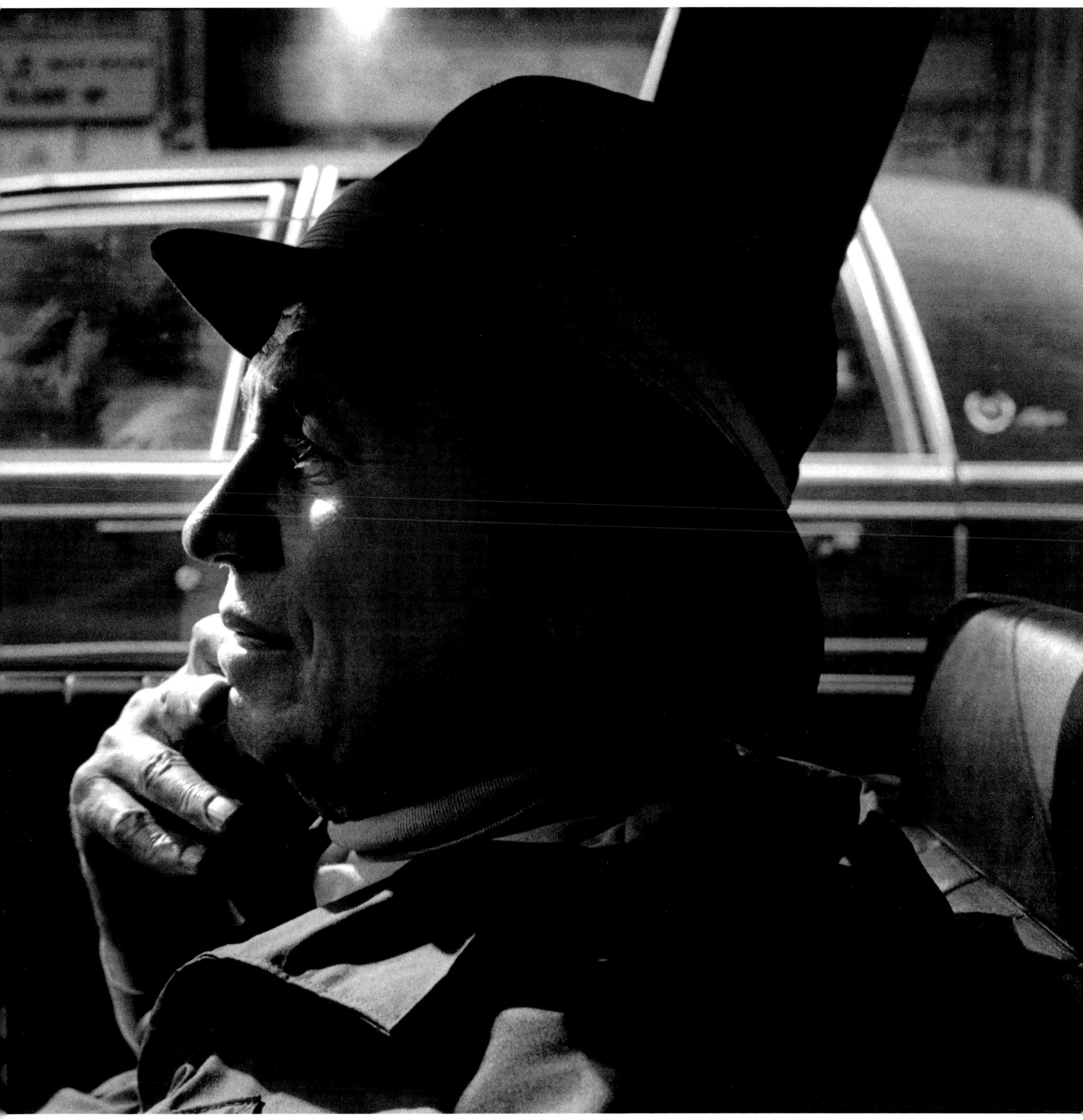

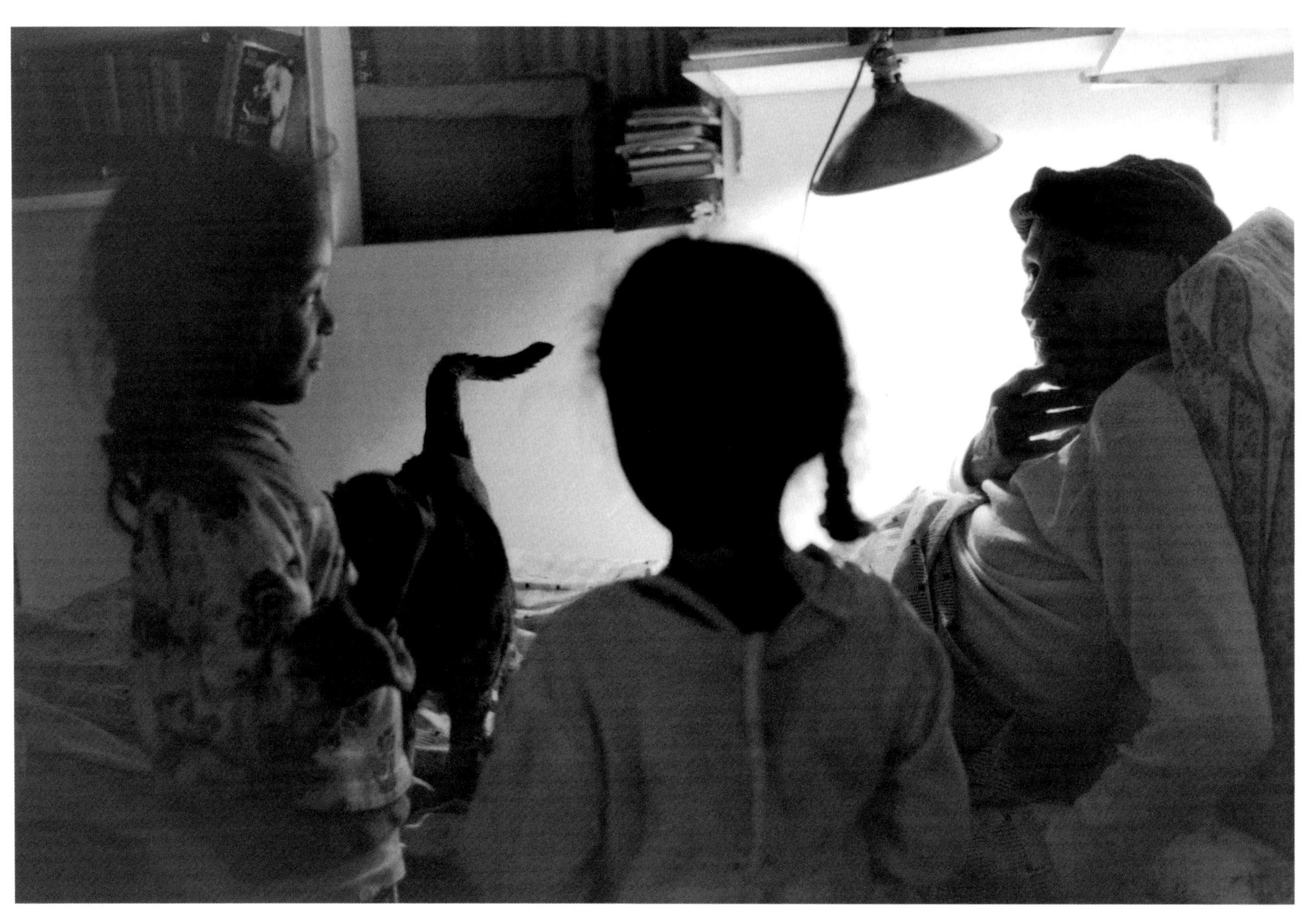

I'd bring my girls, Sing and Bining, to see Romie when he was sick, and he liked that. The cats liked it, too. Romie was down on the second floor of Canal Street by then. That happened around 1986 because he couldn't get up those stairs to the fifth floor anymore. 1987

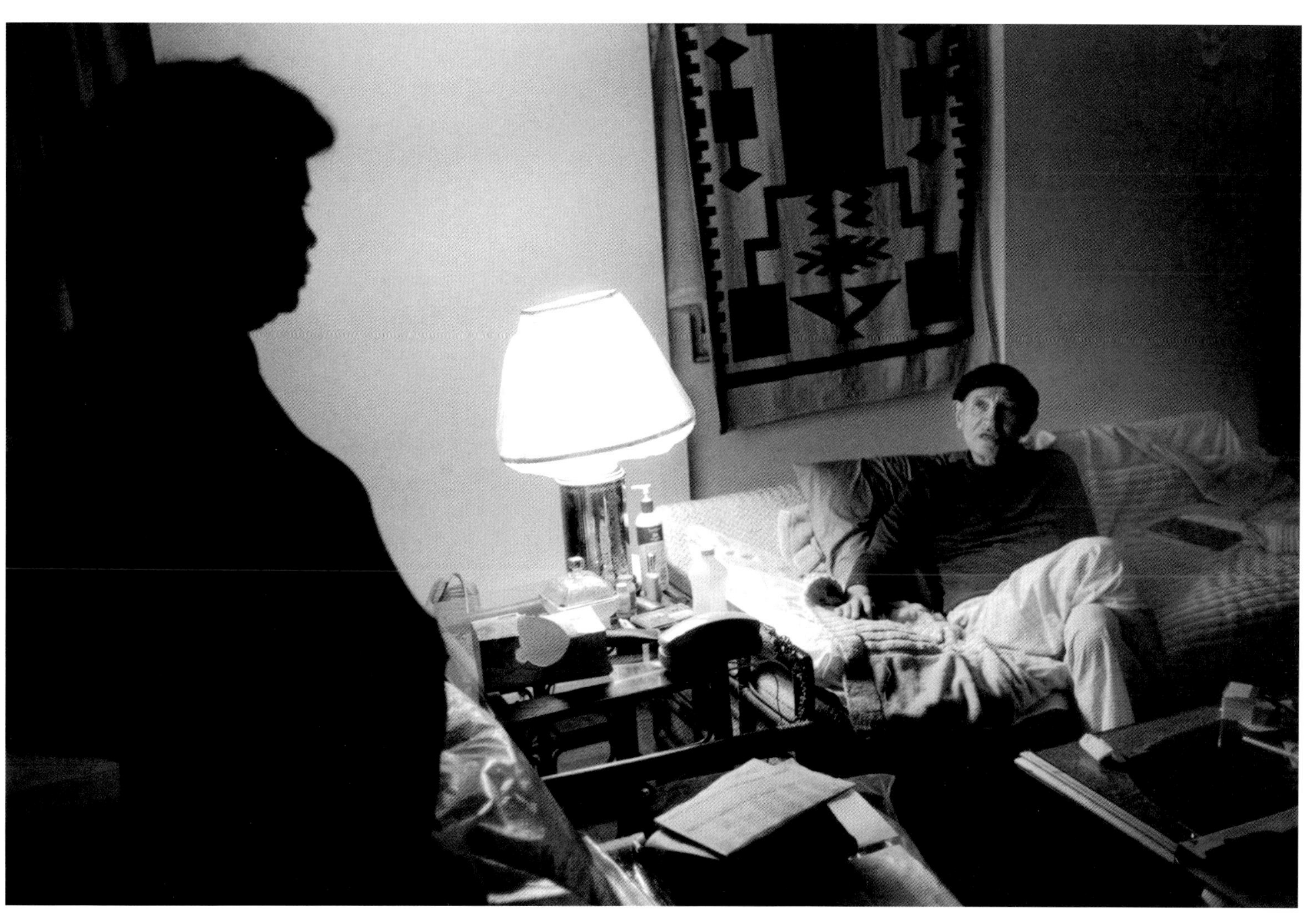

At the end, Romie did a lot of resting. He lost a lot of weight, too. I'd visit, and he didn't say he had bone cancer or anything. Whatever he had . . . I guess it was the cancer. 1987

FACING PAGE
This was near the end. Romie went into a coma for weeks. And then June Kelly called me one day, said if I was standing up I should sit down. And she gave me the bad news. It was on my daughter Bining's sixth birthday, March 12, 1988.

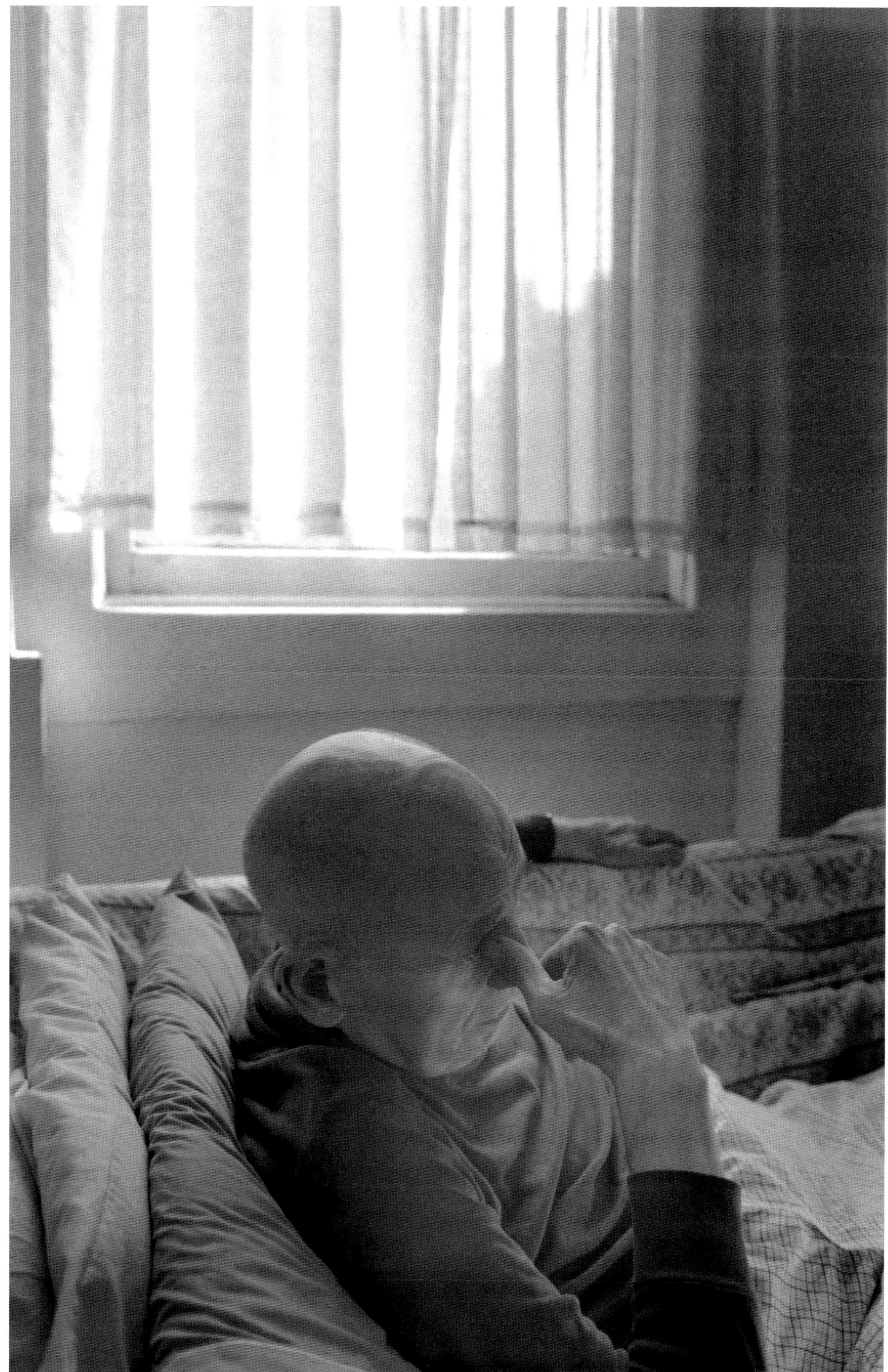

Moutoussamy for loaning me a view camera in the first place, Ruth Fine for convincing me "there is a book here," Susan Sillins for believing and working hard, Tamako Okamura for being a perfectionist, The Bearden Foundation and Sheila Rohan, Dorothy, and Marie for allowing the book to be, Wynton Marsalis for showing me possibilities, Dorothy Johnson for being my mother and being the artist that she is, June Kelly for being with Romie all those years, Johnny Simmons for allowing me to wish, Adrian Jenkins for opening my eyes to the culture, McLain Bennett for saving these negatives from the firemen, Dr. Richard Long for being a lifelong friend to RB, Sing and Bining Stewart for just being, Mertin Simpson for donating a portfolio to the Schomburg, Carolyn Appel for being a friend, Albert Murray for allowing me to listen to the conversations, Katie and Thomas Burke for seeing the light, Lory Ann, Patrice, and our other friends from Pomegranate, Hugh Fierce, Andre K. Guess and all the folks at Jazz at Lincoln Center, Rob Gibson, Halima Taha, Carlton Moss, Tei Sing Smith, Roland Richardson, Walter O. Evans, Ernie Critchlow, Jessica White, Mary Schmidt Campbell, Ntozake Shange, Nelsen Breen, Dan Weisman, Mary Lee Cortlett, Marcie Hocking, Russell Goings, Richard Clark, Terry Gross, Billy Allen, Richard Kaplan, Dr. George N. Preston, Count Rustikoff, Michelangelo, and King Tut for being so faithful, and Jack Fein for the 'house of pain.'